PIETY, POWER, AND POLITICS

Pitt Latin American Series

BILLIE R. DEWALT, *General Editor*

REID ANDREWS, *Associate Editor*

CARMEN DIANA DEERE, *Associate Editor*

Piety, Power, and Politics

RELIGION AND

NATION FORMATION

IN GUATEMALA

1821–1871

Douglass Sullivan-González

University of Pittsburgh Press

Published by the University of Pittsburgh Press,

Pittsburgh, Pa. 15261

Copyright © 1998, University of Pittsburgh Press

Manufactured in the United States of America

Printed on acid-free paper

10 9 8 7 6 5 4 3 2 1

Sullivan-Gonzalez, Douglass.

   Piety, power, and politics : religion and nation-formation in
Guatemala, 1821–1871 / Douglass Sullivan-Gonzalez.

      p.   cm. — (Pitt Latin America series)

      Includes bibliographical references and index.

      ISBN 0-8229-4057-4 (alk. paper)

      1. Catholic Church—Guatemala—19th century.   2. Church
and state—Guatemala—History—19th century.

      3. Guatemala—Politics and government—1821–1945.

      4. Guatemala—Church history—19th century.   5. Carrera,
Rafael, 1814–1865.   I. Title.   II. Series.

   BX1438.2S85   1998   97-45346

   972.11′044—dc21   CIP

   A CIP catalog record for this book
is available from the British Library.

For Maribel, Frances, and Renée

Contents

Figures, Maps, and Tables

Preface

I FIRST DISCOVERED an unusual collection of sermons while I was browsing through the "F" series of the card catalogue in the Benson Latin American Collection at the University of Texas at Austin. Little did I realize that the chance unearthing of these anniversary sermons commemorating Independence in Guatemala would lead me to fruitful research and to an invigorating journey into the heart of Guatemala's nineteenth century. With my colleague and friend Milton Jamail, I loaded up my pickup to travel to Guatemala for a year's worth of dissertation research.

As we crossed the border from Mexico to Guatemala in La Mesilla, Huehuetenango, the customs officials descended upon us like locusts on corn. Before all my goods were spread on the ground in their "routine" search, I waved my award letter from the U.S. Department of Education in the hopes that I could save myself some trouble and "fines." An older ladino (mestizo), evidently in charge of this brigand, halted the search and called us in to chitchat about the finer aspects of life in the United States and in Guatemala. "Look at these eyes," he demanded as he pointed at his blue pupils. "En el Oriente, hasta los puercos tienen ojos azules!" (Even the pigs have blue eyes in eastern Guatemala!) The historic continuity with Guatemala's nineteenth century overwhelmed me. The power-wielding ladino class, struggling to overcome historic barriers to real economic and political opportunity, ultimately identifies ethnically with the white elite over and against its indigenous neighbors.

As I combed the archives in the Catholic church and in the Archivo General de Centro América (AGCA), I saw time and again how this emerging ladino class in eastern Guatemala put fear in the hearts of the white elite in the capital city, Guatemala City, simultaneously disdaining any identification with the indigenous peoples. The letters I read revealed a popular and fiery religiosity from the rebellious hearts of the inhabitants of eastern Guatemala who feared the "foreigner" and the capricious white elite in the capital, who had bargained away Guatemala's resources and its Catholic religion. Foreigners? To this emerging group, foreigners threatened its livelihood. Protestant colonizers from a fly-by-night land company in Great Britain had been granted huge tracts of their land by the less-than-disingenuous officials in the capital, while Guatemala's neighbors in Honduras and El Salvador frequently crossed into eastern Guatemala to inflict damage on towns and crops. This xii anonymous mass of men and women from Guatemala's central and eastern high-lands comprised a minority compared to Guatemala's largely indigenous population. But they became the critical political force in mid-nineteenth-century Guatemala. One of their own, the former pig-herder Rafael Carrera, emerged as the crucial leader and strongman for nearly three decades during their siege. A crude under-standing of Guatemala emerged among these peoples. Motivated by both religious piety and realpolitik, Catholic priests and leaders deftly cultivated this understand-ing of nation to create a buffer from the anti-Catholic federal sentiment among lib-eral opponents. Without the church and its ability to work with its religious con-stituency, Carrera never would have dominated eastern Guatemala; he would have been consumed by the anarchy that threatened the nation in the late 1840s.

Although this fascinating story focuses largely on eastern Guatemala, one can-not overlook the role of the majority indigenous population resident in western Guatemala. Records indicate that the indigenous peoples of western Guatemala identified with the caudillo Carrera because he granted them more autonomy than his liberal predecessor and he did not identify himself with the white elite in the cap-ital. Even though members of the five predominant linguistic groups never roman-tically envisioned a "nation" of Guatemala, they nonetheless identified with this leader and responded when summoned. This strange alliance was thus built upon the individual charisma and political savvy of Carrera who granted the indigenous peoples, by choice or by default, the space to re-create their own communities. Taken together, the caudillo and his indigenous allies, combined with the emerging politi-cal force of ladinos in eastern Guatemala, by the 1850s proved unshakable in battle. Indeed, a rudimentary sense and experience of nation emerged in the conservative era.

Since my initial discovery of sermons praising Guatemala as the New Israel, I have embarked upon my teaching career at the University of Mississippi. As I look back now over all the trips to Guatemala and long conversations with Central Amer-ican historians, I cannot take sole credit for the successful research and writing of this project. I am grateful to the dedicated people and institutions who enabled me to complete this work. A Tinker Foundation grant funded my summer venture to Cen-tral America in 1989, where I explored archives and discussed with regional scholars the real possibilities of researching religion in nineteenth-century Guatemala. A Ful-bright-Hays Dissertation Grant in 1991–1992 made possible a yearlong investigation of the recently opened Francisco García de Peláez Catholic Archives in Guatemala City; and funding through a faculty research grant from the University of Mississippi enabled me to wrap up my research.

Key people in Guatemala City were crucial in cutting through the bureaucratic impasses that so often slow research. First and foremost, I am grateful to the Rev-

erend Archbishop Próspero Penados del Barrio, of Guatemala City, who changed   xiii
decades of Catholic policy by making the Catholic church's precious archives open
to researchers. The archive's able and confident director, Lic. Ramiro Ordóñez
Jonama, and his assistants, José Chaclán Díaz and Héctor Aurelio Concohá Chet,
became my professors of nineteenth-century Spanish calligraphy and proved impressive creative thinkers in rediscovering their people's past. Lic. Edelberto Ci-
fuentes Medina, rector of the History Department of the University of San Carlos,
provided essential administrative support, and Professor Julio Pinto Soria always encouraged me in my historical research. Carmen Valenzuela de Garay and Aréli Men-
doza graced me with their undivided attention while researching the University of
San Carlos César Brañas Library. Guillermo Náñez astutely steered me toward key
documents at Tulane University's proud Latin American collection. Last, without the
unyielding support of the fine staff of the Benson Latin American Collection at the
University of Texas at Austin none of this research would have been possible. Thanks
also to Scholarly Resources Books for granting me permission to utilize my contribution published in Virginia Garrard-Burnett, *In Heaven Above and on Earth Below:
Religion in Modern Latin America,* and to *The Americas* for allowing me to use a version of my article published in the July 1997 journal.

The daily encouragement of my colleagues at the University of Texas at Austin
and in the history department of the University of Mississippi and the sustaining
love from my family enabled me to complete the research and writing. My graduate
colleagues and my Latin American and U.S. history professors challenged me in
seminars, and Richard Graham, my dissertation chair, firmly but compassionately
guided me in my academic pilgrimage.

I must also thank the many professors from Samford University and Princeton
Theological Seminary who played crucial roles in my intellectual formation. My
Samford mentors cultivated my curiosity for religion, politics, and Latin America,
while my seminary professors challenged me to come to terms with the historical
and ethical role of the Christian church in today's world.

Special thanks to Larry Bethune, Jeff McEwen, Terry Minchow-Proffitt, Carlos
Roca, Thomas A. Sullivan, and the good folk of Sumner Presbyterian church who
were critical allies in Guatemala and in the United States. Thanks also to Jane Flan-
ders and the staff at the University of Pittsburgh Press and to my Mom and Dad,
who never stopped believing in me. Most of all, I dedicate this work to the three
loves of my life—my daughters, Dora Frances and Ginger Renée, and my dear companion and spouse, Maribel.

Piety, Power, and Politics

Piety, Power, and Politics

BARELY FIVE YEARS had elapsed since the famed military caudillo from the eastern highlands of Guatemala, Rafael Carrera, had triumphed over his liberal enemies, in 1839, and set in motion a series of events that led to the establishment and consolidation of an independent republic of Guatemala. Now, neighboring El Salvador through military intervention threatened to reintegrate Guatemala to the Central American federation. During the events surrounding this 1844 military contest of wills, the Salvadoran president tried to entice the famed guerrilla priest Francisco González Lobos to join his forces in their goal to oust Carrera. One of Carrera's principal allies during the earlier successful insurrection, González Lobos had, since June 1841, served the Catholic parish in Jalapa, in eastern Guatemala, a potential battle line as Salvadoran troops advanced onto Guatemalan soil. In his response, González Lobos refused the Salvadoran's entreaty and reaffirmed his loyalty to Carrera and his willingness to die for *la patria*. A priest accompanying the Salvadoran president, who identified himself as the "Vicar of the Army," tried again to convince González Lobos to join up with the Salvadoran forces to liberate the Guatemalan people from its oppressor. González Lobos curtly responded, "I am Guatemalan, I love my country and for her I will risk my life, especially when her rights are threatened."[1] González Lobos gave vent to his "irritation" (caused, he said, by the enemies of his patria who committed wrongs in its sacred territory) and concluded that he hoped to see the invaders receive their just punishment. He had clearly taken "Guatemala" as the focus of his loyalty.[2]

Less than two decades later, the influential Guatemalan bishop Juan José

2   de Aycinena would cultivate a theology incorporating views not dissimilar to these popular sentiments expressed by González Lobos and other rural clerics in Guatemala. Aycinena reflected on Guatemala's covenant with God in an 1861 sermon commemorating independence from Spain. Unscathed by the fires of Independence while firmly defending the faith of the Catholic church, he claimed Guatemala had been divinely chosen and protected like the biblical Israel, so long as it defended God's laws. Aycinena asked rhetorically:

> What more could a nation desire than what this magnificent promise offers? . . . God is no less just nor less liberal with us than for the Hebrew nation who served as an example of what the Christian church had to become. The church is a chosen people, redeemed from slavery worse than that suffered in Egypt and sanctified with the precious blood of its Divine Liberator. Behold the reason why our republic, being a Catholic congregation, has the right to appropriate the divine promise, and if we fulfill the divine condition—and time will tell—God will not change the rules: He will reward the good and punish the evildoers.[3]

Religious discourse during the Carrera years explicitly evolved an understanding of nation. A faith-based piety among the clergy served as the catalyst for this emerging nationalist spirit, and political circumstances pushed the religious leaders toward such a position. Capital city and rural clergy cultivated a nationalist sentiment in order to create meaning out of a fluid political situation and they sought to protect their weakened institution from the continuing secular offensive by Central American liberals. Theology affected the political spectrum, and Guatemala's political struggles shaped the clerics' theological understanding of events.

Since the first moments of the insurrection against the Central American federation in 1837, the issue of religion became a crucial question identifying the protagonists in the contest for social transformation. In his formal platform of grievances against the liberal government, Carrera listed the restoration of the church and the protection of its religion as his desiderata. Other contemporary Guatemalans played down the role of religion and focused on local complaints as the prime mover of revolt. Clearly, the clergy played some role in the insurrection and subsequent consolidation of the republic; but to what degree?[4]

"Religion" and "popular religiosity" by themselves do not explain the so-

cial upheaval that eventually undermined the Central American federation.
Religiosity—interwined with the historic ethnic and political struggle between Spanish conquerors and indigenous peoples—made Guatemala's nineteenth century distinctive. The Spanish drive to conquer the indigenous peoples of Guatemala set in motion a historic religious struggle between Spanish Christianity and the Maya religious understanding of the world. Records indicate that some of the diverse linguistic communities eventually adopted and shared many of the basic Christian tenets, whereas others rejected wholeheartedly any attempt to yield their religious understandings to those of the European conqueror. Given the liberal measures against the Catholic church in the first decades after Independence, clerical presence and authority declined in many of the indigenous communities. Many now witnessed open rebellion to the Catholic church among the indigenous peoples. In some areas indigenous religious leaders even donned Catholic clerical apparel and performed services to the Sun God within the Catholic church buildings.

If these indigenous communities rejected Catholicism, what linked them to the emerging Guatemalan nation? Certainly no religious discourse emanating from Spanish descendants could have convinced them to be loyal to a greater community. Rather, their ethnic identification with the mestizo leader Rafael Carrera created a powerful alliance. Rafael Carrera's predisposition to favor the Indian peoples in return for their support created a formidable link with his program. For example, he did not hesitate to yank out of the highland communities any clerics who provoked displeasure among the indigenous peoples. Carrera sought out the right recipe to brew an alliance between the indigenous communities of the western highlands and the growing ladino populations of the east.

Children of Spanish and Indian unions—mestizos—emerged as a third distinctive ethnic group in the post-Independence struggle. Popularly known as ladinos, this middle group also included indigenous peoples who spoke Spanish and who gradually lost an identifiable sense of common cultural past. First language, then class and color distinguished this emerging political force.[5] As Spanish speakers, ladinos were quickly identified (and stereotyped) by European travelers in the early nineteenth century as a distinct social group yielding considerable power. One such traveler, Henry Dunn, anticipated the coming showdown between the white creoles, children of Spanish colonists, and the ladinos. Ladinos, Dunn asserted, were "the physical force" of the nation, capable of uniting "an energy to which the simple Indian is altogether a stranger," and that "inflated with new ideas of liberty

4   and citizenship, and at the same time shut out, both by colour and character, from the councils and society of the Whites, [they] must be dangerous
to the state."[6]

When Carrera's largely mestizo force first occupied Guatemala City in
February 1838, the white elite in the city saw only "barbarians" and "Indians"
who shouted "Long live religion!" and "Death to foreigners!" Carrera had co-
alesced the nascent political force of the emerging mestizos with many of his
indigenous admirers. Understanding how Carrera nourished and accom-
plished the multiethnic coalition among Indians and ladinos is crucial to any
understanding of the influence of religion upon the development of the
Guatemalan nation. A peculiar and fascinating blend of power politics and
religion unique to Latin America in the nineteenth century merged to construct a multiethnic and multiclass alliance and assured the emergence of the
Guatemalan nation. Understanding this phenomenon requires both a look
into the historical context of the Carrera period and a review of some of the
theoretical issues inspiring these questions.

Background

Various indigenous kingdoms were etched upon the territory that now
comprises contemporary Guatemala, long before Spanish conquerors
reached its shores in 1524. Descendants of the ancient Maya Empire—
Quiché, Cakchiquel, Mam, Tzutuhil, and Kekchí peoples—settled amid pic-
turesque volcanic mountains and valleys, fighting each other and forming alliances when necessary. The arrival of the Spanish conqueror Pedro Alvarado
heralded one of the bloodiest chapters in the conquest of indigenous groups
in the Americas. Protected by its steep mountain precipice, a large homogeneous highland population was protected from the depopulation that occurred among their counterparts in the lowlands, who were either decimated
by disease or shipped off to labor in the mines of South America.

The Catholic church played a critical part in the conquest. Early missionaries made a name for themselves, especially the Dominican Bartolomé
de las Casas who set about defending the integrity of indigenous peoples
from the avarice of Spanish colonists while working for their peaceful submission to the crown. Catholic officials established Guatemala's bishopric in
1534, suffragan to Seville, and later, in 1547, to Mexico. In 1743 Guatemala's
Catholic church became independent of Mexico's bishopric, and the other
churches in Central America now answered to ecclesial authorities in
Guatemala.[7]

The Catholic church struggled desperately for the loyalty of one of the   5
largest concentrations of Indian peoples in Latin America. Franciscan, Mercedarian, and Dominican missionaries combed the hills and valleys in the sixteenth and seventeenth centuries, consolidating the indigenous communities into manageable towns. Inga Clendinnen's *Ambivalent Conquest* clearly demonstrates that resistance flowered among the ancient Maya. It did not take the form of open confrontation but assumed more subtle forms. Many Indians took refuge in the popular religious sodalities, *cofradías,* to ensure a certain degree of autonomy and popular religiosity, while others openly challenged Catholic hegemony.[8] When, in the mid–nineteenth century Father Vicente Hernández went to Momostenango to recommence the work of the church, the Indians balked at his attempts to win them over. When informed that Hernández planned to baptize the Indians there, they curtly refused: "the turkeys and other animals were fat and healthy, and hadn't been baptized."[9]

Ever since the conquest, two groups had vied for power in the area: Spanish and Indian communities. Children of Spanish colonists, creoles, wavered between their father's homeland and their own birthland, while Indian communities resisted, shared, or acquiesced to the dominating Spanish presence. Spanish-speaking ladinos (or mestizos), the emerging political force of the nineteenth century, did not hesitate to identify with Guatemala against Spain.

These social groups clustered according to the geographical limitations and resources of the territory. While Spanish-speaking communities settled in the central and eastern highlands, the indigenous communities survived the political and cultural invasion in the western highlands. In turn, geography affected patterns of settlement with respect to the mountain highlands and the humid lowlands. Creoles and ladinos came to dominate the central and eastern highland areas of Guatemala City, Sacatepéquez, Jalapa, Santa Rosa, El Progreso, and Chiquimula (see map 1). The majority of the indigenous peoples lived in the western mountainous areas of Huehuetenango, San Marcos, Totonicapan, Quiché, Quezaltenango, Sololá, Chimaltenango, and the central highland area of present-day Alta and Baja Verapaz. Difficult climatic conditions impeded large concentrations of Spanish-speaking and indigenous people in the humid lowland areas of Retalhuleu, Suchitepéquez, Escuintla, Zacapa, Izabal, and El Petén.

During the colonial era, regular and secular clergy followed these settlement patterns. Regular clergy, those who were bound by vows and who lived in community according to the rules of the monastic body, migrated to

6   higher concentrations of indigenous peoples. The secular clergy, those priests not bound by vows who lived in the world and owed canonical obedience to their bishops, settled with the growing Spanish-speaking peoples of the east.[10]

These divisions deeply shaped the political and religious history of Guatemala. Spanish and creole elites searched long and hard for an export product that would enable them to link up to the world market and share in

Map 1. Geographical Regions of Guatemala

international trade. After the collapse of the indigenous slave trade and the   7
few gold mines in Honduras, settlers invested in cacao as their principal
product. But a sporadic market played havoc with the entrepreneurs on the
Central American isthmus.[11]

Another answer to this historical quest rested with the export of col-
orants. By the late seventeenth and early eighteenth centuries, indigo and
cochineal (supplemented by cattle and sheep) formed the basis of the economy. Merchants within the colonial jurisdiction *(Audiencia)* of Guatemala
traded through New Spain (Mexico) until the eighteenth-century depression
forced them to link with Europe by other avenues. The late eighteenth-century indigo boom enhanced commercial ties to Europe through the
Caribbean, thus fostering a certain economic independence from New
Spain. With the creation of the Consulado de Comercio (merchant guild) in
1773, Guatemalan merchants could now deal directly with their European
counterparts rather than through intermediaries in New Spain. But the market for indigo also disappeared. Cochineal in the nineteenth century and coffee and bananas for the late nineteenth and twentieth centuries were produced with similar hopes of finding a viable export product to produce
sufficient wealth for the merchant and elite class.[12]

The whole Central American territory, governed by the Audiencia of
Guatemala, remained an appendage to New Spain's economy and political
life during the colonial period. With the reform instituted under the Bourbon king Charles III (1759–1788), separate administrative districts (inten-
dances) were formed in Nicaragua, El Salvador, and Honduras, while
Guatemala retained the superior rank of a captaincy general. These administrative districts eventually formed the basis of the emerging nations of the
nineteenth century. With the coming of independence from Spain in 1821,
Spanish and creoles struggled to create new alliances to govern the territory.

For a brief stint the Central American territory remained loyal to the
Iturbide regime of Mexico. But upon the collapse of the Mexican empire in
1823, the Central American elite formed an all-too-fragile Central American
federation. Wars soon tested this alliance, and not until the victory of the
Honduran Francisco Morazán in 1829 did the federation secure a certain stability essential to its governance.[13]

The years of Morazán's federation have received much attention from
historians. Classic liberal policies and incipient state formation characterized
nineteenth-century Latin America. Guided by the European notions of citizenship and representative government, Morazán and his ally Mariano
Gálvez in Guatemala sought to bring the Central American federation into

8   the league of nations through modernization. The colonial religious institution felt the immediate blow of Morazán's policies of secularization as he exiled the archbishop to Havana, closed down most male and female regular
orders, suspended the collection of the tithe, and expropriated clerical property. Marriage soon became a civil ceremony, with divorce proceedings permitted in civil court. A modern judicial system was implemented in
Guatemala with the hopes of promoting trial by jury. Development of the
nascent state's infrastructure—road and jail construction—fell too quickly
on the underclass of poor ladinos and Indians.[14]

One of the most devastating chapters of this story, when combined with
other top-down policies, led to the 1837 insurrection. With hopes of further-
ing Guatemala's ties to Europe and attracting more European settlers to the
isthmus, the Gálvez administration gave away large portions of Guatemala's
arable land to a fly-by-night British colonization company. The company
failed miserably, but this could not overshadow the implication of the state-
initiated policy: foreigners—Protestant by faith—were making headway in
an area where arable land was growing scarcer by the day.[15]

The 1837 cholera epidemic became the flashpoint for popular demands.
Rising from the eastern mountains of Guatemala, rebels from Mataquescuintla led by the former pig-herder Rafael Carrera challenged the legitimacy
of the Gálvez state in June 1837. Although the capital elite attempted to calm
the fears of the insurrectionists through last-minute legal measures ceding to
the demands of the rebels, Carrera's insurgents continued their march toward
the capital, occupying it in February 1838. Carrera forced Gálvez to resign
from the presidency. Due to the commotion in the capital city, a sixth Central American state—Los Altos, made up of Quezaltenango, Totonicapan,
Sololá, and the province of Soconusco in Mexico—declared its independence from Guatemala.[16]

From February 1838 through March 1840, much blood was shed in
Guatemala. Morazán rallied his forces from El Salvador to regain control in
Guatemala, challenged Carrera successfully through 1838, and forced the
peasant's army into retreat and surrender by December. But following this retreat to his home base in Mataquescuintla, Carrera rebuilt his force and re-
took Guatemala City in April 1839, driving Morazán's soldiers back into El
Salvador. Morazán's last military effort to overcome Carrera came in March
1840, when he and his troops made up principally of Salvadorans and Hondurans attacked Carrera's forces in Guatemala City. With his final defeat in
the plaza of Guatemala City, Morazán's hopes of a Central American federation folded. As Morazán fled the country toward El Salvador, Carrera turned

on the breakaway state of Los Altos and brutally suppressed the white elite 9
into submission.[17]

Although Carrera did not formally assume the presidency until 1844 he basically ruled Guatemala. He initiated the restoration of the Catholic church, invited the exiled archbishop to return from Havana, made way for the return of the regular orders, and approved the recommencement of the dreaded tithe. Still, relations between Carrera and church leaders were quite shaky during the first decade of his rule.

Carrera's supporters grew weary of the caudillo's politics, which appeared to favor the city elite, and by October 1847 open rebellion erupted once again in the eastern highlands. In August 1848 Carrera exiled himself for a year to the indigenous highlands of Mexico in Tuxtla Gutierrez while Guatemala began to disintegrate. The department of Chiquimula became an autonomous military district; several mountain caudillos vied for power in the eastern highlands. A shaky coalition governed the capital of Guatemala and soon fell prey to warring factions. Los Altos again briefly attempted to break away, but all such plans were scuttled by the returning Carrera who, backed by a strong indigenous force, reentered the capital and took control in August 1849, this time for good. By the beginning of 1851, Carrera had soundly defeated the various factions, although some of his disgruntled opponents joined forces with the invading troops of El Salvador and Honduras for a final showdown at La Arada in February 1851. Carrera's impressive military victory silenced most opposition for the next fifteen years.[18]

The early 1850s were boom years for the cochineal industry in Guatemala, and Carrera's popularity soared. By 1854 he had been appointed president for life and had arranged a concordat with Rome granting him patronage rights over the Catholic church. The caudillo consolidated control over the whole country, and even the devastating 1857 cholera outbreak did not catalyze any popular movement to oust the military dictator. The pinnacle of Carrera's presidency came with the resounding defeat of liberal El Salvador in October 1863, when Carrera attacked his ideological opponents, invaded El Salvador, and removed its president from power. Carrera returned in triumph as his achievement was hailed as a glorious victory for the country.

Carrera's life came to an abrupt end by natural causes on Good Friday; in April 1865 he was buried amid much pomp and circumstance.[19] His successor, Vicente Cerna, who had governed Chiquimula as its chief magistrate, moved to carry forward a country that was now switching from a colorant-based economy to one relying on the export of coffee. Military challenges

10 based in the western highlands soon threatened the conservative government, as liberal elites led by Serapio Cruz, Justo Rufino Barrios, and Miguel
García Grenados led a series of efforts to oust the government. Although
Cerna's forces fought loyally in battle, his charisma was no match for the
newly imported repeating rifles that carried his opponents to victory.[20]

The conservative decades ended as liberal ideologues resurrected the
failed hopes of the Morazán years. Once again liberals suspended the tithe,
closed down most regular religious orders, and exiled the archbishop. The
Barrios state moved quickly to assure secure land for coffee growers and a reliable, coerced workforce. The Indians, who had enjoyed a limited autonomy
in Guatemala under Carrera's supervision, were now forced to accommodate
to changing circumstances. Communal land suffered a systematic attack as
the Barrios government definitively linked Guatemalan economy to the
world market. Integration, not autonomy, became the political creed as the
dominant group sought to transform the Indians into Spanish-speaking ladinos. Yet Barrios's dream of unifying Central America never materialized. The
conservative contribution remains unaltered to this day: the formation of the
Guatemalan nation.[21]

Historiographical Analysis

The role of Carrera in nineteenth-century Guatemala and the working
relationship Carrera maintained with the multifaceted Catholic church has
evoked much passionate and at times demagogic historical analysis. By his
vitriolic critique of the Carrera period and the clerical role in that conservative regime, the nineteenth-century Guatemalan Lorenzo Montúfar determined how much of Guatemalan history would be written with a negative
eye toward Carrera and the Catholic church.[22] In the last twenty years a
number of insightful studies of the Carrera insurrection in the late 1830s have
reappraised the Carrera phenomenon and, thereby, reshaped much of nine-
teenth- and twentieth-century Guatemalan historiography. Ingersoll, Miceli,
Palma Murga, Solórzano, Woodward, and Burns have challenged those
Guatemalan histories that bury the insurrectional and popular character of
the Carrera revolt. They shed new light on Carrera's victorious challenge to
the liberal federation, which had instituted reform with little popular support and alienated a majority of the indigenous and growing ladino population.[23]

This historical research has also raised more questions concerning the
role of the church, challenging the traditional anticlerical perspective ac-

cording to which the "ignorant" Carrera was a mere tool of the priests.[24] Ingersoll contrasted the rural clergy's support of Carrera with the hierarchy's fearful and resistant acquiescence to the powerful caudillo. Woodward and Solórzano expanded Ingersoll's analysis by focusing on the religious dimension of the popular 1839 insurrection, but they did not examine the multifaceted nature of clerical response. Woodward noted that the priests "were in the vanguard of the uprising" of a "revolution that became a religious crusade"; Solórzano concluded that religion served as the uprising's "catalytic ideology." Palma Murga undermined Montúfar's image of a powerful church and subservient Carrera by focusing on the church's shaky economic recovery during the Carrera years.[25]

Other studies of the Catholic church in Guatemala have bypassed the conservative years. Mary Holleran's 1949 analysis of church-state issues merely noted the resurgence of Catholic power during the Carrera years. Hubert Miller's *La iglesia católica y el estado en Guatemala, 1871–1885* initiated his research with the advent of the second repression endured by the church under Justo Rufino Barrios in the 1870s. David Chandler studied the elite Juan José de Aycinena and delved into some of the theoretical underpinnings of this influential priest's work but provided no overall analytical framework necessary for an understanding of the Catholic church during the Carrera years.[26]

Other historical works have filled some missing holes. Agustín Estrada Monroy's three-volume work on *Datos para la historia de la iglesia en Guatemala* provides a perspective on mission activity and conflicts in the Guatemalan Catholic church. Portions of rare church documents published in his three volumes facilitate an apologetic history of the church.[27] Despite these pioneering works, the quantity of historical analyses dealing with the Catholic church and the Carrera regime is remarkably small. One new perspective anchored in liberation theology has produced some valuable contributions to the study of the church in Central America. Enrique Dussel's series on the *Historia general de la iglesia en América Latina* includes an invaluable volume dedicated exclusively to the Central American church from the colonial period through the revolutionary 1970s and 1980s.[28] Recently opened Catholic archives provide the opportunity to address anew the many historiographical questions associated with the nineteenth-century Catholic church.

Past research has dealt with the question of the emerging nation and national discourse in Guatemala by focusing on either the 1830s liberal Gálvez administration or the triumphant Barrios regime in 1871, bypassing the Car-

12   rera regime altogether. The Guatemalan Julio Pinto Soria tackled the failed liberal project of the Central American nation. Pinto Soria's work embodied certain "Morazanic" aspirations by analyzing state-formation within the large territory of Central America and not delving into why the fragmentation of this geopolitical space led to the formation of seven different states. Severo Martínez Peláez in his classic *La patria del criollo* completely skipped the Carrera years in his concluding analysis. In his significantly titled work "A Liberal Discipline: Inventing Nations in Guatemala and Costa Rica, 1870–1900," Palmer pondered why "nationalism did not occupy a privileged realm of political and cultural discourse in either Guatemala or Costa Rica until nearly fifty years of post-colonial existence had passed." He concluded that creoles made no effort to "foment a sense of shared identity in a translocal manner" because they had no nationalist vision.[29]

Although Ralph Woodward accepted "Central America" as his unit of analysis, in *Central America, a Nation Divided,* he initiated the break with classic liberal ideology by proposing that the foundation of the Guatemalan nation rested with the conservative Carrera period. Woodward concluded that "Carrera's emphasis on state nationalism and autonomous government survives to the present day, the one great victory of nineteenth-century Conservatism."[30] Carrying forward this initial insight, Woodward later completed his exhaustive study of *Rafael Carrera and the Emergence of the Republic of Guatemala, 1821–1871.* In this monograph he accounted for the balkanization of Central America and the development of authoritarian and militaristic patterns common to contemporary Guatemala. He argued that the political power of the regime hinged almost exclusively on the caudillo and a force of rural peasants. Limited by the inaccessibility of archives in the Catholic church, Woodward could only sense the religious fervor cultivated in eastern Guatemala during the Carrera years.[31]

Juan Carlos Solórzano determined that a "proto-nationalism" was at work in the 1837 insurrection when "a nationalist sentiment accompanied a religious emotion."[32] Lowell Gudmundson picked up on this notion and pondered just why members of the Liberal party were so incapable of developing "a series of images, an identity, a discourse capable of galvanizing mass support." Gudmundson concluded that "Catholic discourse appeared more credible" and that church leaders and conservatives developed a "rudimentary national consciousness."[33] Carol Smith asserted, in her "Origins of the National Question in Guatemala," that Guatemala under Carrera was unified nationally as never before in Central America.[34] Through coercive methods and popular support, she argued, Carrera impeded complete creole con-

trol of the political economy. Still, Smith claimed that Carrera did not de-   13
velop a coherent populist ideology. She missed Gudmundson's insight that
many of the leading Catholic clerics did this for him, developing a nationalist discourse during the thirty-year conservative regime, especially after the
bloody confrontations of 1847–1851 in Guatemala's eastern region.

Carrera came to depend upon, even demanded, that clerics occupy
parishes in war-torn areas in order to pacify the region. He assumed that the
priestly message and vision would convince and unify the disparate factions
dismantling Guatemala. In response, the clergy invented and elicited a nationalist notion of Guatemala during the Carrera period, especially among
ladinos in eastern Guatemala.

Several important theoretical issues arise as a part of this investigation,
and they require clarification, especially since an essential part of the historian's task is to arrive at some general conclusions based on the evidence of
the particular. Reading the historical text, specifically society's text as it occurred one hundred and fifty years ago, requires historians to engage in
hermeneutics, that is, in interpretation, "not a simple return to the past, but
a *new* event of disclosure."[35] Historians do not "objectively" reconstruct the
past, but they engage the past and bring to the engagement many presuppo-
sitions. These operating assumptions become the very bridge through which
communication takes place. The old notion of a subject-object dualism that
posited a pristine, unbiased event beyond the historian and the social text has
long been challenged. Today, historians must acknowledge their prejudices
and use them positively to enter the multiple layers of meaning embodied
within the historical event.[36]

The theoretical dualism that long sustained historical and sociological
research consequentially reduced religion to its source in order to understand
the "true" nature of the forces gripping the individual. The classical theoreticians of religion Marx, Durkheim, and Weber, each wrestling in diverse ways
with the task of explaining the nature of the religious event, fundamentally
agreed on their common goal: to discover the basis of religion in economics,
society, and ethics. Religiosity reflected individual attempts to understand or
cope with large social forces. Religion thus became a "false" or "naive" understanding of the forces affecting the individual. Other theoreticians, bas-
ing themselves on philosophical hermeneutics, have rejected this reduction-
ist approach and considered religion integral to humanity's quest for
meaning. Striving for the "thick descriptions" of symbols in the societal text,
theoreticians such as Clifford Geertz, Paul Ricouer, and Victor Turner refused to reduce symbolism to any other aspect of reality and ventured in

14   quest of interpretations that explore the wealth of meaning contained in each particular situation.[37]

Yet some pitfalls surround the investigation of meaning. Consistency and replicability have been the hallmarks of empirical positivism, where the work of a historian withstands the cross-examination of colleagues as they work with the same texts. Those concerned exclusively with meaning fall short in this respect. As Robert Wuthnow wrote, one individual's understanding of an event changes often and is too idiosyncratic. Unless they can be linked to broad trends, generalizations based on individuals do not hold much weight. How then do historians move from the individual to the more observable features of culture? Wuthnow suggests in his analysis that "discourse, communication, and the dramatization of power through the symbolic aspects of social institutions" provide an appropriate means by which one can enrich and deepen the search for meaning.[38] In a similar vein Roger Chartier concludes in his analysis *Cultural History: Between Practices and Representations* that historians are thus freed to ponder "how, in different times and places, a specific social reality was constructed, how people conceived of it and how they interpreted it to others."[39]

This investigation proposes to do just that: to study how elite religious discourse and ritual constructed and imparted meaning to the masses during the crucial nation-building period; and to examine how and to what extent that message was popularly appropriated, shared, or rejected. Methodological questions immediately arise in light of such a proposition. How can one talk of observable features of popular appropriation or rejection if a majority of the populace was illiterate or did not have the technological means to communicate through the printed medium? To be sure, empirically verifiable written material produced by the masses does not exist. Yet the nature of conflict and elite response to any type of social breach becomes itself a medium of expression. Revolts against the relocation of cemeteries outside the village become the focal point of protest during the implementation of the Gálvez social policies in the 1830s. Riots and destruction of the new cemeteries are themselves "texts" written by the masses. Cholera epidemics become the match for the combustible fuel of tense social relations in 1837 but do not bring about a similar sustained revolt in 1857. In the same way, Carrera's ability to mobilize an army to invade El Salvador in 1863 becomes another expression of popular support. Even though no one will ever know just exactly what a peasant soldier was thinking on the eve of battle, the fact that he participated represents a certain victory for the dominant group who welcomed his support.

E. J. Hobsbawm analyzed "nations" and "nationalism" in light of the "invented tradition."[40] Hobsbawm wanted to uncover how dominant groups create a link with the past in order to legitimize the present through rules and rituals. "Historical novelty implies innovation" and the historian's task is to delve into the dynamics of this social invention.[41] Ernest Gellner concluded that such innovation may imply the destruction of other communities. "Nations," added Gellner, "as a natural, God-given way of classifying men, as an inherent political destiny, are a myth; nationalism, sometimes takes pre-existing cultures and turns them into nations, sometimes invents them, and often obliterates pre-existing cultures; *that* is a reality."[42] Gellner and even Hobsbawm weakened their formulation by implying that the exercise of nation formation requires in all instances a certain fabrication, that true community is not the nation.

Here, Benedict Anderson's definition of the nation goes beyond their conceptualization. Anderson perceived the nation as an "imagined political community."[43] Anderson thus emphasized the act of creation in nation formation and did not limit it exclusively to an act of falsification. The community is imagined, since no single member can know every member, and it is imagined as communal because, "regardless of the actual inequality and exploitation that may prevail in each, the nation is always conceived as a deep, horizontal comradeship."[44]

In his study of nations and nationalism Anderson queried why "over the past two centuries, so many millions of people have been willing to die for such limited imaginings?"[45] Florencia Mallon responded indirectly to this question in her work "Nationalist and Antistate Coalitions in the War of the Pacific." She analyzed how peasants from the central highlands of Peru fought the foreign invaders from Chile in order to defend their homes and fields. She defined these movements as nationalist because "they fought against a foreign invader, calling on an alliance of classes to join together in defense of a common interest they termed Peruvian."[46] Mallon concluded that a sharpened sense of belonging to a community occurs when one group wishes to appropriate its neighbor's resources.

In *Creating the Nation in Provincial France: Religion and Political Identity in Brittany,* Caroline Ford pondered why historians have been so quick to accept the implicit bias of modernization theory, which posits an urban elite modernizing the backward and rural population into "modern forms" of political behavior. Also building upon Anderson's thesis, Ford demonstrated how peripheral regions in France did not uniformly adopt ideas emanating from the capital. Rather, the peripheral region contributed, through the im-

16   petus of religious values and leaders, to the creation of new political and cultural forms grounded in local tradition, and it thus redefined the republic.[47]

For the purpose of this work, Anderson's definition of nation as an imagined political community enables the historian to understand the formation of the Guatemalan nation during the Carrera years. The essential dynamic relevant to this analysis becomes the community's identification over and against the foreigner, whether it be a Protestant colonist seeking land or the Salvadoran foot soldier threatening to pillage a village's resources. Ladinos in eastern Guatemala, motivated by fear and religious conviction, participated in the making of the republic.

The current geopolitical boundaries of the Guatemalan nation are not an unquestionable fact. The social groups who imagine political communities often make claims to territories that exceed the boundaries of their real communities. In short, the relationship between those people who identified themselves as Guatemalans and the geopolitical territorial unit known as Guatemala varied. During the Carrera years, multiple claims by different social actors were made upon the territorial resources in Guatemala. Yet those who engaged in battle against El Salvador and Honduras originated principally from the central and eastern highlands and developed a keener nationalist sense of being Guatemalan. The indigenous communities did not participate in overwhelming numbers against the Salvadoran troops. Rather, their territorial claims pitted them against creoles and ladinos. These communities saw in Carrera an ally against the white settlers, and they proved the backbone of Carrera's troops in the 1837 insurrection and in Carrera's pacification of the rebellion during Guatemala's civil war (1848–1851). Carrera, a "man-god" figure for many of these groups, became the medium by which these groups identified with a larger space than the one they lived in. A "protonationalism" and a "nationalism" developed jointly in Guatemala. Two different regions, with different but similar pressures, were linked to the caudillo in the formation of the Guatemalan nation.[48]

One last theoretical consideration concerns the sociological dynamic of secularization and sacralization. Anderson sees secularization as an innate part of the nation-building process. Dynastic realms and religious communities lost their cohesiveness when impacted by economic changes, social and scientific discoveries, and technological innovations (for example, the printing press). The written script was no longer a possession of the privileged alone but became more available to the common person; hierarchical orders were subverted with notions of common citizenship; and the inseparability

of cosmology and history gave way to competing understandings rooted in   17
the notion of progress.[49]

With the fall of the Spanish crown, and the rise of social groups looking to form some type of political community, liberals who defended the Central American federation of the 1820s and 1830s heralded the commonality of all citizens, public discourse, and the secularization of the state apparatus previously so closely allied with the Catholic church. Indeed, the sacred gave way to the secular. But the collapse of this political community and the rise of several nations from the ashes of the Central American federation suggest a sacred/secular dialectic. Although religion as an institution loses its hegemony to the emerging secular state, religion as a cultural force continues to wield power in society. The shift from a kind of theocracy (the Spanish monarchy ruling with divine sanction over an empire) to a nation that is divinely chosen evidences this fascinating dialectic between secularization and sacralization.[50]

This investigation will show the influence of religion on the formation of the Guatemalan nation by examining the relationship between Carrera and the church and the religious discourse supporting Carrera's nation-building regime. A topical approach to the research illuminates the historic dynamics of continuity and discontinuity within the institutional church, among indigenous and ladino peoples as they responded to the cholera epidemics of 1837 and 1857, within religious discourse itself over a forty-year period, and in a crucial analysis of caudillo politics and religious fervor in Guatemala's eastern highlands. Chapter 2 is an institutional analysis of the Catholic church's attempt to revitalize itself after a decade of repression prior to Carrera. The church was partially successful in reconstructing its institutional base in the key eastern highlands where Carrera, tested by the civil war of 1847–1851, came to depend upon the pacifying message of the clergy. Chapter 3 addresses popular protests during the liberal and Carrera years by examining cemetery revolts and cholera rebellions. In most instances, liberal failure and Carrera's success depended upon the relationship between the church and those in power. Whereas the liberal federation alienated itself from popular religiosity, Carrera and the clergy worked toward a creative blend of religious "revivals" and caudillo politics. Chapter 4 examines how the Guatemalan clerics invented and evolved the nationalist notion of Guatemala during the Carrera period, how elite and popular challenges to this discourse emerged, and how the church propagated its religious and political message through pastoral visits. Chapter 5 examines how church work-

18 ers, who initially resisted an alliance with the caudillo, moved to provide the military strongman the backing essential to the preservation of the republic in the face of external liberal threats. The crucial constituency within the eastern highlands demonstrated a nationalist fervor when confronting the "foreigner" in war and responded favorably to Carrera and to the church. Building upon the previous chapters, the final chapter examines how the conservative regime fell to a liberal regime of "Remingtons and Winchesters" in 1871. Although defeated, the ladinos in eastern Guatemala never yielded their popular religiosity. Bishops and clergy would soon be exiled, but the liberal regime was forced to repress and hold in check the "religious fanaticism" of Guatemala's eastern highlands.

The Catholic Church Regroups

RAFAEL CARRERA'S open letter to the vicar general Antonio Larrazábal in December 1840 questioned with measured indignation the church's lethargy and inability to fill the vacant parishes that now dotted the Guatemalan landscape. Part of the Carrera movement's unquestioned esprit de corps had been based on the commitment to vindicate a repressed church; now, less than a year into his administration, the needs of many of his constituents still went unfilled. Not only did the lack of ministers perturb the caudillo but the sheer incompetence of those remaining pushed his manic temperament to the edge. Carrera's frustration led to suspicion of Larrazábal's intent. Striking hard, Carrera charged "it certainly seems to me that you have arranged for many towns to be priest-less, possibly with the goal of returning the people to their primitive state of idolatry and barbarism."[1] Indeed, parish after parish had written the vicar general requesting a minister for the village church.[2]

Why the slow response? After a decade of repression the Catholic church had begun to rebuild its institution, reinviting the entry of regular orders, and looking to strengthen the authority of aged, secular priests. Almost two decades would lapse before the state-sponsored tithe would be fully operating throughout the country. Could the church rebuild itself and regain its colonial prestige? An examination of the results of the Catholic church's attempts to recapture its power base during the Carrera years demonstrates a drastic decline of beneficed appointments, a simultaneous rise of the interim priests, and a rekindled colonial struggle between secular and regular clergy.

20   Finally, the regional economic base of the church can be explored through an examination of the *diezmo* (tithe) and the *cuartas* (the yearly parish contributions to the general operating expenses of the Guatemalan archdiocese). Earlier research concerning the revival of the Catholic church during Carrera's military rule has focused on two events: the easing of state restrictions on secular priests and regular orders and the reinstatement of the state-sponsored tithe. Up to now statistics on the number of clerics serving parishes during the Carrera years have been derived from a single document published by Guatemala's vicar general Antonio Larrazábal, as he entrusted the Guatemalan church's authority to the new archbishop, Francisco de Paula García Peláez, in 1844.[3] Larrazábal's *Memoria* does provide a point of reference in our analysis of the church's decline and recuperation from 1829 through 1868; but additional statistical reports prepared by the Guatemalan Catholic church itself enable us to reconstruct in much more detail the decline and return of the religious institution.

No greater issue touched the hearts of the everyday faithful within the emerging republic than the availability of competent priests to administer the holy rites of the church. Marriages, baptism, penance, communion, and funeral rites required the presence of ordained clergy. Yet these basic religious duties provoked greater questions: who should appoint the clergy and designate the appropriate parish for a particular priest? The power of appointment of bishops and priests in Latin America had been entrusted to the Spanish crown since the colonial conquest through its patronage of the church. The sixteenth-century Hapsburg monarchy of Spain went to great lengths to ensure its control over these crucial religious workers in the growing empire. With the advent of reformist Spanish Bourbons in the mid–eighteenth century, the crown slowly cut its links to the religious leaders and preferred to develop its military and administrative might as an effective means of control. Nonetheless, the Bourbon rulers never relinquished patronage rights over clerical appointments. With the collapse of the Spanish empire and the successful revolts in the Spanish American colonies, the emerging national governments were quick to assume these rights, thus instituting decades of power struggles between the state and the church. John Lloyd Mecham's unsurpassed analysis of this contest in Latin America details how Central America fared no better than other nations in the region.[4]

The Central American federation that emerged after the collapse of the Iturbide's Mexican empire assumed national patronage over the Catholic church, much to the dismay of Rome. El Salvador's renegade assembly voted to recognize its own diocesan bishop in the early 1820s—thus severing ties with the mother church in Guatemala—and eventually, by the late 1830s, won recognition for this act from Rome.[5] The memorable conflict of the Central American church with liberal forces in 1829 over such issues as the right of patronage resulted in an exiled archbishop, the closure of regular orders, and the constant shuffling of beneficed and interim priests. To compensate, Catholic leaders began to depend on interim appointments (which did not require state sanction) in order to soften the political blows suffered from the liberal exercise of patronage. The church would never recover from this strategic decision. The nuances of this political wrestling match cannot be overlooked if we are to understand the shifts in power between church and political leaders. State approval of parish appointments became a political chess game: the church's influence among the popular sector was too great and too mistrusted to be left in the church's hands alone. Political leaders moved quickly to assume patronage in order to control clerical appointments in troubled areas.[6]

Secular clergy took possession of parishes in two ways. The most coveted was the beneficed parish *(cura propio),* a permanent appointment, theoretically for life, removable only by Rome's command. These permanent appointments came after a *concurso,* a competition among the qualified aspirants.[7] Potential candidates would submit their resumés, noting how many years they had pastored and if they spoke an indigenous language common to the parish, and why they sensed a calling to this particular parish.[8] After a nominating board appointed by the archbishop made its recommendations, regal and ecclesiastic authorities would usually confirm the decisions of the board. With the emergence of nations, continued state affirmation of clerical appointments came to be seen as a threat to the church. Through such a practice the state could easily place clerics sympathetic to its political cause in permanent appointments and thus assure a certain political continuity. The 1829 crisis with the liberal Guatemalan state brought to a boil the simmering conflicts of power.

On the eve of the 1829 church-state debacle, 75 percent of Guatemala's parishes were filled by permanent appointments. An 1828 concurso had filled thirty-seven churches with beneficed parish priests.[9] Almost forty years later, in 1868, only 8 percent of the parishes would have permanent priests whereas 92 percent were merely interim appointments. Table 1 presents a detailed picture of the forty years of change within the Catholic church from 1829 through 1868 affecting the total number of clergy, both regular and secular, serving parishes, and the number of permanent and interim appointments to parish churches (see also figure 1).

22   These statistics reflect just an II percent drop in the number of priests serving Guatemala's churches from 1829 through 1844, hardly a radical change in the makeup of the church. But these numbers in no way demonstrate the despair that gripped the vicar general Antonio Larrazábal, when he wrote despondently in 1841 to the exiled archbishop Casáus y Torres that "our situation is pitiful: many parishes abandoned and from every part of the country we receive requests for someone to come and care for their spiritual needs."[10] The church's perception was of great loss. More significant, the sum total of clergymen does not shed light on the dramatic drop in beneficed appointments from 1829 (74 percent) to 1844 (31 percent). What had happened, and why?

Liberal political success and resulting measures against the church were largely responsible for the dramatic change, but administrative decisions made by clerical leaders reinforced a worsening situation. With his military and political base assured in 1829, Morazán quickly asserted patronage rights over the church by shuffling clergy who opposed him to less desirable parishes and favoring clergy who had supported him. He sent most clergy to parishes other than their permanent appointments "in the interest of public order,"[11] and within two years almost half the parishes were being served by interim appointees. By 1844 they occupied over 66 percent of Guatemala's parish churches.

These measures tarnished the general attractiveness of being a priest, and ultimately threatened job security. Only seven men were ordained from 1829 to 1841, yet over the same period thirty-five priests who had been serving

Table 1. Clergy Serving Parishes in Guatemala, 1829–1868

	Beneficed Clergy	Interim Clergy	Total Serving Parishes
1829	81	29	110
1831	3	48	111
1844	30	8	98
1852	14	83	97
1868	9	98	107

Sources: "Lista de 13 curatos que se administran en propiedad," Guatemala, January 1829, AHAG 1829.32, Box T1 93; "Lista de 1831," Guatemala, 1831 AGCA B Leg 1112 Exp 2488; Antonio Larrazábal, Memoria; "Catálogo General," Guatemala, 1852, AHAG 1852.40.9; and "Lista de las parroquias," Guatemala, 188, AHAG 188.175, Box T4 79. The 1829 and 1831 rosters were chosen because they precede and follow Morazán's measures regarding the Church.

parishes in 1831 had died.[12] At this rate, the church was facing complete ruin.   23
This quantitative contrast with the colonial church could not be more no-
table: in 1756 no less than 105 candidates had applied for the beneficed parish
in Asunción Mita.[13] Now no beneficed parishes were being distributed.

Church leaders—especially the newly appointed archbishop, Francisco
García Peláez—made the tough strategic decision to avoid appointing priests
to permanent livings in order to limit the potential political harm suffered at
the hands of the volatile and ever-changing governments. In a confidential
letter to the papal representative in Mexico in 1852, García Peláez confessed
his political decision, which left the church with only fourteen beneficed
parishes. First of all, García Peláez admitted his "well-founded fear that the
civil government would attempt to use the right of patronage" for beneficed
appointments.[14] The archbishop defined the issue at hand: the very liberty of
the church would be compromised if the civil government controlled the
placing of beneficed priests for its political ends.[15] Second, after a decade of
rule by Carrera's forces, including three years of civil war from 1848–1851,
García Peláez still had misgivings about the current government's stability.
Even though one concurso was held in 1861 to place nine priests in beneficed
parishes, the number of permanent appointments plummeted (see figure 1).[16]
By 1868, only these nine appointments survived.

The archbishop's final reason for limiting the number of beneficed

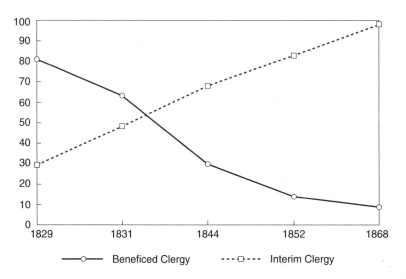

Figure 1. Beneficed and Interim Priests, 1829–1868

24   parishes was even more of an eye-opener than the others. The archbishop stated that "the lack of ideal subjects for beneficed parishes" inhibited his willingness to create them. First, he lamented that many members of the current clergy serving in Guatemala were or had been members of the regular orders. Second, many were foreigners, immigrants from other dioceses.[17] Both comments reveal historic continuities and discontinuities.

The age-long struggle between regular and secular clergy so well analyzed by Adriaan C. van Oss in his *Catholic Colonialism in Guatemala* had not abated. Distrust and competition at both highest and lowest levels of clergy continued to undermine a weakened institution. The archbishop was not alone in his myopic vision of the church's interest in this intra-institutional conflict. Both regular and secular clergy often appealed to their separate roots when confronted with political decisions in the heat of battle.[18]

The regular orders—Franciscans, Dominicans, and Mercedarians—had been the first to the conquered territories, but during the eighteenth century their missions were increasingly incorporated into the growing dioceses administered by secular bishops and priests. This change occurred with much resentment on the part of the regular orders as well as the populace. Adriaan van Oss mentions that troops were even required to escort one priest into San Pedro Solomá in order to "separate" the Mercedarian priest from the parish.[19] The regular orders were specifically targeted by liberal forces in the late 1820s since their role in fomenting opposition to liberal forces was notorious. All orders save one were closed during the purge of 1829.[20] Table 2 gives an indication of the numerical strength of those regulars serving parishes over the four decades. The regular orders certainly suffered under liberal political measures, but by the early 1840s they had made a definite comeback. The aforementioned remark by García Peláez to the papal representative in 1852 grew out of the fact that almost a third of his clergy had ties to the regular orders.

Besides García Peláez's hostility toward priests linked to regular orders, he expressed a reluctance to admit priests from other dioceses to permanent parishes. Such a stance challenged the theological notion of the organic unity of the Catholic church and reflected a growing nationalist sentiment within Guatemala. Yet the entry of foreign priests to Guatemala had come at the request of García Peláez's forerunner, Larrazábal, and had been continued by García Peláez himself. Beset by solicitations from numerous parishes and pressured by the popular caudillo, Larrazábal had turned for help to exiled priests from Mexico and Europe "as the last resort in order to avoid complete ruin of this congregation."[21] Nevertheless, priests from other dioceses were

viewed first as foreigners and only then as members of the same religious cor- 25
pus. Table 3 gives us a look at the nationality and percentage of "foreign"
clergy serving in Guatemala from 1829 through 1868.

This table shows a dramatic change in the makeup of Guatemala's parish
clergy over the four decades. First of all, foreign clergy nearly doubled their
proportion, from a meager 9 percent at the high point of liberal policies directed against the church to nearly 20 percent in 1852. García Peláez's antiforeign stance doubtless also grew out of this significant change. More important, the 1829 and 1831 data show that the majority of these clergy were
from neighboring dioceses of Central America and Mexico whereas, in 1852
and 1868, Europe and especially Spain accounted for two-thirds of the foreign clergy. This historic change contrasts with the colonial church when, in
1770, the episcopacy reported that 95 percent of the diocese's priests were na-
tives of the diocese.[22] Archbishop García Peláez's reservations highlighted a
certain discontent with the growing presence of European clergy and certainly the dormant and historic colonial tensions between the creole and the
Spaniard. He was not disposed to give the foreigners the privileges of a
beneficed parish.

If not beneficed parishes, then what option remained for the
Guatemalan clerical authority? Interim appointments *(encargados)* became
the option, not by default but by design. As García Peláez wrote to the papal

Table 2. Regular and Secular Clergy Serving Parishes in Guatemala, 1829–1868

	Regular		Secular		Total
	(N)	*(%)*	*(N)*	*(%)*	*(N)*
1829	23	20.91	87	79.09	110
1831	20	18.02	91	81.98	111
1844	29	29.59	69	70.41	98
1852	29	29.90	68	70.10	97
1868	29	27.10	78	72.90	107

Sources: "Lista de 136 curatos que se administran en propiedad," Guatemala, January 1829, AHAG
1829.32, Box T1 93; "Lista de 1831," Guatemala, 1831, AGCA B Leg 1112 Exp 24886; Antonio Larrazábal,
Memoria; "Catálogo General," Guatemala, 1852, AHA 1852.40.9; and "Lista de las parroquias,"
Guatemala, 1868, AHAG 1868.175, Box T4 79.

Note: To measure continuity, figures for 1831 and later include as regulars those members of the orders
who had initiated secularization procedures or who had completed the process to comply with the
government on religious orders. Legally, there were no members of the regular orders ministering in
Guatemala in 1831. After the Carrera insurrection, most of these ex-regulars returned to their orders.

26   representative, the church could nominate interim appointments without any intervention from government authorities. If the civil authorities have any problem with an interim parish priest, they "do not take matters into their own hands but work through church channels."[23] For all practical purposes the church hierarchy had little influence on civil decisions affecting beneficed parishes but was the critical channel through which the government worked when it wanted to challenge an interim appointment. Yet what seemed to be a triumph for the church in a test of wills with the state would eventually become a pyrrhic victory.

    Guatemalan parish records provide an insight into how much the churches enjoyed relative stability or were rocked by chaotic change from the time of Independence to the latter 1850s. Two separate mandates from Archbishop Francisco García Peláez, in 1849 and in 1862, called on parish priests to submit a roster of all those who had served their parish from 1820 through 1849 and from 1837 through 1862, respectively.[24] Each parish submitted a list of those clergy who had pastored there, listing the dates of each priest's arrival and departure. Partial and complete listings submitted by a hundred

Table 3. Foreign Clergy Serving Parishes in Guatemala, 1829–1868

Origin	1829	1831	1844	1852	1868
El Salvador	2	2	—	2	0
Honduras	1	1	—	2	0
Nicaragua	2	1	—	0	0
Costa Rica	2	1	—	0	2
Mexico	1	1	—	0	4
Cuba	0	0	—	1	0
South America	0	0	—	1	0
Spain	2	2	—	12	12
Italy	0	0	—	1	1
France	0	0	—	0	1
Total	13	10	17	19	20
(%)	(11.8)	(9.0)	(17.3)	(19.6)	(18.7)
Total excluding Central Americans	6	5	—	15	18
(%)	(5.4)	(4.5)	—	(15.5)	(16.8)

Sources: "Lista de 136 curatos que se administran en propiedad," Guatemala, January 1829, AHAG 1829.32, Box T1 93; "Lista de 1831," Guatemala, 1831, AGCA B Leg 1112 Exp 24886; Antonio Larrazábal, Memoria; "Catálogo General," Guatemala, 1852, AHAG 1852.40.9; and "Lista de las parroquias," Guatemala, 1868, AHAG 1868.175, Box T4 79.

parishes, supplememnted by data from baptismal records, netted over two   27
thousand entries for the period ranging from 1819 through 1871. This information made it possible to calculate the median stay of priests in each parish
and to test two hypotheses: (1) the Catholic church in central and eastern
Guatemala suffered severely under Morazán yet recovered significantly during Carrera's rule and (2) the shift from beneficed to interim appointments
during this fifty-year period diminished long-term parish assignments.

An analysis of parish tenure during this fifty-year period reveals two
dominant patterns in the time served by parish priests. Table 4 and figure 2
break down the parish assignments into groups by the number of years
served, to see the overall picture of parish tenure. These figures reveal that almost 31 percent of parish priests served between one and five years; 41 percent served less than six months. Nearly 60 percent stayed less than one year;
only 10 percent served more than five years. Taken by themselves, these figures present a bleak picture of the Catholic church. If these figures are broken down by regions and by time, a different picture emerges.

In order to get a sense of the dynamics of this period, I have broken it
down into five decades to mirror the changing relations between church and
state. The first decade, 1819–1828, includes the final years of the colonial administration and the first uncertain years of Independence; the second
decade, 1829–1838, embraces Morazán's policies against the church and the
culmination of the Carrera insurrection; the third decade, 1839–1848, en-
compasses the first decade of Carrera's rule and ends with his self-exile in the
face of Guatemala's erupting civil war; the fourth period, 1849–1858, com-

Table 4. 2,024 Parish Assignments and Tenure in Guatemala, 1819–1868

Years Served	No. of Parish Assignments	Percentage	Cumulative Percentage
20 years or more	15	0.74	0.74
10–20 years	49	2.42	3.16
5–10 years	140	6.92	10.08
1–5 years	624	30.83	40.91
6 months–1 year	363	17.93	58.84
Less that 6 months	833	41.16	100.00

Sources: Francisco García Peláez to Clergy, Guatemala, 1849, AHAG, box T4.89; Francisco García Peláez to
Clergy, Guatemala, AHAG 1862.305, box T3.78; Francisco García Peláez to Clergy, Guatemala, AHAG
1863.29; and Family History Center of the Church of Latter Day Saints of Jesus Christ microfilm
collection of the parish archives of the Guatemalan Catholic Church.

28   prises Carrera's return, the consolidation of his regime, and his strategic alliance with church clerics; the fifth and final period (limited to central and eastern Guatemala), 1859–1868, marks the final decade of the conservative regime.

The geographical grouping of the observations significantly affected the results. Guatemalan parishes were clustered into administrative divisions or vicariates, which closely mirrored the evolving departmental structure of Guatemala. Thirteen vicariates comprised the archdiocese in 1844, and these rose to seventeen by 1868. Yet these divisions by themselves revealed no meaningful pattern of change in Guatemala during these formative years. But if one follows the linguistic divide between Spanish and Indian communities (suggested by Murdo Macleod), the results are significantly different. Spanish speakers dominated Guatemala City, Sacatepéquez, Jalapa, Santa Rosa, and Chiquimula, whereas indigenous peoples prevailed in the western mountainous areas of Huehuetenango, San Marcos, Totonicapan, Quiché, Quezaltenango, Sololá, Chimaltenango, and the central highland area of present-day Alta and Baja Verapaz.

Table 5 and figure 3 analyze the median stay of parish priests in Guatemala and confirm the conclusions that churches suffered under Morazán's policies and benefited during the Carrera years. Taken together, the median stay of a parish priest in Guatemala was one year and one month during the 1820s, but beginning with Morazán's rise to power in 1829 parish priests stayed at their parish just a little over six months. During the next two

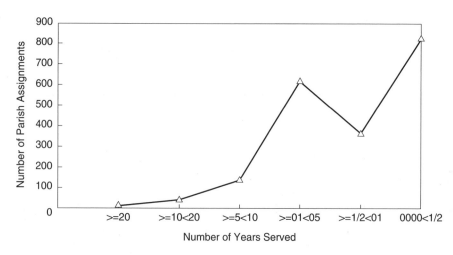

Figure 2. Number of Parish Assignments and Tenure, 1819–1868

Table 5. Median Stay of Parish Priests in Guatemala, 1819–1868 (in years)   29

	_1819–1828_	_1829–1838_	_1839–1848_	_1849–1858_	_1859–1868_
Overall median stay	1.08	0.58	0.67	0.83	0.50
Spanish highlands	1.66	0.41	0.58	1.08	0.75

Sources: Francisco García Peláez to Clergy, Guatemala, 1849, AHAG Box T4.89; Francisco García Peláez to Clergy, Guatemala, AHAG 182.305, Box T3.78; and Francisco García Peláez to Clergy, Guatemala, AHAG 183.29. Statistics do not reflect median stay from the capital.

decades, parish tenure increased from eight months in the 1840s to eleven months in the 1850s.

Analyzing regional variations of the median stays of parish priests sheds light on significant differences. Parishes in the Spanish highlands (figure 3) endured the severest change from a median stay of 1.66 years in the 1820s to less than 5 months in the 1830s; the Indian highlands dropped from 1.33 years in the 1820s to just less than 7 months in the 1830s. Parish tenure in the lowlands declined relatively little. Yet median parish stay almost tripled in the Spanish highlands from the 1830s to the 1850s, from 5 months to more than 13 months. Parish tenure increased significantly in the Indian highlands from the 1830s to the 1850s; the lowlands experienced a continued decline to the 1840s to recover only somewhat in the 1850s.[25]

Thus, through the 1850s, both hypotheses are confirmed. The Catholic church suffered severely under Morazán's anticlerical policies. Church lead-

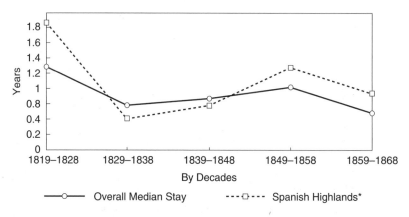

Figure 3. Median Stay of Parish Priests, 1819–1868

30   ers moved frequently and were not able to develop long-term relations with parishioners. The institutional church, especially parishes in the Spanish highlands, rebounded during the Carrera years but never to match the stability of the 1820s.

Data from the Spanish highlands concerning the last decade of the conservative regime, 1859–1868, demonstrate a sharp reverse to the gaining strength of the Catholic church during the 1840s and the 1850s. In the Spanish highlands, median stay reverses for the final decade from an average of thirteen months to one of nine months. If we included data from parishes within Guatemala City, median stay dropped from eleven months to six months. What had happened? The reversal merits attention, especially when written records indicate a more confident church and leadership that underwent institutional changes to enhance its effectiveness and organizational efficiency in 1860. A quick look at the Catholic church's *Book of Deceased Clergy, 1844–1874,* provides evidence that from 1856 to 1865, eighty-seven clergymen died. The church suffered severely during the cholera epidemic of 1857; from 1856 to 1858, thirty-six clergymen (40 percent) yielded to the severity of the plague. The church leadership could not adequately adjust to the quick depletion of its clerics, and the net result was volatility in parish tenure.[26] More important, to adjust to the rapid depletion of its clerical ranks, the church relied even more on short-term interim appointments to handle the crisis.

What was the net effect of short-term interim appointments for the Catholic church? Archbishop Cortés y Larraz, during his pastoral visits of the 1770s, had worried about the effect of priests, especially parish assistants (coadjutors), who had no benefice to root them into communities. Priests moved from one parish to another as they pecked their way up the ecclesiastical order. He disparagingly called them "mercenaries" as they wandered to and fro throughout the Guatemalan countryside.[27] Van Oss noted that most nonbeneficed priests changed posts frequently, searching for better coadjutorships or looking for ways to strengthen their chance at a beneficed parish.[28] By the 1840s a combination of war, disease, economic attrition, and church politics had produced an institutional chaos within the ranks of the Catholic church. What effect did these multiple changes have upon popular support?

Numerous letters from parishioners demonstrate that the faithful were unhappy with the interim arrangements and preferred a beneficed appointment. The faithful from the town of Don García requested a proprietary priest in 1858 because they were tired of sharing their priest with the town of

Santa Lucía Cotzumalguapa. The distance between the two towns made it impossible for the priest to attend both regularly.[29] The municipality of Cuajiniquilapa requested that the archbishop send a priest at least for Lent and Easter, while the mayor of Sacualpa said the people were demoralized without a pastor.[30] The parishioners of Petapa asked for a priest for the coming festival days in 1862; the faithful in Tejutla begged the archbishop not to transfer their priest in 1856.[31] Indigenous parishioners of San Pedro Carchá, in Verapaz, thanked the archbishop in 1858 for sending a priest who spoke their language and implored him never to remove him. Archbishop García Peláez thanked them for their support but stated frankly that "as with the other interim appointments your priest will be with you [only] as long as the circumstances warrant it."[32] Faced with the shortage of priests and bound by his conviction not to appoint beneficed clergy for the time being, Archbishop García Peláez transferred priests from one parish to another in the hopes of sustaining some symbolic presence of the church in nearly abandoned communities. Although he checked government influence in spiritual matters, the archbishop had restricted the long-term impact of his religious subordinates among the faithful.

In the aftermath of the civil war, Carrera sought to push for the reestablishment of a priestly presence among the war-torn areas of eastern Guatemala. Many religious and political officials expressed the popularly held belief that the lack of ministers in eastern Guatemala created the opportunity for anarchy and lawlessness. Commenting on the causes of the civil war that racked Guatemala from 1848 through 1851, Cuajiniquilapa's corregidor Justo Milla concluded that "the instability of public functionaries, principally the parish priests, brought about the last uprising of the *montañeses*."[33] Carrera believed that competent ministers in the troubled areas would resolve the tensions; he maintained regular contact with the archbishop and selected clerics in his efforts to pacify the eastern mountains. With such institutional and military support, clerics were able to return to the eastern Spanish highlands and settle for longer periods of time. As reflected in table 5, the median stay of clerics doubled in the 1850s from its 1830s' low.[34]

In what way did the economic strength of parishes affect the parish priests' mobility? An analysis of the *cuartas episcopales,* or the bishop's fourth, gives us an idea of the financial strength of Guatemala's parishes. The episcopacy had determined the standard income of each parish and expected 2 percent of yearly parish income to be sent to the general vicar's office and 3 percent to the seminary. Parish priests were expected to pay these amounts

32   and had to receive a special dispensation if they could not. Data are available for only the period 1832–1853. Examining the receipts of the cuartas episcopales for this period gives a sense of the regional economic strength of the Guatemalan parishes during extremely chaotic years.

Both the Spanish highlands and the lowlands suffered overall losses in the 1840s in comparison with the 1830s but showed slight gains during the 1850s. The Indian highlands parishes endured a moderate loss from 1832 to 1848 then regained a substantial portion in the late 1840s and early 1850s. Historic events explain this financial ebb and flow: by the late 1830s and late 1840s civil wars terrorized the Spanish highlands, and the surrounding economy suffered dearly. Yet the Indian highlands, which suffered similar instability, provided a more constant bulwark against the changing economic tides.

Since the available data on the cuartas episcopales are not complete beyond 1853, a look at the tithe records *(diezmo)*, restored in 1841 and fully operational by the late 1840s, allows us to get a sense of regional income for the 1850s.[35] The Spanish highlands dominated in absolute terms from 1848 through 1859 (except for 1854), while the Indian highlands and lowlands were almost even from 1855 and onward. Historically, indigenous peoples were exempt from the diezmo, and among them only those who had purchased land previously taxed were called on to give their portion. The 1854 peak in the Indian highlands most likely represents cochineal income from the vicariate of Chimaltenango, located on the border with the Spanish highlands. With the channeling of cochineal income through a specific governmental office in 1855, receipts from the Indian highlands returned to normal levels. There was an overall increase in the Spanish highlands despite a setback during the cholera years of 1857. This increase would then suggest that the basis of the Guatemalan economy was expanding in the Spanish highlands and lowlands. In addition, the Guatemalan economy in the 1850s confirms in part the reasonable decrease in parish turnover in the Spanish highlands from 1849 through 1858.

In a pastoral visit to the vicariate of Chimaltenango in 1860, the visiting Honduran bishop Juan Félix de Jesús Zepeda y Zepeda wrote Guatemala's archbishop Francisco García Peláez about the ruin of so many parish houses in the region. According to Bishop Juan two basic problems gave rise to this problem. A beneficed priest committed to a parish on a long-term basis and would have a reason to take care of his property. An interim priest lacked the influence, power, and respect among his constituents to motivate the community to care for its church property. The bishop was deeply troubled by

the absence of a profound love between the interim priest and his congregation, one that he had seen bind the *cura propio* with his parishioners and that
made him the "true father of his family." From his perspective the bishop
noted that the parishioners resisted the interim priest by refusing to comply
with the mandates of the church. Second, the bishop yearned for the triumph of the past and, overcome with nostalgia, reflected on the past triumph of the regular orders. Members of the regular orders had been pious,
had spoken the languages of the indigenous peoples, and had not been
tempted by personal possession of property. With a certain brashness, the
bishop pointed to the rise of the secular clergy as cause of this situation as
well as their attempt to minister singularly to a flock when the work required
many. The bishop lamented the postcolonial revolutions, the audacity of
some in making the Indians equal to other classes, the demoralized and impoverished towns that had once secured a certain level of civilization and
prosperity. "Three centuries of work has been lost for the most part."[36]

Church leaders, beset by an aging clergy and unable to find recruits willing to take the risks of a job that provided minimum and uncertain benefits,
scrambled to meet the demands of a temperamental military leader and the
sincere cries of a despairing flock. The call for assistance from foreign clergy
and the move to interim appointments so that churches might have a mass
every now and then was certainly a short-term solution to the critical long-
term problems. By the mid-1850s, Archbishop García Peláez had begun to
control the situation: the chaos of the 1830s and early 1840s had abated, appointments to parishes were more stable though still not permanent, and the
church had begun to recover economically. But faced with an uncertain political future he had chosen a way that guaranteed the church hierarchy's control over appointments. In doing so, he had unwittingly limited the long-
term effectiveness of his religious institution.

3   *Popular Protest and Religious Commotions*

CHOLERA EPIDEMICS INTENSIFIED the life and death drama that held captive the people of Guatemala and severely tested the ability of any administration to withstand the challenges to its integrity during a plague. The most famous epidemic of Guatemalan history, the cholera epidemic of 1837 catalyzed the initial insurrectionary movements of the 1830s, undermined the legitimacy of the Gálvez administration, and opened the way for Carrera and his followers to move into power. Whereas the 1837 cholera epidemic made way for the collapse of the Gálvez liberal administration, the 1857 cholera epidemic did not undermine the Carrera regime. Why not? The conservative government's hegemony—its capacity to rule through coercion, persuasion, or both—was threatened many times by devastating epidemics, by clashes between village traditions and urban visions, by landowner–tenant farmer confrontations, and by foreign threats from neighboring countries. Conflict situations probed the depth and integrity of Carrera's support base in the indigenous highlands and provided a historic opportunity for the development of a nationalist identity in the Spanish highlands in Guatemala.

In the next three chapters we shall examine the popular response to the Carrera regime in the Indian-dominated highlands and among the Spanish-speaking peoples of the eastern highlands and lowlands. We simultaneously explore religious discourse and the degree to which the church was able to reconstitute its base in these territories. A variety of conflicts that emerged during the Carrera years reveal how the caudillo managed these tests and how clerics responded to them. Within Guatemala's indigenous highlands, cemetery revolts, epidemics, and millenarian movements tested the govern-

ment's strength. In eastern Guatemala, a peculiar religious awakening began
in Escuintla and peaked months later in Santa Rosa, resulting in a fiery commitment to the church and to Carrera. Encouraged by this religiously inspired loyalty to Carrera's Guatemala, Spanish-speaking mestizos later responded to external threats from El Salvador and Honduras. These "foreign"
invaders pressured for a return of a government more favorable to their liberal interests and ended up fortifying the conservative Carrera more than
ever before. These multifaceted responses to his hegemony will enable us to
gauge the nature of the support for Carrera and the Catholic church, the
seedbed of emerging nationalism within Guatemala.

Cemetery Revolts

The departmental magistrate *(corregidor)* of Totonicapan Rosendo García de Salas wrote Archbishop García Peláez in 1855 requesting funds for the
new chapel to be built on the cemetery grounds now located outside San
Miguel Totonicapan. Emphasizing the importance of his request, the corregidor recounted the recent history of this indigenous village in the western
highlands. In 1834 the previous liberal administration had attempted to san-
itize the village and prevent any possible contamination from corpses buried
in the traditional burial plots located in the churchyards by relocating the
cemetery to the village perimeter. Resistance to the cemetery's relocation by
indigenous groups led to armed conflict with the recently immigrated ladinos. After Carrera's triumph, he acquiesced to popular demand and allowed
the cemetery to return to the village's church cemetery in August 1840. In
1846, however, the corregidor again attempted to move the cemetery, but the
"repugnant obstinacy" of the Indians prevented its relocation. Given that
Carrera recognized the indigenous community as the ultimate arbiter in its
final location, the cemetery remained in the village churchyard. But by 1855,
with a smallpox epidemic looming, the Indians—now "submissive to the authorities"—agreed to move the cemetery to the outskirts of the village.[1]
This story, repeated numerous times for other villages, sheds light on
both the nature of the revolt against the Gálvez regime and the extent to
which the Carrera administration ably understood and responded to the political temper of his constituents. The Gálvez government failed in what appears to have been a noble experiment, while the conservative Carrera was
more successful at classic liberal policies. To understand what role the clergy,
or religion, played in these tenuous circumstances requires a look at the various revolts surrounding the relocation of cemeteries and a look at the

36 church's capacity to respond to popular religiosity in the periphery during the Carrera years.

Epidemics that ravaged Guatemala translated into numerous bodies being crammed into small public spaces adjoining the local church buildings, and fetid conditions for the priest who daily inhabited these walls. Under normal burial circumstances, bodies were placed beneath church floors and in adjoining patios with the appropriate measures taken to ensure that the floors would not sink. Usually the buried corpses were crushed beneath the blows of a pounder replacing nearly all the removed dirt so that the church floor would not sink. But even this ritual was too violent for many people. Stephens narrated a horrifying scene of the burial of a child:

> The floor of the church was earthen, and the grave was dug inside, because, as the sexton told me, the father was rich and could afford to pay for it, and the father seemed pleased and proud that he could give his child such a burial place. The sexton laid the child in the grave, folded his little hands across its breast, placing there a small rude cross, covered it over with eight or ten inches of earth, and then got into the grave and stomped it down with his feet. He then got out and threw in more, and going outside of the church, brought back a pounder, being a log of wood about four feet long and ten inches in diameter, like the rammer used among us by paviors, and again taking his place in the grave, threw up the pounder to the full swing of his arm, and brought it down with all his strength over the head of the child. My blood ran cold. As he threw it up a second time I caught his arm and remonstrated with him, but he said that they always did so with those buried inside the church; that the earth must be all put back, and the floor of the church made even. My remonstrances seemed only to give him more strength and spirit. The sweat rallied down his body, and when perfectly tired with pounding he stepped out of the grave. But this was nothing. More earth was thrown in, and the father laid down his hat, stepped into the grave and the pounder was handed to him. I saw him throw it up twice and bring it down with a dead, heavy noise. I never beheld a more brutal disgusting scene. The child's body must have been crushed to atoms.[2]

Stephens was not alone in his disgust. Some indigenous peoples prevented the crushing of the bodies of their loved ones during burials in church floors

and courts and this complicated the sanitary conditions of the church still   37
further. Father Pedro Gutierrez wrote from Santa Clara la Laguna in 1868 to complain that village inhabitants still continued to bury in the church cemetery and these bodies were poorly interred since "the people were not accustomed to compacting the earth with a pounder because they believed that the corpses conserved sensibilities."[3] Even the simple burial process of pounding the earth threatened the strong link between the living and the dead. Tampering with any ritual associated with the dead provoked protests.

Moving the town cemetery to the village perimeter triggered such a response in the 1830s. Guatemala's liberal government led by Mariano Gálvez imported a number of political and social policies during the decade-long rule in order to bring the state into line with its European counterparts. Gálvez's legislation ranged from the imposition of a new legal code and trial by jury to civil marriages (see chapter 1). One important change sought to improve the sanitary conditions by relocating the town cemetery away from the local church. Gálvez's overall goal to modernize Guatemala required this move to protect the people's health. Although well-intentioned, Gálvez's top-down administration eroded his regime's capacity to govern. Within a short period a good portion of Gálvez's subjects revolted.

In line with new European enlightened policies, the Guatemalan legislature decreed in 1834 that cemeteries be built outside of towns. The new scientific thought coming from Europe, the doctrine of miasmas, held that a poisonous atmosphere resulted from the vapors of decomposing bodies. Relocating church cemeteries prevented deadly contamination with the infected air. In order to pay for the new cemeteries, funds for the new cemetery would be drawn from the church *fábrica* or municipality funds.[4]

Reaction to the new decree was swift and signaled ominous dangers to the Gálvez government, and priests equivocated in their stance on the new policies. As in San Miguel Totonicapan, Indian leaders from Momostenango lodged a protest against their priest because he forbade them to bury their dead in the church patio. The new cemetery was a mile away from the town. Local officials, defending government policy, threatened the Indians with machete blows and placed their town mayor or alcalde in jail. The Indians sought the aid of the church hierarchy in restoring their old cemetery.[5] In 1836, a municipality of Quiché fined its priest when it discovered that he was burying bodies in the church and not in the new cemetery located at the periphery of the town. The priest replied that the new cemetery was not sufficiently protected by walls and that animals and birds were eating the bodies. Although the government ordered him to improve and bless the new ceme-

38   tery, the priest refused. The priest's obstinateness led to rumors that he was fomenting insurrection against the government.[6]

The village elder in San Martin asked for the cemetery to be returned to the churchyard because the air that blew into town came from the cemetery side and carried with it disease and because the cemetery, located on rocky land, did not lend itself to deep burials. Animals were desecrating the bodies. His request was also denied.[7] From San Pedro Chipilapa at the height of the cholera epidemic in 1837 residents begged the government to move the cemetery back to the church because the unfinished cemetery walls were now crumbling, and lions, tigers, and coyotes were eating the bodies. The government denied their petition.[8]

Such decisions on the part of the Gálvez administration led to popular resistance. Writing from Cahabón, the priest wrote that more than seven hundred had died of cholera in 1837, and only two had requested funeral rites. The priest investigated the causes of this open resistance and discovered that when burials were relocated to the new cemetery animals desecrated the bodies. In response, the people buried bodies in the grounds of their own houses.[9]

Escuintla's priest, Antonio Carrillo, concluded that good intentions had surely inspired the 1834 law. Protecting the health of a town was judicious. But the authorities were out of touch with the realities of life in the countryside. To bury outside a town, the priest wrote, residents had to rip trees out of the ground just to be able to bury a body. By the time the mourners returned to their homes, pigs had already dug up half-buried bodies and were dragging them through the town streets, "trespassing on the heart of the child, the mother, the husband or relative of the deceased."[10] Secret burials were now occurring in the homes. Only reparation of the church cemetery, located in the town center, would restore the dignity of the Christian burial.

Rarely did clerical correspondence mention similar revolts among other Spanish-speaking peoples in the eastern highlands and lowlands. Most protests occurred where the indigenous populace dominated. Where sizable ladino populations outnumbered the indigenous community, no such intense protest followed relocations of the cemeteries. For example, relocation of the cemeteries in Zacapa proved to be uneventful.[11] Records indicate there was some lowland protest over the change, but not as much as in the indigenous highlands.

Evidence from research into preconquest Maya burial rituals explains part of the nineteenth-century proclivity to revolt among Indian peoples. Commenting on the remarkable continuity between preconquest and post-conquest Maya society, Linda Schele and David Freidel described how "both 39 the powerful and the humble buried their dead under the stones of their courtyards so that their ancestors could remain with them and hear the sounds of their descendants' children playing over their heads."[12] Moving the cemeteries to the outskirts of town would destroy that fragile link between the living and the dead, between the past and the present. Descendants of the great Maya empire in Guatemala would not permit such a fundamental rupture without protest.

Gálvez's policies had failed at several levels within Guatemala. Politically, his administration dictated legislation in a top-down manner and alienated a significant portion of Guatemala's inhabitants. Imposing European health standards without popular support only reinforced his isolation, and long-term resentments intensified between indigenous peoples and the descendants of Europeans. His policy also failed because there was no practical way of uniformly implementing the policy. If towns were asked to relocate cemeteries and fund them also, the financial burden by itself impeded the policy's success. A political policy rooted in the Enlightenment tampered with the people's religiosity and eventually led to the downfall of the Gálvez administration.

Rituals surrounding death and burial were filled with intense passion and gave meaning to the community. By themselves, the cemeteries reflected the nature of the community that sustained them. During his 1837 visit to Chiquimula, the U.S. diplomat John Stephens visited the old church, previously destroyed by earthquake and now located on the edge of town. The ruined church, first built by the Spanish upon the site of the old Indian village, was now holy ground. Inside the church, remarked Stephens, were the bodies and bones of the town's "principal inhabitants." Priests' and monks' bones filled the niches of the walls. Outside the church walls were the graves of the "common people, untended and uncared for with the barrow of laced sticks which had carried the body to the grave laid upon the top and slightly covered with earth. The bodies had decayed, the dirt fallen in, and the graves were yawning."[13] The very construction of the Chiquimula church and cemetery reflected the social structure of the community. It also linked the past with the present and the future. Any policies emanating from Guatemala's capital that sought to establish new cemeteries away from inhabited zones would divide a people from its past and thus erode its own power base.

Why had the people revolted over the relocation of the cemeteries? João Reis examined the results of similar social policies instituted in the 1830s in

40   Brazil. To understand the nature of the cemetery revolts Reis traced the evo-
lution of the town cemetery in Europe and in Brazil. In seventeenth- and
eighteenth-century France, relatives and friends maintained close proximity
with the dying. Once dead, the living buried the remains of their loved ones
in the local church or in cemeteries that were unquestionably integrated into
the community. Reis observed that the sacred and the profane mingled together in popular fiestas and celebrations. Buried within churches, or in plots
attached to the cathedrals, death was a festive, community event, and members of the town remained a part of the community even after death.[14]

With the advancement of the Enlightenment in the eighteenth century,
an increasingly secularized society progressively divided this cohabited world
of the living and the dead. Public funerals gave way to private funerals, and
medical interests overtook religious interests in dealing with the dead. Reis
comments that "a hostile attitude" challenged the nearness of the dead with
the living. Doctors were quick to point out that the corrupt, decomposing
body represented a medical threat, and so cemeteries were moved to the outskirts of towns. During the 1760s and 1770s, laws were passed forcing the relocation of cemeteries outside of towns, away from plots attached directly to
churches. After the French Revolution, in 1804, strict regulations prohibited
church burials, distanced cemeteries from towns, and regulated the space between burial plots within cemeteries.[15]

Though urban peoples accepted the new laws in France, many rural
groups resisted and revolted. In a small French town in 1778, a group from
the village attacked the new cemetery, destroyed its walls, and transferred the
religious relics back to the old cemetery. Similarly in Bahia, Brazil, when in
1836 a law went into effect prohibiting burials in churches, the townspeople
attacked and destroyed the new cemetery. During the melee, shouts of
"Death to the cemetery!" were heard throughout the crowd.[16] So too in
Guatemala's Totonicapan. Relocating the cemetery was all that was required
for Totonicapan's Indians to challenge the ladino class with armed conflict.

Ostuncalco's priest told the visiting archbishop the history of the cemetery ordeal in his village. Before Father Chinchilla arrived in Ostuncalco in
February 1835, no priest had successfully relocated the cemetery. Within two
months, however, Chinchilla built the new cemetery and, five years later,
completed a chapel for the funeral mass. But in 1840 four different towns,
including Ostuncalco's indigenous leaders, requested General Carrera to
reestablish burials in the old cemetery, and their request was granted. To re-
inforce this victory in 1848, the Indians burned the new chapel to the

ground.[17] Once again, the new cemetery had been killed, and Carrera's gov-   41
ernment had aided the effort.

Carrera pressured the Constituent Assembly in October 1839 to suspend
the earlier law moving cemeteries outside of towns until new cemeteries were
built "that satisfy the opinion of the people."[18] Carrera's political move solidified his popularity among Guatemala's diverse constituency by empower-
ing them. The result was not only a temporary reprieve from the outlying
cemetery but was an acknowledgment of the strengthened autonomy of indigenous peoples and their religiosity.

With the political opening created by Carrera's success, many Indians
began relocating the cemeteries to the churches and resisted any priestly ma-
neuver to block them. Writing from the Cahabón in 1847, Father Baldwini
told how the Indians had been burying their dead in the church since Carrera's insurrection, and he reported that the bones of those previously buried
outside the town in the new cemetery, during the Gálvez administration,
were brought and reinterred in the old church cemetery. Two years later,
Baldwini founded a new cemetery on the outskirts of town to "disinfect the
church," but the Indians abandoned that one also, "destroying the church's
brick floor in order to bury the dead."[19] Evaluating the funeral rituals among
the Indians in 1848, Father Muñoz told the archbishop that the Indians in
Sacapulas were not accustomed to church funeral rites but did pay for the
church bells to be tolled, three times for the death of a male, two times for a
female. When he arrived in Sacapulas, he discovered that the Indians were
burying within the church's old cemetery adjacent to the sanctuary and continued to do so if he was not present in the town. Muñoz verified similar difficulties in Cunen and San Miguel. When the old cemetery was locked up
tight, the people made holes in the wall and tore off the lock in order to gain
entrance and light candles over the graves during mass.[20] The interim priest
in Tejutla complained in 1848 to the archbishop that no one was using the
cemetery located on the outskirts of town. All preferred the cemetery adjacent to the church. He had endured insults in his attempt to persuade the
Indians to bury outside of town, but his explanations of the unsanitary conditions and of the holy and civic laws were not compelling. "The Indians tell
me that they are not dogs to be buried in the cemetery outside of town."[21]

Reverends Baldwini and Muñoz typified church clerics in this conflictive
dynamic between Enlightenment policies and popular religiosity. Some
priests resisted moving the cemetery, while others refused to bury within the
church. Clerics were caught between loyalty to their parishioners and obedi-

42   ence to religious and public officials. When village elders petitioned for the return to the traditional cemetery in June 1839, San Martin's *cura* charged that the Indians were taking advantage of the political circumstances. Prior to Carrera's triumph, the priest remarked, there had been no problem associated with burying in the new cemetery. Rabinal and Momostenango won a reprieve and returned to burying inside the church. The October 1839 law only reinforced Carrera's growing popularity among the multiethnic peoples of Guatemala and served to alienate rural clerics from their indigenous parishioners.[22]

Father Francisco Lemus wrote of his terror in Santa María Chiquimula when he received news of the coming cholera epidemic in 1837. He told how he begged local officials to move the cemetery outside of town to prevent the spread of cholera. Local officials responded to the priest's plea by saying that "they had not obeyed General Gúzman's orders, and even less could they respond to his request." The governors of Santa María Chiquimula defended their intransigence on the basis that they buried in the cemetery traditionally used by their ancestors. The priest explained that he risked contamination, since his parish house was located within this very cemetery, and "he begged them with love exhausting all words of persuasion for them to obey governmental orders."[23]

People living in the surrounding area of Santa María Chiquimula soon heard of Father Lemus's plea to move the cemetery, and a group went to the parish house to talk with the priest. Unanimously, the group confronted the priest and warned him that if town officials were forced to move the cemetery to the outskirts of town, they were prepared to bury on their own land and would not be needing any priest. This group went on to insult the priest, branding him as "useless," and accusing him of poisoning the waters with cholera. Father Lemus concluded that the result was that many parishioners refused to take any sacraments for fear that the holy oil contained poison. The padre tendered his resignation.[24]

The priest in Santa María Cahabón, Father Eugenio Cordova, experienced similar accusations and rejection, and he also resigned. During the 1837 cholera epidemic, the cura searched for the dying so that he could administer the last rites. But, the priest despairingly remarked, this "inhumane and indolent" people rejected him outright. His parishioners told him that "we do not want a priest for any reason because the priest has killed the people of the town." Refusing to accept this rejection, Father Cordova searched in houses looking for the sick and dying and realized that his parishioners were hiding the dying from him or locking the doors and refusing him entrance. The priest confessed to church authorities that just a few hours after his failed entreaties he saw the people pass by with their dead heading off "to plant in the atrium of the church and parsonage the cadavers with depraved intention while others bury the bodies of their loved ones in their own houses."[25] Soon thereafter, Father Cordova fled Cahabón to avoid personal injury.

Later, with continued disease periodically ravaging Guatemala, many of the clerics begged authorities for the burials to be transferred out of the village. The Momostenango clergyman reported in 1847 that the commonly used burial ground was just five or six yards from the church sanctuary, and cadavers recently sepulchered were touching each other. The corregidor approved with a stern warning: be aware of the "irrational resistance" of the Indians and their respect for their ancient customs.[26] Indeed many of the clergy feared for their lives for two reasons: if they did not move the cemetery they might die from contamination; if they did move the cemetery their actions might spark a revolt from which personal injury could result.

In 1848, the cura from Cajolá lamented the complete rejection of his spiritual help during burials from "these disgraceful parishioners." He was completely powerless, unable to prevent the burial of bodies in the church cemetery, "just a few yards from my bedroom."[27] Although Carrera's triumph translated into an immediate victory for some church interests, priests were jeopardized by the popular victory. For centuries clerics had profited from popular religion and its fortuitous convergence with many Catholic practices. The padres had encouraged such church burials, but now their scientific knowledge outdated that of their followers. Now many priests believed that the cemeteries threatened their health. The clerics' inability to control their flock bred both contempt for and well-grounded fear of the Indians. Other clerics expressed similar feelings. These Indians, according to the future archbishop Bernardo Piñol who pastored in the region of Quezaltenango, were "blood-thirsty" in character and "inclined to revolution."[28]

The dangers associated with the continued burials in churches were complicated by the nearly complete rejection of priestly authority during funeral rites in the western indigenous highlands. Empowered by Carrera's triumph, and taking advantage of a weakened clergy, many indigenous communities began a spiritual reconquest of lost traditions within the barest framework of Catholicism. From the late 1830s to the early 1850s, this triumphant spirit was evidenced most notably in funeral rituals. The drop in the number of priests in the countryside provided the essential opening for the emergence of this religious lay leadership. In 1844, fewer full-time minis-

44 ters pastored parishes in the indigenous highlands compared to coveted parishes in the eastern highlands.[29]

Because of the rapid decline of priests in the countryside, local indigenous leaders assumed more religious authority and carried out many of the rituals associated with the Catholic church. Chanters *(cantores)*, Indian officials *(fiscales)*, and choirmasters *(maestros de coro)* directed most of the burial rituals within the indigenous communities and sometimes even directly challenged the priest assigned to the village. During the crescendo of Carrera's insurrection in 1837, Father Cordova sought to update church records on deaths in Cahabón but the community responded by threatening to kick him out of town: when the cura implored them to help him comply with the government's wishes, the Indians sarcastically told him, "If you want to know who and how many are dead, go to the cemetery, count the graves, and ask them for their names."[30]

In Cajolá Father Sabino de Leon related to the archbishop in 1848 how the Indians performed their own burials. From the house to the church, with the cross and the scepter raised, the choirmasters chanted and sprinkled holy water on the procession, and the priest did not even realize the funeral was taking place. Father Sabino de Leon complained to the archbishop that these choirmasters were themselves blessing the holy water; he demanded an end to these abuses and disorder because the "Indians were very daring."[31] In Momostenango, the priest struck out against the cantores who were performing burials. The church was in such ruin, the priest lamented, that the "great truths and observances of Religion had been mutilated by other divinities, other priests, other rituals, refusing to acknowledge the honesty and virtue, the advantages of grace and spirit."[32]

Nancy M. Farriss, in her study of the Yucatan Maya during the colonial period, suggested that "*maestros cantores* and their assistants presided over the burials of all but the wealthiest Indians, who alone could afford the curates' fees for an elaborate funeral."[33] In Guatemala, some evidence indicates that during the colonial period Indians conducted burials. In San Pedro Carchá, the priest noted that "since time immemorial" the fiscales directed the burial services, and with new laws governing burial sites many people buried bodies covertly so as to bypass the restrictions.[34]

As early as the pastoral visits of 1846, religious workers appealed to the sixteenth-century Mexican Councils, which had forbidden such lay participation, to condemn the role of Indian officials and chanters in performing burial services.[35] But protests from the clerical ranks in many parts of the indigenous highlands in Guatemala during the nineteenth century reflected a

church struggling to regain control of basic Catholic rituals recently lost to   45
the lay leaders. What had been a nuisance in the colonial period appeared to
be pandemic in Guatemala's nineteenth century.

In 1852, the Tactic priest offered to perform burial services for free
among the indigenous peoples, hoping this would resolve the church's
dilemma. But the Indians refused his pro bono offer; only the Indian fiscales
performed the services. The 1848 civil war had unleashed a series of reprisals
against ladinos, as in the neighboring village of Chamiquin, so the cura
yielded his priestly role in burials to the Indian officials since he feared vin-
dictiveness and rebellion.[36]

During the late 1850s and early 1860s many vacant posts were finally
filled with more permanent appointments, and with Carrera's support many
church clerics were now more successful in controlling and performing
church burials. As the cura from San Pedro Carchá in the Verapaz region reported in 1864, the church clerics were performing the majority of the funeral rituals. Whereas only four of every eight adults who died in this community had been buried with church sanction between 1846 and 1856, and
only one of eight did so between 1856 and 1858 (when there was no church
cleric), since 1858 six out of eight adults who died received church sacraments.[37] The turnaround points to a somewhat revitalized clergy in
Guatemala's countryside, and the church's increasing ability to monitor burials.

The provincial vicar Muñoz informed the archbishop in 1866 that in
Huehuetenango his campaign to relocate church cemeteries had been successful only in the principal city, for it was impossible to go against traditions
in the countryside. In Chimaltenango, two cemeteries were established along
racial lines: one for ladinos in the north part of town, and one for Indians,
located south of Chimaltenango. In San Andrés Itzapa, the cemetery was relocated out of town without provocation in 1856. After successfully relocating the cemetery to the outskirts of town in Momostenango, one priest complicated this victory by burying a wealthy member of the community in the
adjoining church cemetery.[38]

Yet victory was still not complete in the struggle to locate the village
cemetery outside of town. In Retalhuleu, Father Fernando Aguado relied on
authorities to prevent more burials. By the time of the 1857 cholera epidemic
the churches had become "foci of corruption" and the priest threatened not
to aid the dying. When his parishioners defied his threat, Father Aguado
called in government officials to enforce his request. In Chichicastenango, a
town of between eighteen and twenty thousand inhabitants, the priest called

46   for the cemetery to be moved outside of town. Each year, the priest complained, constant fevers ravaged the town despite the cool climate. And Father Abella reported from the Verapaz region that many Indians were still burying their dead in the mountains and refusing to inform the priest, so as not to pay for the funeral rituals.[39]

    The impact of the cemetery revolts was twofold. Popular protest over the cemeteries' locations was integral to the liberal state's unraveling in the late 1830s. Carrera had built much of his regime's prestige on his ability to respond to community complaints and to construct a regime that empowered its people to assume control of their communities, which thus ensured the integrity of the state. Second, the cemetery rebellions encouraged lay religious leadership in the western indigenous highlands. The diminishing numbers of clerics in the countryside gave cause for local religious leaders to assume more control in the religious rituals of death and burial.

Religious Revolts

    When the historic conjuncture in Guatemala provided more space for political expression, especially through religious movements, church and state responded to co-opt or repress the threat if that popular religiosity challenged their hegemony. In November 1859, the first mayor of Solomá reported that five miles from Santa Eulalia, a boy "proclaiming himself to be God" was causing quite a stir among the Indian peoples. This man-god was causing a perpetual fiesta among the people, collecting large amounts of money, with many of the Indians lighting candles and venerating him. More than sixty armed men now accompanied the boy. The command post of Los Altos sent orders to capture the boy and asked the local priest to work to "extirpate the foreign ideas" that this "impostor" was inculcating among the indigenous peoples.[40]

    At the end of the civil war in Guatemala's eastern mountains in 1851, a similar man-god movement had already been snuffed out by Carrera's loyal troops. The first mayor of the village of Jocotán reported to Carrera's regional leader Vicente Cerna that a group of Indians were preparing for armed confrontation with the government. An Indian named Pio Perdido claimed that the Apostle James (in Spanish, Santiago) had appeared to and spoken with his son Angel Perdido and called on him "to liberate" the mountaineers from the cruelties that besieged the people. In Jocotán, the Perdido family was celebrating the apostle's arrival when the military commander Vicente Cerna captured and jailed them and twelve Indians, also confiscating sixteen rifles.[41]

On the site of a long-standing conflict between indigenous communi- 47
ties, the church became embroiled in a struggle over priestly authority in a
community spiritually reconquered by preconquest traditions. From the first
pastoral visit to the region (Sololá and Totonicapan) in 1846 came the reports
of widespread and uninhibited preconquest religious practices among the Indians of Santa Catarina Ixtahuacán and neighboring villages. The faith was
"a mountain of ruins," proclaimed one priest. From the perspective of the
Catholic clerics "native superstitions and popular European errors transmitted by the conquerors" gave rise to diverse and errant practices among the Indian peoples. As if admitting defeat, the cleric confessed that the faith of the
indigenous people "was the same as that before being conquered with some
very small Christian notions and practices added on." The cleric wrote to the
archbishop in his report that Indian officials Miguel García and Diego Chox,
to add insult to injury, prayed to the Sun God in front of him![42]

In the adjoining canton of San Miguel one Indian religious leader,
Miguel Solzon, entered the church, dressed himself in the sacred vestments
of the priests, and danced in the church. The choirmaster Tomás Ahpop was
also accused of this sacrilege, and in 1844 Miguel Soom was fingered as the
choirmaster who used baptismal waters for his "exorcisms." In 1848, Soom
was surprised by a visit from Father Hernández who discovered the physical
impression upon Soom's brow to fit the priestly crown. After these two particular incidents, Father Hernández removed the church ornaments and vestments and locked the chapel doors in San Miguelito.[43]

These two particular incidents followed another more prominent challenge to Catholicism. Hernández recalled that in 1838 Don Nicolás Dubón
was returning from the coast with his spouse around midnight and saw the
door of the oratory opened. Inside one of the Indians had dressed himself
with the church vestments of an alb and chasuble. Standing in front of a
cross the Indian burned copal and let it fall into a hole and then began to say
mass with the village people lighting a large quantity of candles. Hernández
expressed his confident opinion that these ceremonies took place from 10
P.M. to 12 midnight, and that the midnight mass in church followed a large
procession through the village.[44]

Through the informer and current governor of Santa Catarina Ixtahuacán, Manuel Tzoc, Hernández discovered that the priest Ali-Chiam
from the canton Payajul had dedicated a cave for his sacrifices and had sup-
posedly sacrificed an unbaptized child. The brothers Chiam were thrown in
jail, and Governor Tzoc attempted to verify the accusation. The brothers
Chiam countered by accusing Father Hernández of causing a fever in the vil-

48   lage. Father Hernández and the governor spent three days deliberating with the townspeople in order to pacify their fears. The record does not indicate the fate of the brothers Chiam.[45]

A couple of months later, Lucia Quiq accused Antonio Tambris before Santa Catarina Ixtahuacán's governor of killing her eighteen-month-old child with a spell. She discovered his spell by consulting with three "priests of the God of the Sun"—Juan Tay, Miguel Suc, and Diego Con—who confirmed Tambris's actions. When the governor called the three priests before him, they denied any role in the alleged death and the governor made them perform the same ritual to identify the culprit. Upon its conclusion, they said that Tambris was innocent. The governor then forced the Sun priests to perform their ritual in front of Father Hernández. Juan Tay "bowed before him and begged the governor to excuse him from the shame of performing the ceremony in front of Hernández." Since Tambris's life was at stake, the governor forced Tay to perform the ceremony.

Tay placed the lid of a china vase at the head of a row of pieces of crystal rock. In front of the row of crystal rocks, he placed a handful of colored beans, blew on three fingers, and made the gesture of taking them, but did not touch them. Instead, he made several signs over them at least three times, concluding fearfully by taking a portion of the beans with four fingers and placing them in two rows, two by two, leaving one bean unpaired. Over each bean he pronounced the name of a day of his almanac (tenth of *toj*, thirteen of *tijar*, ninth of *cat*) until he finished with the tenth of *tzii*, and declared the man innocent.[46]

Hernández considered his efforts almost successful in order to rid Santa Catarina Ixtahuacán of its ancestors' pagan religion. He realized that he confronted a "hierarchical order of priests and ministers of the Sun" in his battle and thought he succeeded for the most part except in the legendary hamlet of San Miguel.[47] In a letter supporting Hernández's work in Santa Catarina Ixtahuacán, Pedro Valenzuela reflected on previous political measures carried out by civil and religious authorities who had struggled equally with the people of San Miguel. The resistance was so strong "in previous times" that both civil and religious leaders tried to disperse the people away from San Miguel, forcing their incorporation into adjoining towns. Valenzuela cynically remarked that the great epidemics that swept this part of the country "cooperated" through the lack of ventilation and poor sanitation in San Miguel by decimating the village more so than others.[48]

Hernández reflected in a letter to the archbishop the sadness that overcame him to see "the indifference and ridicule he endured from the practice

of the most refined native religion." Hernández wrote that he feared "for the   49
luck of the Catholic clergy in this country where Catholicism is barely sustained by tradition and good appearance."[49] As mediators of the faith, the
clerics confronted an invigorated religious tradition that had not acquiesced
to their priestly persuasion. Only with the supportive arm of the state behind
them did these religious professionals succeed in subduing the followers of
the Sun God. In their age-old reliance on force, the priests had become
agents of control once again.

Cofradías

Not all popular religious movements manifested such an open confrontation with the dominant culture as did the man-god phenomenon and
the religious revolt of San Miguel. Various methods emerged among the Indian communities to protect and enhance their religious autonomy. Some
indigenous groups worked within the formal Catholic structure of the religious brotherhoods, the cofradías, while neglecting to comply with the or-
ganizing rules laid down by the Catholic hierarchy, and others sought the intervention of the popular caudillo to block forced participation. Still others
took advantage of tensions between clerics and corregidores in order to ac-
complish their goals.

As the Catholic church moved to restore its institutional base during the
Carrera years, the archbishop tried to get a picture of the strength of the religious cofraternities.[50] Most had suffered financially during the 1830s and
1840s but some recovered quite well during the economic boom years of the
1850s. No clear regional pattern emerged in an analysis of the cofradía
strength as recorded in pastoral correspondence from the 1830s through the
1860s, though two variables did consistently interact to produce financially
solvent cofradías: an improving local economy and committed priests who
watchdogged their investments and expenditures.

Scattered reports throughout the country in the 1860s indicate many
cofradías were struggling to survive or even closing due to insufficient funds
or lack of popular support. Curas reported that the religious sodalities in
Cuyotenango did not have a cent while those in the highland Olintepeque
were on the verge of closing. The number of cofradías in Villa Nueva had
been cut in half, and those in Chimaltenango region were nearly broke. In
1848 Cuilco's cofradías had a combined total of 1,258 pesos but by 1861 this
had dropped to 894 pesos.[51]

To conclude that all cofradías were at the brink of collapsing throughout

50   the country, however, is to overstate the case. Some parish cofradías dramatically increased their capital savings during the Carrera regime. The cofradías in San Pedro Sacatepéquez, tucked away in the western highlands near Quezaltenango, more than doubled their capital assets from 2,000 pesos in 1848 to more than 4,000 pesos in 1861. Coban's eighteen cofradías possessed 2,500 pesos in 1831, but twenty cofradías tripled its assets to more than 8,000 pesos by 1856. Neighboring Rabinal experienced similar growth with 2,635 pesos of capital in 1841 compared to 3,029 in 1864. In Guatemala's core, Conguaco's cofradías guarded 800 cattle in 1852 and cared for more than 1,200 head of cattle just seven years later.[52]

    Many of the cofradías hesitated to turn over records (if they even kept any) to the visiting archbishop's entourage or to newly arrived priests for inspection or for verification of their officers in elections. Resistance to outside meddling in the lay-led organization ranged from impeding priestly supervision to utilizing the corregidor to halt unfair demands made by the priest. In 1838 cofradía leaders in Coban, by completely abandoning their bookkeeping, successfully fooled the interim priest into believing that their organizations were in financial ruin. The Ostuncalco cleric complained in 1848 that the archbishop's pastoral visit did not rectify the cofradías: they continued to keep their own disorganized books. The archbishop critized the Momostenango cofradías for irregularities in elections and in management of funds and for indifference toward clerical authority. The ladino cofradías kept the amount of their savings secret while the Indian brotherhoods' records were so obtuse the priest could not understand them. After his pastoral visit to Huehuetenango, the archbishop discovered that neither Indians nor ladinos prepared their records for his visit and ordered the cleric to take charge in organizing them.[53]

    In 1853 Padre Juan Raull sought to resign his post in Totonicapan because of the climate and his incompatibility with the Indians. Raull complained that the Indians held elections for their cofradías without notifying him and distributed its money secretly. He affirmed that if he dared intervene he would only stir up their hatred. Writing from San Jacinto near Chiquimúla, one of the principal centers of Catholic support, the Indians protested against turning over their cofradía books since to do so would "change their traditions." Another cleric writing from the Mita region complained that the Indians blocked his free access to the cofradía records "pushing me out of the way several times in the process." And from San Cristobal Acasaguastlán, the interim cleric bitterly declared that the Indians believe they are "the exclusive owners" of the cofradía's properties. Conguaco's cofradías' successful increase in their capital assets led to conflicts between the parishioners and the town cleric, who charged in 1855 that the cofradías were being robbed by their drunken overseers.[54]

Many different triangular relationships emerged surrounding disagreements and mutual expressions of disgust among corregidores, priests, and the people. Some parishioners implored a corregidor or Carrera to rein in their abusive priest. Others encouraged church authorities to use their influence to remove unjust judges in local towns. Many corregidores supported popular petitions to Carrera imploring him to halt the removal of a town priest when all appeals to the church authorities had failed.

In an interesting twist of power politics during the first, unstable decade of the caudillo's regime, a number of parishioners from Mataquescuintla begged the corregidor to intervene in their behalf because they could not fulfill all their financial obligations to the parish priest. The priest countered that the majordomos were disposing of cofradía assets without seeking the approval of the clergy.[55] Evidently, these parishioners and others sought the intervention of their townsmen who held the reins to power in Guatemala City in order to counter clerical authority. A legislative decree ordered church officials not to compel the people to participate in the cofradías. The priest in Mataquescuintla received a letter from the Supreme Government preventing clerics from obliging Indians to participate in any cofradía against their will since the cofradías "were ruining the towns."[56]

This conflict in the cofradías highlights the fascinating relationships emerging in postcolonial Guatemala between church officials, state authorities, and parishioners. Each cofradía operated under written agreements to hold a certain number of masses and patron saint celebrations during each calendar year. These masses and celebrations were in large part funded by cofradía investments in land and its rental, the sale of cattle or other domestic animals, or loans. Where cofradía funds were short, wealthier leaders were expected to make up the difference. By virtue of its attachment to the institutional Catholic church, cofradía members de jure could not dispose of its property or wealth without the consent of Catholic officials. With the weakening of the Catholic church and the diminishing numbers of priests in the 1830s, Catholic sodalities either disappeared or invigorated a confident lay leadership. When the church began to reconstitute itself in the 1840s, priestly intervention in the affairs of cofradías became a reality once again. As in the case of Mataquescuintla, correspondence indicates that cofradía members resisted the return of clerical interference and appealed to the state to protect their autonomy. The state, by virtue of decree, annulled the written agree-

52 ment between the Catholic church and its cofradías. Church officials acquiesced to the state's demands and lowered financial obligations and eliminated
certain cofradía celebrations but only on a case-by-case basis.[57]

Some cofradías took advantage of Carrera's decree designed to give them
breathing room from the financial demands placed upon them by clerics. Indians from San Cristobal Acasaguastlán in 1855 appealed to the 1847 law in
order to resist clerical demands to verify cofradía records and funds. And understanding all too well the explosive political potential of indigenous
groups, the Catholic hierarchy was more than ready to comply with indigenous demands. One cura mediated with the Indians from Nejapa who were
insisting on being relieved from the financial duress of cofradía obligations.
The "repugnancy" these Indians felt was cause enough for the church to realize that political opponents could easily take advantage of the Indians' dis-
satisfaction, and the church agreed to lower much of the financial require-
ments upon the Indian cofradías in Nejapa.[58]

Other Indians used the cofradías as a shelter from the labor demands of
a growing capitalist society. Town officials from Tecpan Guatemala complained to the corregidor about the "abandoned state" of the Indians due to
the "abusive" demands of their cofradías, which reduced them to "drunkenness and hatefulness." These authorities emphasized their disgust with the
cofradías by stating that rarely did a day go by without some sort of celebration emanating from the cofradías. With each fiesta, eight hundred pesos
were spent to fund the celebration, thus bankrupting the participants and
forcing others to flee the town to avoid the financial obligations. "Who suffered because of these religious demands of the cofradías?" they asked. The
town officials concluded that the ladinos lost money because they advanced
salaries to the Indians, which they never repaid in labor, and that public
works projects remained unfinished. The Indians defended themselves by reminding their bosses of the revolutionarily charged slogan emanating from
Carrera's movement: "You can't take away our traditions."[59]

In his letter to the government in Guatemala City, the corregidor verified the town officials' claim that the "traditions of the aborigines" proved
detrimental to the town's well-being. The cofradías' traditional celebrations
sucked away the Indians' savings, dismembered the towns, debilitated the
people, and contributed to "in a word—the moral and material destruction
of the people." What really perturbed the corregidor was the Indians' justification for their fiestas: tradition. Tradition was "a magical word among them
which enabled them to sustain their capricious celebrations with tenacity."[60]

What becomes clear in this analysis of popular religiosity in the indige-

nous highlands is that the church was the weakest link in the triangular   53
forces of state, church, and society. Caught up in the swirling vortex of political and social changes brought on by liberal policies, clerics faced difficult
choices between loyalty to one's parishioners and obedience to government
officials. Political expediency and deference to popular will with regards to
the location of the town cemetery placed clerics in precarious positions with
liberal governmental authorities. With Carrera's successful insurrection, clerics now were forced to reconcile popular will with the doctrine of miasmas.
By the 1850s and 1860s, clerics in larger towns were finally successful in relocating the town cemetery to the periphery.

Strong lay leadership emerged during the decline of priestly numbers in
the 1830s and 1840s. Clerics, preempted by indigenous religious leaders, attempted to gain control of the community's religious rituals. Only when
popular religiosity threatened the state's hegemony did Catholic officials
reconquer their lost religious authority. In most cases, where popular religiosity thrived within the Catholic structure, the padres were continually
frustrated by the sodalities' increasing autonomy. When Catholic leaders attempted to reestablish control over the cofradías by monitoring the sodalities' economic strength, then parishioners turned to the popular military
caudillo for state support and protection. Catholic officials relinquished final
authority in these new circumstances to the state personified by the caudillo,
Rafael Carrera.

Carrera, not the church, became the critical link between the peripheral
indigenous highlands and the capital. A weakened church with depleted
numbers never convincingly reestablished itself as the crucial mediator of indigenous claims. Church officials expended much energy in quelling the rising religious autonomy of the indigenous communities. Claims arising from
the indigenous highlands looked to the charismatic Carrera to vindicate indigenous interests against an encroaching ladino population, and Carrera
readily complied. During the 1857 cholera epidemic in Guatemala, both Carrera and church workers teamed up to stave off revolutionary threats.

The 1857 Cholera Epidemic

The cholera epidemics of 1857 tested Carrera's political hegemony
throughout the country. Whereas the 1837 cholera epidemic had served as the
catalyst to spark Carrera's successful insurrection against the liberal Gálvez,
the 1857 cholera epidemic did not spark widespread rebellion against Carrera's government. Why did the 1857 epidemic not give cause for similar up-

54 heavals in Guatemala? A brief look at both epidemics and at the institutional response to the epidemics suggests the nature of Carrera's support and the role of religion during both periods.

Gauging a government's popularity by measuring a population's response to an epidemiologic crisis offers the historian a chance to analyze various factors and influences pressuring a small country linked in some way to the world market. Internal and external pressures were present in both 1837 and 1857 cholera crises, and both the Gálvez and the Carrera governments took similar measures to check the spread of the disease as well as to contain any spread of panic associated with the mass numbers of dead in the larger cities. Church officials were directly involved in medicinal measures to control the spread of cholera and to prohibit the gatherings of large numbers of people. In both instances many people died, and panic spread among certain sectors of the population, and both governments were accused of poisoning the water. Yet Carrera's successful ability to link up with the popular sectors and the church's improving capacity to provide meaning to the people during the crisis enabled the government to survive the second epidemic.

Both 1837 and 1857 cholera epidemics devastated Guatemala. The few figures we have remaining demonstrate that both crises took their toll on the people. Clerics were responsible for yearly censuses of the church's population. With the absence of many clerics in the 1830s, pastoral reports fell way short. Scattered reports from parts of the country, however, provide an insight into the devastation. Comparing the death figures in 1837 and 1857, it seems twice as many died in Quiché, whereas Villa Nueva on the outskirts of Guatemala City was devastated in the 1857 cholera epidemic.[61] Witnessing the suddenness of the disease and the immediacy of death terrified the population.

Charles E. Rosenberg studied the cholera years in the nineteenth-century United States. He observed that the onset of cholera was "marked by diarrhea, acute spasmodic vomiting, and painful cramps. Consequent dehydration, often accompanied by cyanosis, gave the sufferer a characteristic and disquieting appearance; his face blue and pinched, his extremities cold and darkened, the skin of his hands and feet drawn and puckered."[62] Quoting the diary of a young man in Albany, New York, in 1832, Rosenberg noted that "to see individuals well in the morning and buried before night appalled the boldest heart."[63] Cholera unleashed an existential terror in individuals and potentially threatened the integrity of a government.

In response to the devastating effects of both epidemics, Guatemalan political and religious figures demanded that the church prohibit the tolling of church bells in memory of the dead and limit the number of masses in churches. With the church at loggerheads with the government in 1837, some resistance to limiting the number of people attending mass took place at that time; no similar protests occurred in 1857. Letters from government officials in 1837 repeatedly warned the church against violating emergency provisions, whereas no warnings were apparently issued during the 1857 epidemic. Additionally, some churches continued to ring bells in memory of the dead in 1837 and were threatened with a hundred-peso fine. The Gálvez government used quarantines to isolate villages affected by the disease, though no similar actions apparently took place in the 1857 epidemic. In short, some church clerics resisted full compliance in 1837 and attempted to subvert the government's authority, while no similar complaints were lodged in 1857 under the Carrera government.[64]

What were some of the key differences between the two crisis periods? In 1857 Archbishop García Peláez prohibited the placing of cadavers for viewing in churches, although many churches in 1837 were struggling to prevent the burying of bodies in church floors or adjacent patios. Remember that a good number of churches in Guatemala's periphery had successfully relocated the cemeteries to the outskirts of town by 1857. For example, the parish priest assigned to Santa Clara la Laguna reported that the cemetery on the outskirts of town was used during the 1857 cholera epidemic, and the Totonicapan corregidor informed his superiors that since 1855 the indigenous people had complied with authorities in burying outside of town.[65]

Though many villages had resigned themselves to the relocation of the village cemetery on the outskirts of towns, in 1857 many people still believed that cholera resulted from governors' and priests' poisoning the waters. Recall that during the 1837 cholera epidemic many in the eastern mountains held the Gálvez government responsible. Father Aqueche was pointed out as the instigator of this rumor, which mobilized forces soon to be loyal to the caudillo Carrera.[66] But the cholera epidemic gave cause for other prominent accusations too.

Priests were the favorite target of the accusations in both epidemics. At least six different priests throughout Guatemala were accused of poisoning the waters and were held responsible by the local community for the 1837 cholera epidemic: Anselmo Llorente in Santiago Atitlán, Juan José Solis in San Luis Xilotepeque, Ysidro Menéndez in Jutiapa, Francisco Lemus in Santa María Chiquimula, the parish priest in Jalpatagua, and Eugenio Cordova in Santa Maria Cahabón.[67] These multiple accusations against the priests gave way to various rumors that priests in general were responsible for the 1837 epidemic.[68]

In 1857 three clerics were accused of poisoning the waters: José María

56   Ycasa in Chiquimulilla, José Antonio Díaz in Mataquescuintla, and Felipe de Jesus Betancourt in Conguaco. Whereas such allegations were more widespread in 1837, the accusations were then confined to a smaller region of the eastern highlands. It is ironic that this particular region was the base of Carrera's 1837 insurrection. In Conguaco, the priest reported that three hundred armed men arrived to murder the cleric, but the heroic and fateful intervention of the governor Aniceto Morán saved the cleric, by unfortunately sacrificing his own life. Rafael Carrera was also accused of ordering a priest to poison the waters in Mataquescuintla, and the Indians in Chiquimulilla thought their priest became a sorcerer *(brujo)* and poisoned the waters by stealth of night. The priest was forced to swallow his medicines and two women and three Indians were killed in the uproar.[69]

Given the similar circumstances in 1837 and 1857, why did Gálvez fall and Carrera survive? First, the Gálvez administration had already lost popular support and could not move to put down the social breaches that occurred during the cholera outbreak. On the other hand Carrera's administration moved effectively to repress the outbreaks. In Chiquimulilla, the Indians accused of murder were put in jail and sentenced to death, and the leader of a similar revolt in the neighboring Guazacapán was executed.[70]

Second, the Gálvez government faced opposition and resistance from many clerics whereas by the late 1850s Carrera and the clergy had integrated their goals and strategies. Teams of regular and secular priests combed the hills and valleys of Guatemala during the mid-1850s seeking to shore up the weakened church. Gálvez and his government had created an environment of hostility toward the church, and clerics such as Aqueche evidently took advantage of the situation to undermine the popularity of the liberal government.

During the Carrera years Catholic priests worked to strengthen the Catholic church and to support the conservative regime. When cholera struck Guatemala in 1857 the Catholic leadership, the rural priests, and the caudillo all worked to ameliorate the situation. For example, the priest of Conguaco, after the murder of the governor and other abuses had taken place, called on the archbishop to send the Capuchins there.[71] Since August 1857, popular protests surfaced in Santa Rosa attacking the Carrera government. Again, some accused the government of poisoning the waters with cholera. Teams made up of regular priests became crucial to the pacification of eastern Guatemala, especially in the Department of Santa Rosa.

The Capuchin order had received authority since 1852 to begin work in Guatemala. By 1856 scores of Capuchin monks had arrived in Guatemala to

respond to the spiritual maladies besetting the nation. Immediate success in   57
Escuintla in December 1856 pushed to the forefront an aged cleric, Esteben
de Adoáin, who began a series of preaching missions to different parts of the
country. Testimonies concerning his sermons arrived in Guatemala City. Escuintla's corregidor wrote the archbishop praising the success of the Capuchins' missions, especially Adoáin's preaching, for they had filled the tem-
ples.[72]

Reflections recorded by the missionaries about their religious campaigns
in Santa Rosa agreed that the preaching of Esteben de Adoáin successfully
persuaded the people of Santa Rosa to pardon their enemies and to submit
to the authority of the government. Markedly old, with a long white beard
about a meter in length, Adoáin visited the majority of the towns in Santa
Rosa, and the people evidently received him each time with popular religious
processions. The preaching of the old cleric caused a "general commotion,"
a religious awakening among the people who crowded into the town
squares.[73]

In his sermons, Adoáin did not allude to the recent protests and rebellions inspired by the cholera epidemic; rather, he focused on the virtue of for-
giving one's enemies. Witnesses recounted that the words moved the ladinos
of Santa Rosa, and more than four thousand people came to hear him the
next day.[74] After explaining the depth of pardon offered by Jesus Christ, Father Adoain warned his listeners of the "divine wrath" for those who did not
forgive and who "spit out poison" at their neighbors.[75] His advice was clear:
the epidemic attacked the people who did not protect their religious faith.
The play on words in Spanish did not escape the listeners. "Divine wrath" *(la
cólera divina)* resulted in cholera *(el cólera)* and "the poisoning of hatred" paralleled the accusations of "poisoning the water." The Capuchin astutely had
taken the key phrases from popular accusations and refashioned them in
favor of the church and Carrera's government. Adoáin had adopted the theological language and insights of the capital.[76]

The most spectacular incident occurred when one of the chief leaders of
Carrera's armed forces publicly repented during the religious campaign in
Santa Rosa. Observers noted that General Antonio Solares was so moved
during the sermon of the aged Capuchin that he threw himself on his knees
in front of the whole crowd:

Spontaneously General Don Antonio Solares stood out, and
climbed the steps of the altar and threw himself on his knees beg-
ging the pardon of the soldiers who were in the church. Overcome,

58   his soldiers responded that they pardoned him. With a breaking
voice, the general asked for everyone to pardon him, included his
political adversaries and those who had taken up arms against him.[77]

Adoáin so succeeded with his preaching in many towns in Santa Rosa
that members of his religious team affirmed that even the coldest hearts of
the bitterest of enemies among families were warmed.[78] Data taken by par-
ticipating clergy indicate that an extraordinary number of people were baptized and received communion as a result of these religious campaigns. Clerical reports also indicate that "all, except for five, put down their arms and
the yearned-for peace was entirely reestablished."[79] From this point on, the
town of Santa Rosa became known for its faith to the church and its popular support of the Carrera government. One Jesuit, commenting on this religious mission to Cuajiniquilapa, Chiquimulilla, and Santa Rosa, reported
that all the religious campaigns were important, "especially Santa Rosa,
where its inhabitants were the fiercest of the army's fighters and at the same
time the most decided and faithful defenders of their religion and country."[80]
Clearly Carrera's administration was able to rely upon its base of popular support cultivated during the previous decade in order to withstand the
social breach caused by the 1857 cholera epidemic. Carrera's troops suppressed rebellions and executed those responsible for the turmoil, while clerics, by professing a convincing theological interpretation, made sense of or at
least created a religious meaning out of the devastating cholera epidemic.
Whereas the 1837 cholera epidemic created an opening for many prominent
clerics to oppose the government and resist any public measure of controlling public unrest, the 1857 epidemic proved the resilience of the political and
religious alliance that now governed Guatemala for mutual benefit.
During the first years of the caudillo's rule, clergy deferred to popular
protests concerning the location of the town cemetery and watched from the
sidelines as lay religious leaders emerged and fashioned the religious life of
the indigenous communities. Empowered by Carrera's victory and ready to
defend the caudillo, the indigenous people of the western highlands represented a formidable force in the internal balance of power in Guatemalan
politics. Carrera, as the final arbiter for the indigenous people, linked the remote communities to the growing nation. His ability to intervene on behalf
of the indigenous peoples created a powerful relationship that frightened the
white elite of the capital. Given the test of the 1857 cholera epidemic, which
devastated the country, Carrera's hegemony was reaffirmed. He and church
workers united to lessen the impact of the natural disaster and to cultivate a

popular loyalty and support base among those who had challenged the con-   59
servative coalition.

Discourse and conflict within the Spanish highlands and lowlands of Guatemala proved to be qualitatively different from that in the indigenous highlands. In these regions Catholic clerics evoked a religious notion of Guatemala's being a chosen nation, most notably during Independence celebrations. Civil war and foreign invasions compelled Carrera and the church to work together for mutual benefit. In the Spanish region, clerics responded by pacifying the internal rebellion and by rallying parishioners to the defense of the republic.

4   The Covenant

N^{O CLEARER TESTIMONY} evidences the social upheaval and
shifting political landscape in Guatemala in February 1838 than the graphic
narrative by the traveling U.S. diplomat John Lloyd Stephens. Recently arrived for the first time in the capital, Stephens witnessed the insurrectionary
triumph of the military caudillo Rafael Carrera and his "tumultuous mass of
half-naked savages, men, women, and children, estimated at ten or twelve
thousand." Stephens described how Carrera's indigenous followers, upon entering the abandoned plaza and within earshot of a terrified white elite,
shouted "Long live religion and death to foreigners!" A political uprising incited by religious concerns had laid siege to the entire pyramid of inherited
power.[1] For the next thirteen years, factions among Guatemala's minority
elite struggled to establish a tactical alliance with the powerful Carrera and
his indigenous constituency. Church leaders, in disarray and weakened by
liberal repression, sought to temper the insurrectionary fever and point the
way out of the spiraling violence that gripped parishioners. Clerical discourse
within the capital reflected on and responded to the social chaos and attempted to steer a course through the rugged political terrain. They offered
hope through an optimistic, theological interpretation of events that made
sense of the political convulsions by fomenting a sense of nation.

Upon Rafael Carrera's return from exile and his definitive defeat of the
montañeses (mountaineers) in the civil war that gripped Guatemala from 1848
to 1851, the clerics sought to establish a political and theological consensus
now backed by Carrera's perpetual presidency. Carrera came to depend upon,
even demanded, that clerics occupy parishes in war-torn areas in order to

pacify the region. He assumed that the priestly message and vision would
convince and unify the disparate factions dismantling Guatemala. During
the Carrera period the clergy responded to this historic opportunity by inventing and eliciting a nationalist notion of Guatemala.

During this thirty-year period clerical sermons systematically developed
a theological understanding of Guatemalan social events. The clergy used
biblical and philosophical criteria to affirm the good in society and prophet-
ically denounced the evils they believed would destroy the fabric of the social order. Their messages demonstrated a history of salvation for those peoples and nations that obeyed divine law and went on to characterize the
bloody revolutions that engulfed nations in horrible conflict as divine punishment for deviating from that law. If they were to be different from the nations engulfed in civil wars and to live in peace, Guatemalans would have to
protect their church and hold dear its sacraments. Guatemala was to become
like Israel, a chosen nation called upon to fulfill the law of God.

September 15, the anniversary of independence from the Spanish crown
in 1821, proved the crucial ritual celebration where religious and political in-
terpreters reassessed the past in order to fashion the future. Anniversary celebrations of Independence were established by the National Constituent Assembly in 1823 (the first one was held in 1824), while Guatemala still formed
part of the newly constituted Central American Federation. Records show
that anniversary celebrations were consistently held on September 15
throughout the nineteenth century.[2] By 1829, departmental heads were called
on to celebrate September 15 with a thanksgiving mass and street celebrations.[3] Even when the Catholic church was under pressure by Morazán and
his allies, religious leaders followed government orders to hold mass.[4] Only
in 1857 was no civic or religious function held, because of the cholera epidemic.[5]

During most Independence celebrations, religious and political leaders
convened for a mass and a sermon reflecting on independence. In the capital and at departmental administrative centers local officials, dignitaries, and
military leaders were the invited guests. For example, in 1845 leaders of the
principal corporations, public officials, foreign consuls, and other prominent
authorities made up the audience in the cathedral. Artillery salutes, the
tolling of church bells, and military bugle calls filled the air as elite capital
residents cleaned their house fronts and sidewalks and lit the streets in celebration. After his military and political triumph, Rafael Carrera was a fre-
quent participant and honored guest at these celebrations.[6]

During the 1830s liberal administration in Guatemala, the majority of

62 published anniversary speeches were delivered by secular political leaders. Thereafter, however, religious leaders' prayers and sermons dominated printed discourse until the successful liberal insurrection in 1871. From the late 1830s to the late 1840s, political speeches in the palace paralleled religious sermons in the cathedral. By the mid-1850s and throughout the 1860s, religious leaders maintained exclusive right over the interpretative significance of the celebration. One prominent cleric, Juan José de Aycinena, preached at least twelve of the twenty-eight sermons commemorating Independence from 1837 through 1864, wielding enormous influence in the yearly ritual. In addition, many copies of these imprints circulated outside Guatemala's capital.[7] Today, three-fourths of the speeches delivered from 1831 to 1871 survive in private and public archives.[8]

During the anniversary celebrations of the 1830s, liberal political discourse severely criticized Spanish conquest and its aggression against native peoples.[9] Liberal ideologues attempted to become the vicarious spokesmen of the fallen indigenous people as they denounced the monarchy and the Catholic church while preaching liberty and progress.[10] The *patria* for these speakers was all of Central America, not just the state territory known as Guatemala. Citizens would be guaranteed equality, but equality would come to mean the transformation of the Indian into a Spanish-speaking creole. The implementation of liberal policies (secularization of the state, colonization projects, unbridled faith in reason and progress) alienated the masses and ultimately translated into an attack on indigenous communities and lifestyles. In summary, as Lowell Gudmundson concludes, "Liberals' inability to develop a series of images, an identity, a discourse capable of galvanizing mass support was a basic problem."[11]

Catholic clerics responded to the religious dimension of the Carrera revolt, evolving a religious discourse that took into account both Carrera's indigenous support and the church's need to reconstitute a religious institution dismantled by liberals. In 1840 the Catholic cleric Aycinena called for the restoration of the peoples' traditions, an appeal that would simultaneously affirm the autonomy of indigenous communities and restore Catholicism to its previous rank. Those "traditions," he said, "were the authentic expression of the will of the people"; they had revolted in order to recover them. General Rafael Carrera was to be praised as the "Restorer of the people's custom."[12] Just three years earlier Aycinena had not been so confident of the rebels' intentions and had expressed an elite fear of the religious fanaticism of Carrera's "savages" as he appealed to the role of reason in molding traditions to the principles of eternal justice. He had commented in his 1837 anniversary homily that the majority indigenous peoples were "swallowed up in the most crass ignorance and didn't even understand our language." He wrote off their religious devotion as nothing but "idolatrous acts."[13] By 1840 Aycinena had changed his tune: not "savages" but "the people"; not "religious fanatics" but "protectors of our custom." Aycinena's reversal probably represented the effort of a fearful, white elite forced to come to terms with a successful insurrection of mestizos and Indians. By accepting this explosive political reality, Aycinena adroitly sought to formulate a tradition that included both Indians and the religious institution in the makeup of a new Guatemala.[14]

Thus the fear of social chaos became a dominant theme in religious discourse. Triumphant liberalism had led to institutional repression of the Catholic church, and now a victorious mass of Indians and mestizos threatened. What could rein in the passions that had led to these unsettling times? Achieving order and peace depended on the restoration of religion. The clerics' reflections were based on growing convictions that Guatemalans must commit themselves to the divine in order to calm the troubled sea of revolution continually threatening Guatemala.

The calls for a restored tranquillity would be based on the primacy of the church. José Nicolás Arellano and Basilio Zeceña joined Aycinena in claiming historical confirmation for the principle that, without religion, neither society nor liberty would endure.[15] Aycinena proclaimed that "a people without religion cannot have morals, and a people without morals are incapable of governing themselves. For this reason, governments, whatever their form may be, ought to protect Religion as a base of public morality, as fundamental to good traditions. Without these elements, Republics cannot survive." Bloody revolutions indicated that a given nation was founded on human interests, not divine. As in the biblical period of the judges, nations were destroyed for departing from the path of God.[16] Francisco García Peláez drove home this point in his 1843 anniversary sermon: like the Hebrews who spent forty years wandering in the desert because of their rebellion, so too Guatemala had spent twenty-two years aimlessly roving since Independence.[17]

These ecclesiastical authorities were not without hope even as they warned of societal doom. Recourse from the horrible epidemic of war lay in religion, the "cement of the social edifice."[18] France, stated Aycinena, was capable of transforming itself into an ordered country out of the carnage of revolutionary war only by reestablishing Catholicism. With the restoration of Catholicism by Bourbon forces in France, religion, the solid rock of society,

64   had produced peace among the French. No institution or political theory, claimed Aycinena, could match the Christian principle of brotherly love, which assured true liberty and kept people united.[19]

The central theological motif that emerged in these anniversary sermons was the divine pact or covenant between God and his people, realized first with the chosen people of Israel through their leader Moses and then for all believing people through Jesus of Nazareth, the Christ. The first hint of this theology can be traced back to what could be called the first anniversary sermon of Independence, preached by Guatemala's vicar general José Maria Castilla in 1821: "We must be virtuous if we desire heaven to protect our liberty." Quoting scripture, Castilla called all to "be faithful to our religion, and we will be blessed; if not, God will turn us over to ourselves, and we will become prisoners of our enemies."[20] The religious historian Agustín Estrada Monroy credits Castilla with turning the tide of debate in favor of independence that very day as Castilla publicly broke with the Guatemalan archbishop Casáus y Torres who had vigorously opposed independence from Spain. Doubtless due to Castilla's continued educational and administrative leadership roles, his theological insight was reflected over the coming decades in the sermons of many fellow clerics.[21]

Prior to Independence most clerics understood the covenant community to comprise the Spanish monarchy and its bountiful lands in the Americas. In a sermon celebrating Spain's supposed liberation from Napoleon in 1808, the Dominican Luis Escoto proclaimed that God had placed Spanish Europe and America under the protective embrace of Holy Mary, the Divine Mother.[22] During the same festive occasion the archdeacon of Guatemala's Catholic church Dr. Sicilia y Montoya compared the Spanish monarchs Charles IV and his son Ferdinand VII to Abraham and Isaac, respectively. Ferdinand's ascension to the throne in 1808 was nothing less than the intervention of the angel of the Lord in favor of the monarchy.[23] Sermons prior to Independence thus reflected a covenant between the Spanish monarchy and God.

Some clerics identified Central America as the "nation" due to their experience with the Central American federation in the 1830s. In late 1839 the exiled archbishop, writing from Havana, mourned the continued wars in Guatemala and the inability "to consolidate a new order, a permanent peace and the union of the states."[24] Manuel Zacarías Velasquez preached during his 1844 sermon that the compassionate God had spared "Central America" from the wars of independence.[25] But the chief political ideologue and elite clergyman, Aycinena, challenged the organic unity of the federation and propagated the theological vision of God's covenant with the Guatemalan nation alone.

While writing from exile in the United States in the 1830s, Aycinena ridiculed the federation's inception as a political idea forced upon its people in a "top-down" fashion. As a representative to the Convention of Central American states in 1839, he authored congressional decrees permitting Central American states to reconstitute themselves, thus formally weakening the federal alliance.[26] With Morazán's execution in 1842 (on September 15, no less) the fragile federation crumbled. In March 1847 Guatemala was declared an independent republic. Now political events forced a recasting of the covenant to fit the emerging nation. The consequences for such a shift would lead to a fateful alliance with Carrera and, implicitly, to a recognition of the loss of Catholic hegemony in an increasingly secularized world.[27]

As Guatemala's civil war drew to a close, Aycinena demanded Guatemalans to see how the law of Moses represented God's covenant with Israel: "God himself called it his Covenant." Therefore, Guatemalans ought to conform to God's law, as did the children of Israel in the time of Moses. Aycinena rejoiced that Guatemalan authorities recognized that the Mosaic law would be the foundation of Guatemala's peace and prosperity. Archbishop García Peláez agreed in 1856 that Guatemala, like Israel, recorded its promises with God in its own covenant of Independence. In 1858, Aycinena prodded his listeners to "persist in our covenant" *(persistais en vuestro pacto)* and uphold it continually and keep its commandments forever."[28]

No wonder Juan José Aycinena became the prime interpreter for this novel theology during the Carrera years.[29] In 1858 and in other sermons he elaborately traced the story of salvation from the fall in the Garden of Eden through the Mosaic covenant. When humanity broke the law in the garden, God castigated and banned humans from its pleasures. The same principle applied to Abraham, Isaac, and the chosen people of Israel: "Blessings if you obey the commandments of our Lord our God; and damnation if you do not obey them."[30] The tablets of the law delivered to Moses formed the basis of the Pentateuch, which Aycinena called Israel's "Magna Carta." If Israel obeyed, God would protect them from calamity and from other vile nations, and heal their land.[31]

The famous archbishop Francisco de Paula García Peláez followed suit: this "holy alliance" was ratified in all the towns and villages, and when alien constitutions provoked revolt the masses, he said, burst forth to present their own constitution. García Peláez saw Carrera's final triumph over Morazán on March 19, 1840, as the triumph of a people who wanted to hold religion sacred and to rid the country of those constitutions that had not.[32] Zeceña and Piñol reaffirmed García Peláez's proclamation: divine obligations fulfilled meant prosperity; obligations ignored resulted in adversity.[33]

The contractual relationship between God and Israel, which reflects a distinctive characteristic of the Israelite religion, has been understood to signify the conscious formation of Israel as a tribal confederacy. In his *Sociology of Religion*, Max Weber commented that, historically, the formation of political associations entailed subjugation to a tribal god. In Israel's case the mutual promise, or covenant, with Yahweh distinguished the Israelite from other ancient religions. Not only was Israel ethically responsible to Yahweh, but Yahweh was obligated to respond and fulfill His part of the bargain.[34] With the destruction of feudal Europe and the emergence of the modern nation, communities continued this conscious process of reformulating their relationship to the Divine. In Geneva the reformer John Calvin spirited the rule of the righteous and influenced a similar tradition developed by the Puritans in revolutionary New England.[35]

In the United States and South Africa, the notion of a covenant community emerged within the reformed heritage. Puritans in colonial North America regarded New England as a New Israel, a covenant community. Governor Winthrop preached, "We are entered into Covenant with [God] for this work" and, if there is any breach of this covenant, "the Lord will surely break out in wrath against us."[36] In South Africa, the victory at Blood River of a small contingent of Afrikaners over a vast Zulu army in December 1838 became the celebrated Day of the Covenant, known today as the Day of the Vow. Paul Kruger, the 1881 president of Transvaal, preached that this 1838 victory at Blood River proved that God had selected the Afrikaners as his chosen people; the loss of Natal in 1843 and Transvaal in 1877 to British annexation were the Divine's punishment for the Afrikaners' failure to honor their vows.[37] In both New England and South Africa, covenant theology formed a national community over and against an indigenous people. Theology created a new history, endowing a nation-building people continuity with ancient Israel while demarcating community boundaries to exclude those they wished to dominate.

Guatemalan clerics went to great lengths to draw out the analogy between Guatemala and Israel. No other nation enjoyed such privileged relationship as did Guatemala. As a chosen nation, Guatemala was called to fulfill its moral obligations.[38] García Peláez testified to Guatemala's covenant with God: as the children of Israel had committed themselves to the ten commandments presented to Moses on Mount Sinai, so too Guatemala should remember its emancipation from the government of Spain with the articles of Independence. Article 10 of this new Tablet, the "religious alliance contracted with God our Lord,"[39] the *Scripsit in tabulis verba fœderis,* stated:

> The Roman Catholic religion which we have professed in the past centuries and which we will profess in the future, will be preserved pure and unaltered, keeping alive the religious spirit which has always distinguished Guatemala, respecting the ecclesiastical ministers, secular and regular, protecting their persons and property.[40]

Reiterating one of José María Castilla's affirmations in his 1821 sermon, Aycinena testified that God providentially ordered the events surrounding the declaration of Independence on September 15, 1821. God had chosen Guatemala since "emancipation cost not one extraordinary effort, nor any painful sacrifice."[41] Guatemala could count itself as blessed and chosen.

To what extent had Independence not cost "one extraordinary effort"? No other single affirmation kindles more passionate debate in contemporary Guatemala each September 15.[42] Aycinena preserved and transmitted this interpretative tradition initiated with Castilla's 1821 Independence sermon. Castilla had proclaimed that "Guatemala had witnessed the birth of its liberty without its cradle being stained by a single drop of blood."[43] By the late 1830s, the clerics Aycinena, Zeceña, and Herrarte and the politician Pedro Molina reaffirmed Castilla's assertion.[44]

By 1844, though, precisely when Carrera briefly distanced himself from the Catholic prelates, other clerical interpretations surfaced, challenging this bloodless narrative of Independence. Friar Manuel Zacarías Velasquez lambasted the Spanish conquerors, venerating Bartolomé de las Casas and lauding indigenous resistance. Zacarías Velasquez confronted the notion of a gratuitous Independence by saying: "I will never forget that in my own cloister some fathers of Central America's liberty were made prisoners!"[45] He was referring to the "Conspiracy of Belén" when, in December 1813, these Dominican friars were captured for planning armed insurrection to liberate Central America from Spanish control.[46] Nevertheless, Zacarías Velasquez's statements were more the exception than the rule. By the 1850s, with the consolidation of Carrera's conservative regime, Guatemala's uniqueness was reaffirmed: Guatemala had become a "rare comet" before many nations.[47]

Many of the clerics purposefully underscored the importance of the peaceful transition from colony to independent state, which contrasted so sharply with events in Mexico. When thousands of peasants had rallied to

68   Father Miguel Hidalgo's cry for independence in Mexico, creoles in general refused to support him and were consequently identified with and slaughtered alongside Spanish officials in the battle of Guanajuato. The painful memory of creoles' predicament during the 1810 Mexican insurrections weighed heavily on the minds of Guatemalan creoles who faced daily the whims of a caudillo supported by a giddy, nonwhite multitude. The Mexican revolutionary experience frightened the Guatemalan creole elite.[48] In contrast, political transformations (like the one in Guatemala) that assured continued order and elite control were deemed wise and prudent. Aycinena praised the people of Guatemala for their "patience" in not provoking senseless revolutionary fervor in order to gain independence from Spain. He then extended his argument by demonstrating through the bloodless events of Independence that God had chosen Guatemala, not the reverse. Just as Israel had responded to its election by preserving the Pentateuch, just so Guatemala must now respond to its election and forever hold to the promises made on September 15, 1821.[49]

With decisive military victories in the 1850s and with Carrera's regime firmly entrenched, history now confirmed the clerics' theological assertions. Now that Guatemala was fulfilling its obligations, God had blessed and protected it from adversity. The liberal governments of El Salvador and Honduras, having agreed in 1851 to reestablish the Federal Republic of Central America, waged war on conservative Guatemala in an attempt to make it join the enterprise. Carrera's troops crushed the invaders and thus maintained Guatemala's independence. This victory was all the proof necessary to confirm the clerics' theological insight. Antonio Larrazábal expressed his gratitude for the divine shielding of Guatemala, noting that the country's religious piety had made this possible. Even Carrera affirmed that Providence had continued to protect those who truly believed.[50]

In 1857 two Guatemalan generals and other military men died of cholera while fighting William Walker's troops in Nicaragua. This North American filibusterer had threatened to invite Protestants to the region. In a funeral speech Aycinena eulogized the Guatemalans for fighting the "intrusive, cruel, and bloodthirsty foreigners who desired to abolish our worship." Aycinena relied on God's "strong arm" since these Guatemalans, like the Maccabees, died in the strict observance of divine law and in their fervor to protect Guatemala's religion.[51]

The 1857 cholera epidemic proved a setback to the church's view that God favored Guatemala as long as its people protected its religion. One Jesuit tried to put a positive twist on the epidemic by proclaiming that the pestilence must be God's way of cultivating their happiness. Another member of the regular clergy attempted to hold fast to the notion that the Guatemalans must have broken the covenant. He pointed out their continued state of sinfulness. Ignacio Cambrils integrated the lessons learned from the historic 1773 earthquake that leveled the Old City in Antigua with the concurrent 1857 cholera epidemic that was ravaging the countryside. He argued that "your sins led you to these tragedies, your brutal passions, your dishonesty, your drunkenness, and other horrible sins provoked the wrath of God to send the earthquake or to send the cholera." Cambrils begged them to call on God to forgive them and release them from cholera's grip.[52] It was, however, the successful Capuchin missions to eastern Guatemala (discussed in chapter 3) that "redeemed" the people from their sins and, in the church's understanding, finally released them from the plague. Archbishop García Peláez thanked the Capuchins for their work, noting that "the hand of the Omnipotent has touched us, sending the cholera epidemic, in order for us to recognize how divine justice weighs in against our straying."[53]

Carrera's imperialistic defeat of El Salvador, the holdout of liberals, in 1863 proved God's definitive favor. Carrera had challenged the leader of El Salvador's government for taking strong measures against its clergy. Through a difficult war, he overthrew the tyrant of the Catholic church. The abbess of the Capuchin Convent, Sister Maria Clara, praised Carrera's triumph over the enemies "of our religion"; Aycinena declared that all Guatemalans must honor Carrera with the title "Father of Our Country." García Peláez congratulated Carrera on his victory and concluded that "Providence had favored our holy cause."[54]

Throughout their sermons, the clerics set apart and denounced those social forces they considered destructive and responsible for social anarchy. Church authorities challenged rival visions, forcefully excluded them from the "good," and thus imposed their own understanding of the meaning of events and their vision of the social world. During the last decade of conservative rule, the Guatemalan clergy openly denounced their opponents and their opponents' ideals. The sermons centered on three predominant concepts that contested the principle of ecclesiastical authority: liberty, separation of religion and society, and the usurpation of ecclesiastical goods.

Consistently and forcefully, Guatemalan clerics argued against a "deceitful liberty" spread by those bent on revolution. As Eve was seduced by the Serpent who promised to make her like a god, so Guatemalans were tempted into unbridled licentiousness.[55] But liberty cannot supersede the regulatory law of God. Those groups that pushed for reform under the guise of liberty

70 were atheists or apostate Christians who did not recognize the head of the church. Aycinena linked political reformers to Luther and Calvin, religious anarchists who had fomented horrible rebellions against the church and thus incited people to licentious lives. As in the days of Israel false prophets deceived God's people with false notions of liberty.[56] The Baptist missionary Frederick Crowe became the "false prophet" of the Guatemalan Catholic clerics in the mid-1840s. The vicar general Antonio Larrazábal demanded that the government revamp the laws that protected people of different beliefs and move quickly against people such as Crowe, who had set up a school in the Guatemalan capital. Protection of religious diversity should not extend to the public sphere; rather, it should protect only private beliefs. The clerics' discourse proved effective and after considerable internal debate Crowe was exiled from the country.[57]

God is the sole author of liberty, and liberty (Aycinena affirmed) was a gift; its good use would be tribute to God. The freer a people, the more submitted it must be to the will of God. The Guatemalan clerics had radicalized this notion to include not only individuals but the nation. Although Guatemala had declared itself independent from Spain, it could never make itself independent of God. Therefore, the nation could make no claim to sovereignty, since only God was sovereign.[58]

What did Aycinena want to communicate with this notion of divine sovereignty? The church and the state had together attempted to expand Christendom throughout the Americas. With the loss of Spanish political hegemony, Guatemalan clerics envisioned a strengthened church supported by the conservative nation of Guatemala. Aycinena's words projected a Guatemala governed by a Christian theocracy, a church tactically allied with a conservative regime, a government guided by Levitic-like priests, indeed, a Catholic rule of the righteous.

No society could dare envision itself separated from religion. The danger of dividing religion from society accompanied the threat of unbridled liberty. "What remains with Society when the power and influence of Religion is subtracted from it? It becomes a chaos of confusion, and an ungovernable tumult," declared Aycinena. The cleric Zeceña concluded that the political and religious orders were so "intimately united and interwoven" that neither could be altered or separated without seriously damaging the other. Prudencio Puertas ascertained that social order resulted from the "empire of religion," where God's commandments were to be obeyed by both governed and governors. The future archbishop of Guatemala, Bernardo Piñol, declared in 1849 that "without Religion, it is impossible to consolidate the liberty of nations!"[59] Nation and Christianity became inseparable. The clergy's personal fate mingled with the nation's destiny in the mortar of Guatemalan society.

The final threat, which knew no political boundary, concerned the usurpation of clerical property. Aycinena graphically described pretended reformers who had brought with them "demagogic tyranny" by suppressing religious institutions and pillaging church property. Governments that attempted to usurp Catholic goods did not "deserve to be called governments, because they are tyrannies subverting the law of God, sinister precursors of communism." Aycinena dogmatically concluded that liberty and property "were sacred rights established in divine law."[60] Aycinena utilized his theological and legal capabilities to challenge even Guatemala City's municipality over the rightful ownership of property in the capital. Faced with a challenge over possession of a small plaza in the city, he confronted the city leaders by comparing them to the biblical villain Ahab, who coveted the vineyard of the simple farmer Naboth. After Aycinena's death, the archbishop continued to utilize Aycinena's *Demonstración del derecho de propiedad* in order to reaffirm legitimacy of title.[61]

The Guatemalan clerics' successful transmission of their unique covenant theology can in part be measured by the response of their vociferous critics. In their elite opponents' jibes one senses their utter disgust with the clerics' theological rendition of Guatemalan history. These elite adversaries held the clerics in contempt for creating a historical narrative that closely linked Guatemala's past struggles with a sacred tradition while unctuously anointing its present administration with divine approval. One anonymous pen unleashed a series of attacks on the famed Guatemalan cleric and novelist José Milla, who had preached on Independence Day in 1846. Calling Milla the "apostle of backwardness," the undisclosed critic attacked Milla for not denouncing the horrors of the conquest and for revising the Independence movement to make it appear that the aristocratic families "spontaneously" favored independence. Angered by Milla's comparison of Guatemala to Israel's captivity in Egypt, the author countered Milla's history by exclaiming that independence was liberation from the slavery of clerical abuses and the colonial inheritance of privilege.[62]

The cleric Prudencio Puertas went so far as to proclaim that Carrera was the Moses who had led his people out of captivity.[63] In a terse published response to his speech a group of Salvadorans expressed their surprise and disgust that the "guerrilla" Carrera had been compared to Moses. In their attempt to humiliate Puertas, they scornfully asked:

Did Carrera divide the sea with his staff so that his army could pass through, and then bury his enemies in its wake? Did he quench the thirst of his army by making water come out of rocks? Did he make manna rain from the skies to feed his hungry people? Has anything similar to this occurred in Guatemala? No; consequently, Father Puertas has played with the Holy Scripture like a child, like a fool, like a wicked man.[64]

In spite of their critics' skillful attacks, Guatemalan clerics continued to preach their theological vision of Guatemala's past, present, and future. Far from being a reformed heritage, yet very close theologically to the spirit of the covenant communities of the United States and South Africa, Guatemalan clerics broke definitively from the spiritual and political boundaries associated with the Spanish crown. New theological and political boundaries created a national consciousness that circumscribed the covenant community of God. Strangely enough, a kind of Protestant position on nationhood developed in response to the distinctive challenge faced by the Guatemalan clerics. Religious leaders in Guatemala no longer identified the "elect" with the Spanish empire; now the nation and its faithful assumed prominence. As the bishop of Chiapas congratulated the Guatemalan archbishop on his 1857 anniversary sermon and his pastoral letter on the war in Nicaragua, he noted particularly that García Peláez had "bonded patriotic feelings and earthly successes with the eternal and holy ideals of our divine religion that we profess."[65]

During the conservative regime, two other ceremonies solemnized the triumphant victory of good over evil. The celebration of Carrera's victory over Morazán in Guatemala's plaza in 1840 was held consistently on March 19. This final battle, which terminated Morazán's influence in Guatemala, took place on the eve of the festive day commemorating Saint Joseph. The coincidence led the vicar general to testify that "Guatemala's very existence was threatened with extermination" and only "extraordinary events" had saved it.[66] Documents indicate that up to the liberal insurrection in 1871, a mass and thanksgiving service were held each year thereafter.[67] Evidence also suggests that similar celebrations were held initially in Chimaltenango, Chiquimula, and in Escuintla, but that over time the principal festive occasion was confined to the capital city.[68] After Guatemala was declared a "republic" on March 21, 1847, governmental officials decided to combine the March 19 and March 21 celebrations.[69] Additional military victories over El Salvador in 1851 and in 1863 generated equal pomp and circumstance in the

capital city and further reaffirmed the geographical and political integrity of   73
the republic.[70]

Another significant ritual confirmed the presence of the extraordinary hand of God in the grand design of history, and His immediacy in the unfolding Guatemalan experience. The dogma of the Immaculate Conception, formalized in December 1854, represented far more than a theological affirmation of the divinity of Jesus through the Virgin Mary. Its proclamation represented a divine counteroffensive to liberal and radical advances in the world. Just as the Guatemalan clerics faced social chaos and anarchy during the resurgence of conflict from 1847 through 1851, so too the Holy See confronted a revolutionary challenge that exiled Pope Pius IX from his protective cloister. From the Guatemalan clerics' perspective, the pope's expulsion from the Vatican in 1848 and his triumphant restoration in 1849 mirrored the upheaval in Guatemala. The chaos endured by the Holy See allegedly paralleled Guatemala's civil war of the mountains. Guatemala's experience converged with global stirrings and gave cause for celebration in the 1850s.[71]

Two foreigners commented on how well established and popular the Catholic church had become once again. The U.S. diplomat Henry Savage, commenting on the increased presence of Jesuits in the country, penned a vicious anti-Catholic message to his superiors in 1853. In his objections one can sense the profound religiosity that had begun to sweep Guatemala:

> A revival of old superstitious ceremonies which had fallen into disuse, has been effected, and it is asserted that the processions of idols and large dolls decorated with an awful display of Jewelry and tussel, during the last Holy Week have never been surpassed in pomp and solemnity, while the female part of the community, neglect their domestic concerns to satisfy spiritual cravings, have sunk into a heathenishlike superstition and expect the attainment of their salvation from mere ceremonial observances. The perversion of a religious sentiment that characterizes the principles of the rigidly catholic party, and which causes the bigot to view with kindred hatred any intellectual advancement, seems here to be on the ascendency.[72]

A traveling French priest and ethnographer, Carlos Brasseur y Bourbourg, remarked that the 1855 celebration in Guatemala of the pope's proclamation of the dogma of Immaculate Conception "was most certainly the most beautiful that I have seen in all of America, for neither in Mexico nor in New York have I witnessed such a splendid illumination of the city!"[73]

74   Later, Guatemala's recovery from the 1857 epidemic of cholera was credited to the Divine Mother's protection. But greater still, the prominent Guatemalan cleric José Barrutia y Croquer pinpointed the significance of the dogma: it demonstrated the continued vitality of the Roman Catholic church against the forces of evil. Protestants, Muslims, and revolutionaries retreated against the resurgence of Catholicism. The forces of secularization had provoked the wrath of the Divine; now, the Catholic church stood ready to redefine itself within the changing geopolitical configuration of Europe and Central America.[74]

In any study of discourse and ritual, especially one concerned with an emerging nationalism, the historian must examine the degree to which elite discourse was appropriated by the community. But complicating this unavoidable query is a question of method: How can one measure popular appropriation or rejection of these invented and adopted traditions if the majority of the populace was illiterate?[75] It will always be nearly impossible to know their hearts and minds. But it is crucial to study the action, the conflicts produced within these communities during the nation-building moment, and examine how the dominant group responded to the challenge.

Victor Turner, who viewed conflict as the essence of the human social drama, pointed out the potential of religious ritual to redress and reintegrate groups who threaten social breach, and at the same time the potential of ritual to escalate crisis moments, giving birth to irreparable schism among social groups.[76] For example, when an explosion at an artillery unit assigned to salute Guatemala City's celebration of the 1837 anniversary of Independence left one person dead and another badly burned, an investigation was immediately ordered to see if the detonation had been purposeful or accidental.[77] Participants clearly recognized that this had been a crisis moment in a ritual with potential significance for the life of a political community. Disturbances in the ritual posed a threat to the government's legitimacy. (Remember that in 1837 popular revolts were surfacing in Guatemala's eastern mountains and in key Indian villages in the western highlands.) Although the investigation claimed that sparks from the third round of artillery fire ignited the ammunition box, popular perception might not have agreed with the official conclusion, thus further eroding the government's credibility. Civil disturbances thus provide a barometer to measure the strength and weakness of state hegemony.

Religious and political celebrations became critical opportunities to show popular disgust with the clerics and their message. "Unfortunate incidents" were reported in Zacapa during the 1840 Independence festivities. In

Santa Lucia Cotzumalguapa, near Escuintla, the priest complained that he was shown disrespect by various drunken individuals during the anniversary celebration in 1855 and Archbishop García Peláez called on authorities to punish the irreverent men.[78] When one priest did not celebrate Independence in Chiquimula in 1865, he was immediately thrown in jail by the chief magistrate.[79]

Father Cayetano Serra caused a public uproar when he challenged García Peláez's theological justification for Guatemala's involvement in the filibuster war of 1856. Evidently Serra had preached that the war was not fought to sustain the Catholic faith nor to conserve the independence of Central America nor to defend the Republic of Guatemala. The theological power houses—José Maria Barrutia, Juan José de Aycinena, Prudencio Puertas, Julian Alfaro, and Bernardo Piñol—complained to the archbishop that Serra's sermon threatened schism and chaos.[80] In 1869, Juan La Canal wrote that the people of Escuintla were scandalized by the behavior of the military authority during the September 15 festivities. The military not only had dissolved the military band but was conspicuously absent from the event. He reported that "they have been severely punished by the general rebuke of the people!"[81]

One of the most humorous scandals to rock religious and political boats took place in Rabinal in Baja Verapaz in 1862. Salamá's parish priest Juan Valdez notified the archbishop that the municipality leader of Rabinal had organized a celebration honoring Independence and had picked a local leader, Nicolás Blanco, to give the honorary speech. However, Blanco literally read word for word a copy of an 1835 sermon written by Matías Quiñones, a priest who had wholeheartedly supported the independence of Los Altos in its brief break away from Guatemala and who had additionally used the 1835 occasion to attack conservative renditions of Guatemala's history. Blanco's speech thus attacked the Spanish conquerors for utilizing Christianity to cover up their ambitions and praised the Mexican hero Hidalgo for initiating the Mexican independence movement. The 1835 speech also concluded with praise for the past federal system heralded by Morazán's ideological descendants. Both Rabinal's mayor and Nicolás Blanco received verbal reprimands: they were "ignorant" and "incapable" of putting together such a speech.[82] Consequently, church officals circulated copies of Bishop Juan José de Aycinena's 1862 Independence sermon to all parish priests in Guatemala in order to avoid future "mistakes."[83]

Religious ritual was also crucial for healing social breaches and dissipating political crises. In the midst of a tenuous political situation for the

76   Catholic church in the mid-1840s, Archbishop García Peláez initiated a series of pastoral visits to examine the nature of the church's strength and to revive dispirited adherents of the faith. To analyze and determine the vigor of
the physical institution, the archbishop and his clerks followed a regular
checklist for each church visited: examine the administrative books; analyze
the appropriateness of funeral rites and accompanying prayers for the dead;
inventory church property; observe the teaching environment and sense its
effectiveness; assess the extensiveness of confession and communion during
Lent; check savings destined for capital improvement on church buildings;
and examine cofradía records.[84]

The prelate's inquiry into the spiritual health of each parish depended
upon a written report submitted by each parish priest, combined with the
prelate's own general impressions gathered during the actual visit. The archbishop's entry into a remote village was usually heralded by the town elders
and the priest, who received the archbishop on the outskirts of town and escorted him to the church. Upon his entry into the sanctuary, a celebrative
mass would commence his two- or three-day visit. Confirmations and con-
fessions of the adult population brought the archbishop into personal contact with the adult population. The pomp and circumstance of the pastoral
event signified authority, legitimacy, and power, whereas the absence of such
regal pageantry translated into weakness and illegitimacy. This reading was
not limited to the elite. When one priest arrived two days early to his new
parish without beforehand notifying the village elders of Nebaj (located in
the highland vicariate of Totonicapan), thus avoiding a properly ritualized
celebration, Indians rumored that the priest had been removed from another
parish because of some crime or that he had been too poor to live in the capital. His spurious arrival could only mean he had come running to Nebaj to
save himself.[85]

During his two-decade reign as the archbishop of Guatemala, García
Peláez succeeded in visiting nearly every clerical district (vicariate) in his
archdiocese at least twice (as demonstrated in table 6). Usually in the drier
seasons of the year, García Peláez chose to make contact first with the key indigenous vicariates of Verapaz, Sololá, Totonicapan, and Quezaltenango.
Only after the pacification of the eastern mountains (and the demands made
upon the archbishop by Rafael Carrera) did García Peláez venture into those
parts. For the Catholic church, recovering from the devastating liberal
reprisals of the late 1820s and early 1830s, the pastoral visit symbolized the
church's attempt to reconstitute itself amid a changing geopolitical
panorama.

The memory of one such conflict in Santa María Cahabón highlighted the frustrated efforts of the church to reincorporate indigenous peoples into the Christian fold and into the nation of Guatemala. Back in 1829, at the height of liberal repression against the Catholic church, the Dominican friar Juan Cabrera was returning to Santa María Cahabón after spending the day at the neighboring village of Lanquin. Sunburned and troubled by a headache, Father Cabrera entered the church sanctuary hoping for some peace and relaxation when he discovered the Indian local religious leaders *(chimanes)* banging away on drums in preparation for the festivities celebrating the birthday of St. John the Baptist. When the Indians refused his entreaty to stop pounding their drums, Father Cabrera grabbed the drumsticks and struck a couple of Indians on the head. His actions led to a furious tug-of-war over the sticks, and to his retreat as the Indians began to strike him physically. The priest hid in a back room behind a locked door until the Indians en masse broke the door down. Cabrera's jump from a window to escape the mad crowd caused him to fracture his leg, and he hobbled to neighboring houses for refuge. For fear of reprisals he was denied safety. He hid in the chapel of San Sebastian, only to be captured when its door was torn off its hinges. One witness stated that Cabrera held onto the altar until he was

Table 6. Chronology of Pastoral Visits, 1845–1871

	Vicariate
October 1845–February 1846	Verapaz
October 1847–January 1848	Chimaltenango, Sololá, Totonicapan, and Quetzaltenango
October 1852–March 1853	Chiquimula, Zacapa, Mita, and Escuintla
November 1854–January 1855	General Vicariate (Guatemala City), Escuintla, and Cuyotenango
November 1859–May 1860	San Jose, Totonicapan, Verapaz, Quetzaltenangô, and Sololá
August 1860–March 1861	Chimaltenango, Zacapa, Chiquimula, and Mitas
January 1864–March 1864	Verapaz

Sources: This data was collected from the archbishop's and parish clergy's records, which are bound into books now located in AHAG, boxes 58.T6, 59.T6, 60.T6, and 62.T6. If these boxes are discarded, the researcher can easily locate the volumes, entitled "Visita Pastoral," by date.

Note: In García Peláez's late years, he sent representatives in his stead.

78   hit on the head with a machete, knocking him unconscious. He was dragged through the streets of Santa María Cahabón and thrown into stocks. That evening, the Indian Joseph Cacul entered the jail and finished off the padre with a blow to the head. Those who interceded in behalf of the padre received equal treatment. Ambrosio Cap and Francisco Coy were beaten and whipped along with a ladino. In addition, the crowd also went on to punish those *principales* and majordomos who had dealings with the padre. The alcalde segundo, Sebastian Cucul alias Chem, was one of the ringleaders of the vindictive crowd, and the alcalde primero discreetly remained on his milpa field when he discovered the cause of the disturbance. Departmental authorities arrested several, but they escaped soon after.[86]

Sixteen years after this murder, church leaders looked for ways to reincorporate the Cahabón church into the Christian community and into the larger nation. The archbishop and his entourage were greeted with extravagant ceremonial events in this remote village to demonstrate the local church's linkage with a greater body as well as to legitimate the local priest's authority in the eyes of the community. The events in this village were seen to represent a microcosm of the larger problems plaguing the church during Morazán's rule and the determined efforts to revive ritual suggested the church's attempts to rejuvenate itself under more favorable political circumstances. Reflecting on this turbulent general history pro-secretary José Antonio Urrutia, speaking for Archbishop García Peláez, explained that only three Dominican friars had pastored the Cahabón parish from 1817 through 1829 (twelve years) including Father Cabrera. After the friar's death thirteen ministers had served as interim priests from 1829 to 1845 (fourteen years).[87] Pastoral effectiveness had been inhibited because no parish priest dared run the risk of facing such a hostile environment. The power of the church had been undermined by such nominal and superficial clerical attention.

What were the ramifications of this institutional chaos? The Catholic church was losing its ability to represent and to re-create itself. Ministers who only preached and baptized for a few months—who did not minister over a long period of time—sowed suspicion among many parishioners. Indeed the faithful began to question the motives of the traveling clergy. Marrying, burying, and baptizing during a few weekends generated substantial income but did not respond to the long-term needs of the faithful. Now it had become the dominant mode of relations with parishioners. In a visit to Guatemala in 1860, the Honduran bishop Juan de Arendal commented that parishioners viewed an interim priest as a "speculator" or a "passerby" who had no interest in the people.[88]

The most significant consequence of parish abandonment was the emergence of indigenous religious lay leadership and the resurgence of preconquest religious traditions. By the mid-1840s indigenous lay assistants (fiscales
and cantores) were fulfilling priestly functions in Santa María Cahabón. The
archbishop's secretary reported that it seemed as if a "new non-Christian
sect" had appeared in the Cahabón church. Traditional doctrinal practice had
collapsed, and no visiting priests could correct the problem within a week or
two. He went on to say that Cahabón was not an exception to the rule.
Throughout the indigenous highlands, priests reported that churches had
fallen into ruin and lay indigenous leaders were performing rituals foreign to
Christianity. In Ixtahuacán, midnight masses led by lay assistants dressed in
priestly robes burned incense to the Sun. And in Ostuncalco the indigenous
cantor performed marriages and divorces for the community.[89]

Archbishop García Peláez's pastoral visit thus sought desperately to reaffirm the authority of the church through discourse and ritual. To commence,
the archbishop led a procession to the church where he was received by the
interim priest. After entering the sanctuary, García Peláez took a seat in front
of the curious crowd and reminded the people through his homily "that they
were part of a celebrated nation [*nación celebre*] in the annals of America, in-
vincible to Spanish weapons, but docile to the voice of their missionaries,
honored by Spanish monarchs, favored by the Holy See with the erection of
a bishopric, and a people praised for their services to Religion." Yet their actions had then made them enemies of God. It was time for the people of Cahabón to restore what they had lost.[90]

The results of the church's actions to reincorporate the Cahabón Indians
were mixed. Most of those implicated in the friar's murder refused reconciliation. Cayetano Zalam confessed to Archbishop García Peláez in Guatemala
City, and Pedro Xae confessed in front of three principales. Cahabón's parish
priest suggested a colonial-style public confession for the penitent in front of
the cross on a Sunday, but no record indicates that this ritual was ever carried out. In addition a few were publicly shamed with the title of "mata-
padre" (priest-killer) by family members. Despite the measures to punish the
accused, many were able to rejoin the Catholic sodalities without the knowledge of the local priests. Upon their death, two had to be buried in the
mountain and not in the church cemetery. Yet one escaped even this ritual
humiliation and was buried under the church floor. The archbishop could
only excommunicate his spirit because any attempt to remove his remains,
the archbishop confessed, could have led to another insurrection.[91]

With elite challenges to the religious nation-building discourse and with

80   the popular indigenous defiance of Catholicism, what evidence might suggest any appropriation of the clerics' religious and nationalist discourse? In the next chapter we shall explore the extent to which the religious and political message was appropriated by popular sectors in the Spanish-speaking eastern highlands. What becomes clear through this present analysis is that a new theology born of experience worked toward developing a national community that would protect the faith.

The Guatemalan clerics attempted to rebuild a devastated institution within a new geopolitical entity. They had fashioned a nationalist discourse during the turbulent years of the caudillo's rule. Grounding their theological understanding of salvation history in the biblical notion of the covenant community, clerics adapted to the changing geopolitical boundaries and beckoned loyalty to the emerging nation of Guatemala. Religious discourse dominated anniversary celebrations of Independence during the conservative period and reflected on Guatemala's sense of election.

To what extent was this discourse successful in cultivating a shared notion of being "Guatemalan" among the diverse peoples of the new nation? In light of some of these narratives, it is hard to imagine how any political discourse appealing to a larger community such as the nation had any profound effect among the entire heterogeneous population of Guatemala. Indeed, Cahabón's parish priest Baltasar Baldwini commented that the Indians of Cahabón "had never formed a political party nor taken part in the wars of Independence nor ever understood what 'republic' and 'liberty' expressed."[92] Even the elite cleric Juan José de Aycinena could see that any pretense to gather twenty-four linguistic groups (remnants of preconquest kingdoms) and to bind them into a common nation would have been quite a political feat.[93] Yet Guatemala as "nation" survived. Two military threats from its neighbors and an internal civil war within Guatemala failed to cloud the elite liberal vision of a nation now championed especially by Catholic clerics.

After Carrera's death in 1865 the conservative regime would soon collapse. The Catholic church would endure another season of institutional repression with the liberal triumph of the 1870s. But all future attempts to unify Central America fell short. Theological discourse had lent itself to the making of a single nation from many.

5

Carrera, the Church, and Nation Formation

ONFLICT IN THE eastern highlands of Guatemala gave rise to independent Guatemala and the demise of the Central American federation during the Carrera years. The caudillo, swept into power by a popular insurrection in 1838, built his conservative coalition on the vindication of popular grievances and the restoration of the Catholic church. During the first decade of his dominance Carrera, in his pursuit of a solid basis of support, jockeyed with the Catholic hierarchy over the lack of parish ministers in the eastern highlands. Within a few short years, relations chilled between church leaders and Carrera. Overall, Carrera's alliances in this critical transition period proved tenuous and unreliable, and Guatemala degenerated into fratricidal war for four years beginning in late 1847. With the threat of foreign invaders in 1851 and 1863, Carrera rebounded from the chaos of civil war and met the military challenge with success. Key to his victory in the Spanish-speaking areas of the eastern highlands were church clerics who responded to Carrera's call and sought to pacify the rebellious and rally their parishioners to Guatemala's defense against liberal intervention.

Understanding the formation of a popular national spirit in Guatemala requires a comprehension of the nuanced relationship between Carrera and the Catholic church that developed in the insurrectionary period, chilled during the 1840s, and rebounded during the 1850s and 1860s to contribute to Carrera's success. The convergence of domestic and external events provided Carrera and the clergy the chance to respond both to a rising antiforeign sentiment in the eastern highlands and to threats from anticlerical governments in Honduras and El Salvador, in order to forge a nationalist discourse that mutually benefited both Carrera and the Catholic church.

A Religious Insurrection?

What role did religion in general and the clergy in particular play in the 1837 revolution that eventually culminated in Carrera's 1839 triumph? Some clergy from Guatemala's eastern mountains were from the beginning implicated in the rebellion. The 1837 cholera epidemic became the catalyst for popular insurrection against Morazán's representative in the state of Guatemala, Mariano Gálvez, and at least one clergyman accused the government of "poisoning the waters" when the government attempted to control the epidemic through quarantines and medicinal measures. One captured guerrilla testified that, during mass,

> Father Francisco Aqueche, along with citizen Pablo Pivaral sent the servant Angel Domingo to check out the spring water and see if it was possessed by bad spirits because the Justice of the Peace, Governor and Lieutenant Colonel, Ignacio Pérez, had thrown a sackful of venom into it. The people who heard this became alarmed and the discontents began to speak out against the government.[1]

Even if accurately reported, however, Father Aqueche's allegation appears more the exception than the rule. Indeed, many clerics were themselves blamed for the 1837 cholera epidemic in both the eastern and the western highlands. The priest in Atitlan—the future archbishop of Costa Rica, Anselmo Llorente—had to flee his parish because the Indians were convinced he had put poison in the water. Other priests were also implicated. As the village leader of San Luis Xilotepeque wrote to the head of the Catholic church, "our people feared that the priest had poisoned the water in ways similar to what has been said about other priests." Other than Aqueche's alleged statement, no other evidence clearly implicates Catholic priests with subverting the liberal government.[2] But as the testimony of the prisoner guerilla indicates, the cholera epidemic opened the floodgates of dammed-up resentment against the government. And some priests were certainly involved directly with the caudillo's military embodiment of this popular sentiment.

Various clergy supported Carrera and his insurrection, and at least two died in the ensuing conflict. The above-mentioned Father Aqueche, parish priest of Mataquescuintla, died after a prison confinement; Father Durán, who had previously served in Esquipulas, was executed by Morazán's troops; and Francisco González Lobos, ex-Franciscan who had served the parishes of

Jalapa and Santa Rosa, became Carrera's major general and led troops in various armed conflicts.[3] Does any pattern emerge in an analysis of those clerics involved in supporting Carrera? Ingersoll's still unsurpassed analysis of the "War of the Mountains" points to a split between the lower and the higher clergy in explaining the different responses among clergy to the Carrera revolt. Her work convincingly describes the well-known opposition of vicar general of the Catholic hierarchy Father Antonio Larrazábal to the Carrera revolt in late 1838, which contrasted with the action of the rural pastors Father Aqueche and Father González Lobos.[4]

On September 9, 1838, Carrera's forces were repelled by forces loyal to Morazán in the battle of Villa Nueva. Prior to the battle, Antonio Larrazábal publicly challenged Carrera and his followers to cease hostilities in the name of religion. Larrazábal recognized that the rustic folk had risen up in the name of religion, but he insisted that no one could defend religion by murdering, stealing, and raping. To continue such actions would make them traitors to God. In stark contrast, the parish priest Francisco González Lobos directed a portion of the troop assault against Villa Nueva and came to the rescue of the wounded Carrera. Morazán's forces captured and executed Father Mariano Durán after this battle.[5]

These priests pastoring in the rural areas were more the exception than the rule: a majority of the rural clergy opposed the caudillo. Larrazábal's challenge to Carrera indicates that some rural priests refused to follow the caudillo's insurrection and abandoned their churches for fear of retribution from Carrera's loyal followers. Larrazábal charged that "many parishes were priestless, persecuted because [the priests] had encouraged their people not to follow any laws contrary to those of Jesus Christ." Evidence supports Larrazábal's conclusion that priests left their churches for fear of Carrera's wrath. Writing from Antigua in March 1838, the parish priest Antonio Velásquez admitted he had compromised his reputation by stating to his parishioners that Carrera was an enemy of the people. Velásquez could not fathom how the majority of the people had "blindly sold out" to Carrera. Padre Florencio Arriasa turned down the liberal government's request for him to serve the parish of Sansaria because, he said, everyone in the town was devoted to Carrera, and he did not want to endure insults and threats. Father Pablo José Casasola described how he was almost murdered after Carrera's troops occupied Tocoy in June 1838. After he fled his parish, his parish house was looted by Carrera's troops and even by members of his own parish. The parish priest of Zacapa, Juaquin Arellano, recounted to Larrazábal in 1839 how the town leaders in Sanarate, Carrera's allies, had threatened him and he begged to be transferred

84   to another village where no Carrera troops frequented. Six months earlier, in March 1839, Father Arellano had lost two hundred pesos after Carrera attacked Salamá. Padre José Maria Madrid, who pastored the church in Santa Rosa during the initial 1837 uprisings, secured a letter in late 1837 from a high-ranking government official assuring its readers that Madrid was not an accomplice to the insurrection.[6] Clearly, then, many rural priests did not support the caudillo and his revolutionaries and did their best to distance themselves from the insurrection. At most, five out of a hundred clergy were identified with Carrera in late 1838, hardly a significant showing.[7]

Ingersoll suggests a capital-rural split among the clergy who opposed and those who supported the rebellious forces. While this hypothesis may account for the radical variance between the vicar general Antonio Larrazábal and those clergy supporting Carrera, it does not account for those rural clergyman who did not support Carrera. Those priests who did support Carrera were not totally unrelated to the eastern insurgents; rather, they had been pastoring for a number of years in the eastern highlands. In an ironic twist of history, Father Aqueche was assigned to Mataquescuintla in 1831 after the beneficed parish priest had been removed, and González Lobos and Father Aguirre also served parishes in the eastern highlands by the mid-1830s (though the duration of their parish tenure cannot be calculated). Although no clear evidence exists to clarify this puzzle, some tentative conclusions can be drawn. This pro-Carrera clerical handful most likely suffered the forced changes brought upon their communities under Morazán: heightened tensions created by English colonization projects bargained away prime eastern lands, and a religious hegemony, already undermined by liberal policies, was further threatened by the presence of Protestant colonists in their parish area.

Observers who witnessed the earliest popular rebellions struggled to understand the motives behind the rebellion. In one of the first attempts to probe the meanings and causes of the insurrection, Alejandro Marure compared the revolt in 1838 to a similar insurrection in the Vendée, France. Marure minimized the religious nature of the revolt and focused on social and economic pressures as reasons for rebellion. A U.S. diplomat traveling in Guatemala, John Stephens during the insurrectionary years affirmed that Carrera was manipulating the people's religiosity. He commented, "Carrera and his Indians, with the mystic rites of Catholicism grafted upon the superstitions of their fathers, had acquired a strong hold upon the feelings of the people by endeavoring to bring back the exiled clergy and to restore the influence of the church." The liberal historian Lorenzo Montúfar scoffed at those who were persuaded to see a religious dimension in the revolt and de-

duced that only a few clerics had been hurt by Morazán's political measures.   85
Montúfar cleverly pointed to the first rebellion against the liberal government, which flared up in Ostuncalco in 1837. After attacking government
troops, the Indians fled, leaving an idol, which was to have released snakes
upon the attackers. According to Montúfar's analysis, the rebellion was a
simple "beans and rice" issue, not a religious one. The Indians had been
forced to work without compensation for state officials. They revolted because they were not paid. Montúfar believed that the idol proved that the Indians did not revolt in order to liberate a repressed Christian church.[8]

Some of the capital elite assumed that a religious overreaction appeared
to be the root of the rebellion. They quickly acted to rescind all laws that
they believed had provoked the masses to rebellion. As one member of the
capital elite saw it, the masses rose up because of "religious fanaticism." The
vicar general, serving as the president of the legislative assembly, spoke in a
horrified manner, saying that "the most disastrous revolution ever was un-
derway, one in which the savage masses were taking a direct part. As Carrera's
hordes increased, the government's troops decreased." All laws that offended
the people's religious sensibilities were then suspended. The ban on religious
orders was lifted and the forced exile of the archbishop was rescinded.[9]

Juan Carlos Solórzano, after deconstructing liberal historiography, has
concluded that the people's religiosity bound them together as a community
and motivated them to action when their religious, economic, and social institutions were attacked by the Gálvez administration. Religion was an "ideological catalyst" in the fight against the Gálvez administration.[10] No immediate alternative social program appeared in the popular demands; rather,
Carrera and his followers called for a cessation of the Gálvez attacks and for
respect for the people's traditions.

In his memoirs published posthumously in 1906, Rafael Carrera reflected on the reasons for revolt. "When the customs of the people are attacked and changed suddenly, the people revolt no matter how noble the intentions may be."[11] In this broader sense, Carrera correctly perceived that the
people's traditions, both religious and political, had been violated. He suc-
cinctly affirmed the reason for revolt in a letter to Salvadorans on the nature
of the insurrection: "The people want [their own] country, a good government, and religion, and do not want anyone to rob them of the fruit of their
labor." In this sense, the revolt in Ostuncalco paralleled the uprising in eastern Guatemala. Both popular rebellions wanted a guarantee of a religious
and social autonomy to preserve meaningful customs. But in their desire to
recover what was lost, the rebels bypassed the authority of the Catholic hier-

86   archy and ignored Catholic leaders' admonitions to halt the insurrection. When the masses sang the "Hymn to the Virgin" on the eve of battle and shouted "Long live religion and death to foreigners!" reformational undercurrents could not have been more prominent: the insurrectionists were in control of their own religious and political destiny. A religious and political identity of the nation was in the making.[12]

Church clerics, both the capital leadership and a majority of rural priests, opposed Carrera's movement for two reasons: the fear of an ochlocracy, the rule of the rabble, instilled fear in the minds of these European descendants; and insurrection, religiously inspired from a popular root, threatened the fundamental hierarchical nature of the church. Even though Carrera's followers proclaimed the restoration of religious rights, capital rural clergy opposed Carrera's forces for fear of their uncontrollable passions. Not until Morazán's execution and the imprisonment of clerics involved in the Carrera movement did clergy in the capital begin to gravitate toward the popular movement. Juan Carlos Solórzano deduced that Morazán's interference in the internal affairs of the state of Guatemala and the challenge of the masses brought about a change of heart in the conservatives and among the members of the religious hierarchy toward Carrera in 1839. Clearly the power and fear of the popular masses pressured the capital elite to reckon with Carrera's followers. For the first time in Guatemala's history, whites were forced to treat nonwhites as equal political partners. But the impact of Father Durán's execution must have weighed heavily upon the hearts of the religious conservatives.

The fear of a repeat performance of the 1829 liberal-inspired repression of the Catholic church stimulated a reassessment of the religious elites' tactical support of Morazán in early 1839. The religious hierarchy and conservative elites abandoned protection from the liberal state when representatives of the state began executing church priests. Lorenzo Montúfar aptly concluded that Aycinena, Batres, Arellano, and Larrazábal feared Morazán more than they feared Carrera.[13] Morazán's imprisonment of Father Aqueche and Father Aguirre in September 1838 and Morazán's execution of Father Durán in late 1838 brought more fear than comfort to the religious leaders. With the removal of the interim president in January 1839 (who, at the request of Carrera, had guaranteed the restoration of some of the church's privileges), the clerics feared another round of 1829 legislative repression against the church. Popular power and an ill-advised execution had moved the clergy toward Carrera.

A Tactical Alliance Falls Apart: The 1840s

After Carrera's decisive victory over Morazán in March 1840, religious leaders maintained a tactical alliance with the caudillo. But two incidents between the caudillo and the church strained the coalition and left the future of the church hanging. The apparent lethargy of the church in filling vacant parishes and the mass refusal of priests to bankroll Carrera's military expedition of 1844 chilled relations between the church and the caudillo.[14]

After Carrera's successful return to Guatemala City in 1839, the religious elite along with Carrera and his forces enjoyed a brief honeymoon of cordial relations. A call for the return of the exiled archbishop had been made and personally guaranteed by the caudillo, the state tithe was reestablished in mid-1841, and the regular orders were looking to reconstruct their convents and ministries among Guatemala's heterogeneous population.[15] New Year's Day festivities in 1840 shattered class and racial barriers momentarily as people filled the church to celebrate the potential of the coming months. A restored church, a hopeful administration, and an empowered mestizo caudillo gathered in the cathedral to demonstrate the unshakable alliance of the new Guatemala. Stephens witnessed the religious mass commemorating the new year and reported:

> The shops were shut as on a Sunday; there was not market in the plaza. Gentlemen well dressed, and ladies in black mantas, were crossing it to attend grand mass in the Cathedral. Mozart's music swelled through the aisles. A priest in a strange tongue proclaimed morality, religion, and love of country. The floor of the church was thronged with whites, Mestizoes, and Indians. On a high bench opposite the pulpit sat the chief of the state, and by his side Carrera, again dressed in his rich uniform. I leaned against a pillar opposite and watched his face; and if I read him right, he had forgotten war and the stains of blood upon his hands, and his very soul was filled with fanatic enthusiasm; exactly as the priests would have him. I did verily believe that he was honest in his impulses, and would do right if he knew how. They who undertake to guide him have a fearful responsibility. The service ended, a way was cleared through the crowd. Carrera, accompanied by the priests and the chief of the state, awkward in his movements, with his eyes fixed on the ground, or with furtive glances, as if ill at ease in being an object of so much

attention, walked down the aisle. A thousand ferocious-looking soldiers were drawn up before the door. A wild burst of music greeted him, and the faces of the men glowed with devotion to their chief. A broad banner was unfurled, with stripes, black and red, a device of death's head and legs in the centre, and on one side the words, "Viva la religion!" and on the other, "Paz o muerte a los Liberales!" Carrera placed himself at their head, and with Rivera Paz by his side, and the fearful banner floating in the air, and wild and thrilling music, and the stillness of death around, they escorted the chief of the state to his house. How different from Newyear's Day at home![16]

In December 1840, barely twelve months later, the alliance between the church and the military strongman was wavering. Rafael Carrera published an open letter attacking the church hierarchy's inability or unwillingness to fill the unserved parishes. Carrera pointed to five difficulties. First, incompetent ministers were employed in the more rewarding parishes while the good priests were assigned to rural and poor churches. Second, Carrera suspected a plot to leave many parishes abandoned so that the people might return to their primitive state of idolatry and barbarism. Third, the caudillo was angered that the archbishop had not returned from exile, and he suspected that Larrazábal or his colleagues were blocking the archbishop's return. Fourth, why pay the church tithe if the archbishop was not even in the country? Last, Carrera was angered that church officials had suppressed a number of fiesta days. A part of Carrera's platform had been to protect the people's traditions, and now the institutional church was subverting his restorationist platform. Carrera proposed a nationalist—almost Protestant-like—church council in which the people could express their frustrations and where authorities could respond to their demands.[17]

In a telling unpublished response to Carrera's letter, Antonio Larrazábal delicately attempted to address the military strongman. Larrazábal thanked Carrera for his service to the church but informed him that he had been given false information, had been lied to, and manipulated. Larrazábal responded to Carrera's first charge by saying that the church's inability to fill parishes resulted from a loss in able-bodied clergy and not from any sinister plan. In the twelve years since the archbishop had been kicked out of Guatemala, 110 priests had died and only 7 been ordained for 111 parishes. Larrazábal could only reiterate that the archbishop had been encouraged to return. Last, he stood firm on his conviction that good parishes were not used as rewards; rather the priests were called to obey and serve the parishes in greater need. Larrazábal never addressed Carrera's recommendation for a national council to deal with the church's difficulties. To do so would have decentralized the decision-making apparatus of the religious institution and ultimately undermined its (and his) authority.[18]

Carrera's public letter caused much consternation among the clergy. One clergyman in particular, José Francisco Ortiz, wrote Larrazábal utterly infuriated over Carrera's pretensions. Father Ortiz told Larrazábal that Carrera's words uncovered his true sentiments toward the church. Ortiz warned that if such perversities and slanderous remarks continued, he and others were more than ready "to take out our swords in order to defend your honor and virtue." Larrazábal thanked him for his concern but merely called on him to pray for the church in "this distressful time."[19]

Internal and external challenges to Guatemala further threatened the already uneasy relations between the clergy and Carrera. Social protests and conflicts erupted within Carrera's eastern constituency in early 1844 and forced the caudillo to reassess the conservative elite governing in Guatemala City. Although the reasons behind the disturbances have been obfuscated by lack of evidence, the negotiated peace brought significant changes to Guatemala in March 1844: the dissolution of the Constituent Assembly, for one, and a legal measure forbidding clergy from holding any political office.[20] Two months later, when troops from El Salvador threatened Guatemala in May 1844, the church distanced itself even more from the military strongman.

Yet Carrera looked for spiritual and financial support from the church to sustain his troops in the 1844 conflicts. He was denied both at first; but through some teeth-pulling negotiations he then received halfhearted support. When El Salvador threatened, Carrera asked for an army chaplain to come to the aid of his troops. At least three out of five priests who were asked refused the honor. Two of the three claimed that physical illness impeded them from rallying to the needs of the country, while a third flatly turned down the offer.[21]

Adding insult to injury, the clergy openly balked at supporting Carrera's troops economically. In July 1844 a presidential decree called for a voluntary donation to the war effort against El Salvador, and the church was called on to pay its share. In order to avoid misunderstandings, government officials encouraged the recently ordained interim archbishop Francisco García Peláez to ask his parish priests for funds. Within days of the formal request, letters poured into the archbishop's office from clerics throughout the country who resisted supporting the civil authorities. Writing from Totonicapan, Father

90   Quiñones refused on the basis of clerical immunity when the corregidor asked for 1,000 pesos. Now he expected García Peláez's formal approval. The cleric José Pablo Casarola described how the municipality of Gualan demanded 100 pesos, and he only had given 50 pesos. "I was threatened with a thousand insults," Casarola wrote. "We, the priests, are the target of everyone's frustration."[22]

In probably what was the first crucial political decision of his historic career as Guatemala's ninth archbishop, Francisco García Peláez convened a meeting of the church council *(Cabildo Eclesiástico)* to discuss the best way of addressing the government's request for funds. The stakes were more than just mere pesos for the war effort. Rather, Francisco García Peláez was being called on to define the relationship between the emerging national government and the church. The church's decision would clarify its obligations to the state, and more important, it would measure its backing of the caudillo who had won social space for the religious professionals.[23]

The council's detailed response to the governmental request was anything but encouraging. The church, it said, was running up a deficit. The structure to collect the state-imposed tithe was still barely functional; there had been a drastic decline in voluntary church offerings over the last decade; the cofraternities were ruined; and the funds for pious works were extinguished; towns were in miserable condition; and parish priests were in arrears even on their *cuartas* contribution. This difficult situation was combined with the outstanding state and federal debt (principal and interest) of 100,802 pesos to the church. The church council concluded that the archbishop could not order his parish priests to loan any more money to the government; he could only encourage them.[24]

The next significant correspondence on September 12, 1844, demonstrates the government's growing impatience with the parish priests. The governmental official in charge of church-state affairs, Manuel F. Pavón, was angered by Chiquimula's small contribution when compared to Zacapa's generous sum. Pavón was beside himself that others who had less had contributed more, and a number of priests had refused to loan any money at all.[25] A difficult relationship became even more troubled during the month.

On September 20, 1844, troops from the Permanent Battalion began looting Guatemala City because they had not been paid. Pavón expressed his disgust at the clerics for not supporting the government and blamed the church for the troops' action. The very harmony between the clergy and civil authority was threatened, he said. Ingersoll concluded that Carrera staged the September revolt to consolidate his power base.[26] Indeed, after halting the violence, Carrera skillfully reached the pinnacle of power as president of Guatemala on December 11, 1844. But more than that, his ascendancy over the church was also consolidated. The clergy's hesitancy cost it dearly.

A second government petition for more money in early March 1845 met equal resistance among some of the clergy. Sebastian Valdez, while pastoring in Ytzapa, challenged the municipality's right to ask for money. This time, church leaders did not formally protest the government's request but moved quickly to sanction the state petition and order clergy to follow suit. García Peláez intervened on behalf of the government and called on Váldez and all of Guatemala's clergy to ante up. Now he saw the government's request as legitimate.[27] The church had already suffered a serious setback in its relations with the Carrera-dominated authorities because of its slow response.

Soon another incident exacerbated the church's relationship with Carrera. The first ship of Spanish and Belgian Jesuits arrived at the Atlantic port of St. Thomas the first week of March 1845. Upon their arrival, government authorities did not allow them to disembark. García Peláez challenged the government's contradictory stance. How could they complain about a shortage of clergy, he said, and then deny entry to the missionaries? Within two months, one of the Jesuits died from the tropical conditions, and the rest soon returned to Europe.[28]

Carrera's response to this situation was even more revealing. Carrera attacked the Jesuits' "insatiable desire to dominate us and return us to slavery with the chains of despotism." In a nationalistic challenge familiar to the insurrection, Carrera denounced the dependency on foreign preachers when "in our Republic priests and monks are teaching and preaching the Gospel." Carrera charged that the Jesuits would try to intimidate and make the people servants: "instead of morality, the Jesuits preach submission to tyrants and the fear of religion."[29]

Relations between the clergy and Carrera had reached their lowest point. The Baptist missionary frequenting Guatemala, Frederick Crowe, observed that by 1844 the priests possessed a very limited share of influence.[30] What had begun as a decade of promised revitalization for the Catholic church was quickly degenerating into institutional isolation and political impotence. From the church's perspective, Carrera was just another Morazán who wanted to use the church for economic and political gain, whereas Carrera, brought to power on the heels of a religiously inspired and antiforeigner platform, had been horrified by the arrival of religious strangers brought to control his constituency.

One way of capturing the tension in this period is to look at one cleric

92 who allied with Carrera from the beginning. No other priest inspires the imagination and creativity of this period as does the ex-Franciscan Francisco González Lobos. Surprisingly little biographical information is known about him. Although he has not been the subject of a systematic investigation, he is publicly remembered as the feared guerrilla priest, "Padre Lobos," who once commanded a significant portion of Carrera's troops. From the initial insurrectionary years through the tumultuous 1840s, González Lobos was drawn almost naturally into conflict situations, never fearing professional or personal consequences. His actions, though, were not guided by a clear ideological vision. Rather his deeds sprang from a complicated mix of values and principles that were neither egotistical nor completely altruistic.[31]

Extant records indicate that González Lobos entered the Franciscan order in 1822 and was ordained to the sacred diaconate on June 14, 1828. He briefly accompanied Archbishop Casáus y Torres to Havana during the archbishop's forced exile in 1829 but then returned to Guatemala in 1831 to initiate measures leading to his secularization and to serve as a parish priest.[32] In 1835 he left Guatemala for Tabasco, Mexico, to recover from his impoverished condition and "to soothe an unhappy mother." He worked for fifteen months in Mexico before returning to Guatemala, "his country," a half-year prior to the Carrera insurrection.[33]

González Lobos served as a parish priest in the war zone. He was licensed to minister in Santa Rosa, on February 3, 1838, and later in Jalapa, in August 1838.[34] One month after his assignment, González Lobos was accused of performing religious services outside of his assigned parish area and working with the insurgency. Antonio Larrazábal, at that time the vicar general of the church, when notified of González Lobos's conduct initiated a legal procedure against the priest within the church. Five government soldiers were brought to testify against González Lobos.

The first soldier, Lino Morales, a twenty-year-old unmarried Nicaraguan who had accompanied Morazán's troops, was captured by Carrera's guerrillas on August 15, 1838. Morales declared that while in captivity he heard González Lobos saying mass in the principal doorway of the church in Jutiapa on August 19, 1838, and was additionally told that González Lobos performed mass and baptized children in Santa Rosa. Morales was later transferred to Mataquescuintla, and there saw González Lobos baptize a child. Margarito Martínez, a sixteen-year-old Guatemalan and a federal soldier, confirmed Morales's version of events. He had also witnessed González Lobos performing mass in Santa Rosa. Sebastian Hernández, a twenty-five-year-old Guatemalan, was also captured in Jalapa and was a personal ac-

quaintance of the guerrilla priest. Hernández confirmed, along with two additional soldiers, that González Lobos had performed mass in Jutiapa.[35]

Additional evidence implicated González Lobos. A printed circular written by González Lobos directly tied him to Carrera's insurgency. The circular, written to the inhabitants of Antigua, was from the "Army of Liberation
and Protector of Order and of Religion Commanded by General Rafael Carrera" and was signed by González Lobos. In this particular pamphlet
González Lobos tried to assuage the fears of the Antigua residents by asserting that Carrera's troops were not barbarians, thieves, and rapists, but honorable men who cherished public morality. In the battle of Villa Nueva on
September 9, 1838, where Carrera's troops were forced to retreat, federal
forces captured a logged book of military orders that had thirteen pages
signed by the priest. Portions of the book were copied into the trial record
and showed that González Lobos, who signed as major general, had given
general orders and rules of combat.[36]

In a passionate and intimate letter to Francisco González Lobos, Antonio Larrazábal confronted the guerrilla priest "as a companion who cherishes
him immensely and is concerned for his spiritual and worldly welfare." Of-
fering González Lobos a way out of his legal difficulties, Larrazábal told
González Lobos that he understood that "unfortunately, the enemy took over
territory in your parish and you were pressured to turn your services over to
the caudillo Carrera against your wishes and to abandon your parish." Larrazábal expressed dismay at the difficulties facing González Lobos since he
had apparently embraced this political faction. Admonishing him, Larrazábal
wrote: "God has given you more than adequate instructions to understand."[37]

Larrazábal assured González Lobos of absolution if he were to abandon
Carrera. Larrazábal called on him to repent and to distance himself publicly
from the caudillo, particularly for the benefit of the state of Guatemala. As
Larrazábal affirmed, the state of Guatemala "looks at you as one of the principal agents of its terrible sufferings. The government does not doubt that
the priestly influence encourages and sustains and pushes forward the most
perverse plans within a class of people who are not sufficiently capable of dis-
cerning just from unjust, truth from lies." Pushing his point further, Larrazábal confronted González Lobos's involvement in the insurrection:

You know, my companion, that our Divine Founder of our Holy
Religion would never allow his ministers to take part in the sedition
of the people. Our inheritance, given to us before he ascended to the

heavens was the conservation of the peace. And our Lord reprimanded [Peter] the head of the church who attempted to defend the Christ with the sword. Suffering, humility, and patience of the faithful were the only powerful weapons that shined forth in the most flourishing age of Christianity, and the most fertile seed in propagating Christianity was the practice of these virtues.[38]

Adding his voice to a historic theological debate within Christianity, Larrazábal attempted to persuade the minister to use peaceful means to further the goals of the church's missions and to dissuade those prone to violence. Larrazábal's choice to condemn Padre Lobos's involvement in the rebellion rather than provisionally to accept the rebellion as a just war suggested the vicar's elitist protection of the status quo.

In a strange turn of events, a possible peace accord to be established through a negotiated settlement in December 1838 pushed the federalist president and military leader Francisco Morazán to write and ask for González Lobos's assistance. Morazán requested Catholic authorities to issue González Lobos the necessary license for the priest to aid in the pacification of the people of Guatemala. Larrazábal conditioned his permission on a face-to-face talk with González Lobos. But then the renegade leader of Los Altos Agustín Gúzman wrote Larrazábal, attempting to pressure the vicar to drop his demand that González Lobos go to the capital. Rather, Gúzman asked Larrazábal to allow González Lobos to minister to Carrera's troops so that peace could be established in the Mita district. Gúzman commented that it was necessary to have someone at Carrera's side who was dedicated to peace.[39]

In his own correspondence with Larrazábal, González Lobos assured the vicar that he had always been true to the Catholic faith. If his actions had detoured from canonical law, "it was due to human nature." He had joined Carrera's forces in order "to aid the unhappy and the disgraced." In partial fulfillment of Larrazábal's demands, González Lobos published a letter to Carrera's soldiers clarifying his role in the insurrection on November 6, 1838. Acknowledging that they had fought for the well-being of the people he said it was now time to pursue these goals by peaceful means. In an amazing clarification, González Lobos admitted that "God had never wanted his dogmas and precepts to be understood or to be supported with the noise of a cannon or with the edge of a sword. Religion is pure and loathes all violent means. If you believe that religion and our country are motives to impel us to a blood battle, be aware: religion rebukes bloodshed and enjoys peace."[40]

González Lobos additionally called on the insurgents to pressure General Carrera to achieve peace through a mutually beneficial treaty. His diplomacy evidently succeeded since the Treaty of Rinconcito was signed a month later, on December 8, 1838. In this treaty, in return for peace Carrera tactically surrendered, returned to Mita, and became the area's recognized district chief. González Lobos was given formal permission to accompany Carrera to the Mita district and ensure Carrera's fulfillment of the peace treaty.[41]

In his formal petition for absolution González Lobos confessed that he had indeed joined Carrera's troops, but he explained that he did so because of a series of events that he could recount only orally to the vicar. González Lobos evidently told Larrazábal that he had been pressured to serve the caudillo for fear of losing his life to Carrera's hordes. He admitted, however, that though his intentions were always just he could not guarantee he had not committed some "irregularity" in his participation with the insurrectionary forces.[42]

To what extent had González Lobos truly distanced himself from Rafael Carrera in the final and uncertain year of the insurrection? Had the famed guerrilla priest denied, even lied about his involvement with Carrera and his role as major general? Or had he tactically distanced himself from Carrera in response to pressure from the vicar? All evidence points to two conclusions. First, González Lobos had not severed his relations with Carrera. Carrera followed through on González Lobos's advice to negotiate a key treaty in December 1838. In all likelihood, Carrera would have been crushed or his forces reduced to insignificant bands if he had not had time to retreat and recuperate. Carrera was quick to call on González Lobos again. The priest was offered the position of major general in June 1841 but declined because of his obligations to the church.[43] And second, González Lobos surely misinformed church authorities as to his real involvement with Carrera. His equivocal stance guaranteed him an immediate measure of professional security but in the long run undermined the famed priest's integrity in future conflicts with the church hierarchy.

A second trial against Father González Lobos reflected not just the continuity of a strong relationship between the caudillo and the priest but also some of the social and economic problems brewing among Carrera's supporters, which led to political rancor in 1844 and eventually to civil war in 1847. A land dispute resulted in the murder of an indigenous leader from San Pedro Pinula in 1842. The leadership of San Pedro Pinula wrote the vicar general of the Catholic church accusing Father González Lobos of murder. Their *jefe político* Juan Ventura Vicente, they claimed, had died at the hands of the famed guerrilla priest.

96   The indigenous community's version of the incidents told how Father González Lobos arrived at San Pedro Pinula in response to a denunciation made by the town officials concerning the Indian principal, Juan Ventura Vicente. According to the leaders of San Pedro Pinula's indigenous *común,* on February 5, 1842, Francisco González Lobos arrived to celebrate the patron saint and, in a drunken state, called Juan Ventura Vicente and other indigenous leaders together and denounced Ventura Vicente. González Lobos then forcibly removed the jefe político's staff and hit Vicente three times in the head and broke the staff in the process. In the melee, González Lobos ordered Juan Valdes to stab Vicente. Then he ordered Juan Ventura Vicente, now almost dead, to be taken to the plaza and executed. The *común* of San Pedro Pinula said that González Lobos subsequently ordered the town's Indians, including women, to be put to death. So the entire indigenous community took to the mountains to escape death.[44]

Antonio Larrazábal ordered an immediate investigation into the charges and, through the testimony of some people closely related to the events, was able to uncover a few more details of the murder. In Larrazábal's eyes these witnesses were honorable and accredited and did not pertain to the plaintiffs and were not involved with the parish priest, Francisco González Lobos. The first witness was Vicente Cerna, the future military leader of Chiquimula and Carrera's successor to the presidency in 1865. Cerna informed Larrazábal that Juan Ventura Vicente, who held the community's staff, had been threatening order with his large groups of Indians. After discussing the particulars with Carrera, González Lobos was ordered on February 2, 1844, to "repress and make an example" of Juan Ventura Vicente and the rest of the mountaineers. Cerna explained that González Lobos sat on the order and did not act.

Two days later, on February 4, Juan Ventura Vicente went to the convent with twelve Indians and González Lobos asked him, "by what authority do you carry that staff? Why did you say that no one has authority over you? And why did you say that the town officials were a bunch of thieves?" Cerna said that Ventura Vicente denied the accusations. González Lobos continued, "Why do you go around saying to the people that they shouldn't obey their priest, but only you?" Ventura Vicente defended himself saying that he had been appointed to oversee their land.[45]

At this point, Cerna recalled how González Lobos lunged toward Ventura Vicente and grabbed his staff, and a riot broke out between the soldiers and the Indians. Ventura Vicente was subdued after being hurt in the head and was taken to the plaza. A shot was soon heard, and when they arrived they found Ventura Vicente shot dead allegedly trying to escape. Cerna concluded his testimony that González Lobos was not drunk; he never gave an order to shoot Ventura Vicente; nor did González Lobos hit him in the head. The troops, affirmed Cerna, were very worked up by the Indian, Juan Ventura Vicente.

Francisco Aragan confirmed Cerna's testimony with a revealing perspective. Aragan claimed that Ventura Vicente was stirring up the people *(andaba revolucionando)* and encouraging the people to obey only him. After the fight over the staff, Aragan said that Vicente Cerna took the Indian leader to the jail where he was shot while trying to escape.

Ygnacio Argueta recalled González Lobos asking Ventura Vicente why he promoted war against the Indians and ladinos of Jalapa. Ventura Vicente responded that "he was empowered by an authority: he was commissioned in the name of the *común* of the people to be in charge of land disputes and land survey." When González Lobos tried to take the staff away from him, Juan Ventura Vicente resisted and was hurt in the scuffle, and was later shot while trying to escape.

The tragic scuffle that led to the murder of the indigenous leader Ventura Vicente pointed to the extent to which the padre González Lobos complied with Carrera's desires in making an example of the rebellious leader and reflected the degree to which Carrera was slowly isolating himself from his eastern supporters who had brought him to power on the wings of insurrectionary fury. The record also indicates that the ethnic conflict between ladino and Indian fed part of the anger between the two parties. As Carrera and González Lobos proved, their combined authority was more than enough to deal with the popular challenge. The apparently popular interpretation among the indigenous people of San Pedro Pinula encouraged many to seek shelter in the mountains for fear of communitywide reprisals. It is interesting that the indigenous community appealed to the vicar general, Antonio Larrazábal, for divine justice against the perpetrators, but church officials supported the version of events put forward by the witnesses sympathetic to González Lobos.

Although the guerrilla priest survived the second trial brought against him, his penchant for military prowess pushed his rapport with church officials to the brink. Archbishop García Peláez was notified that González Lobos's name appeared on a Carrera army battalion list in charge of military operations. Soon thereafter, the archbishop received a letter from González Lobos dated May 1844, requesting that he be nominated the Vicar of the Military *(Vicario Castrense)*. García Peláez chided him, saying that it was ridiculous to those who understood the meaning of the title originally given

98 to the King of Cordestra, Spain: he subsequently denied the request.[46] During that fateful year of 1844, when many clergy distanced themselves from the caudillo, only González Lobos accepted the nomination as chaplain of the army. But as the year came to a close, even Father González Lobos admitted that the job was overwhelming for just one chaplain. Citing his deteriorating health, González Lobos resigned as Carrera's chaplain. Church pressures had taken their toll on the courageous priest from eastern Guatemala.[47]

The Civil War

The outbreak of hostilities again in 1847 led to a drawn-out civil war that weakened the already fragile nation of Guatemala. The threat evolved from within the very base of Carrera's constituency but terminated four years later when El Salvador and Honduras invaded Guatemala in February 1851. Carrera had alienated himself from his people and was eventually forced to turn to the Catholic clergy to renew support and establish the authority of the government. Carrera's remarkable comeback assured his political continuity for the next fourteen years, but it also strengthened the church, upon which he came to rely.

The conflict first erupted in October 1847 when fighting broke out on Carrera's very own hacienda in Palencia. Outraged by the murder of a prominent rancher from Palencia, a significant number of people attacked Carrera's hacienda. Their protest initiated a chain reaction that eventually led to the caudillo's withdrawal from power in August 1848 and his self-exile to southern Mexico. In comparison with the 1837 insurrection, these rebels were highly decentralized and unable to coordinate military actions against government troops. Initially, the insurgents came to be known as *los lucíos,* named after the murdered rancher, but as time wore on and the infighting splintered those opposing the government those groups-in-arms became known as *los facciosos* (literally, the factious).[48]

And divisive they were. These rebels were almost successful in challenging the integrity of the evolving nation of Guatemala. By the end of 1848, Guatemala was in effect splintered into three countries: Los Altos, Chiquimula, and Guatemala, with a good portion of the latter territory held by guerrilla groups loyal to no one else. Furthermore, those challenging the Guatemalan government received considerable military support from El Salvador's liberal elites.

There appear to be at least three reasons that Guatemala erupted into civil war between October 1847 and February 1851: the worsening economic outlook for many of Guatemala's eastern inhabitants, discontent with Carrera's regime, and a growing sense of an intrusive foreign presence. These became the common popular reasons in explaining the multifaceted revolts. An increasing impoverishment in the countryside contrasted with the relative stability of the capital city. Carrera's own personal success evidently exemplified the growing disparity between the capital city and the countryside. He had acquired a renowned hacienda in Palencia for his use and for munitions storage, and his wife was accused of monopolizing the grain market in Palencia. A difficult economic situation followed by the moral outrage at the murder of José Lucio López, who had challenged Carrera, generated the first protests in Palencia in 1847.[49] During one of the many attempts to seek reconciliation with the armed rebels in 1848, even government officials recognized the decreasing availability of lands for cultivation and the increasing appearance of tenant farmers and sharecroppers among Guatemala's eastern inhabitants.[50] Many became exasperated with the failure of Carrera's regime to remedy this deteriorating situation and with his tendency to profit opportunistically from their plight.

Given these difficulties, a xenophobic response to foreigners festered beneath the surface. Not since the failed attempts at colonization of the Atlantic coastal lands in the 1830s had any government attempted to attract European settlers to Guatemala. Although nearly two decades had passed, many eastern inhabitants continued to fear foreign takeover of arable lands. British interests were maneuvering to secure lands on Guatemala's Atlantic Coast, and such fears intensified. One member of the "Plebeian Army" that fought against Carrera wrote of his disgust with Carrera's government for not curbing the Protestant heretics and merchants who were increasingly present. This writer desired a Christian government that did not oppress the poor, called for the burning of evil books infiltrating Guatemala, and opposed any treaties or alliances with Protestants or heretics, demanding that all international trade should be restricted to the port area. Frustrated over his inability to convince the insurgents to lay down their arms and enter a dialogue for peace, Father Arellano could only report the reason for their rebellion as the "story of the foreigners."[51]

Liberal ideologues who had long opposed the Carrera regime took advantage of the political difficulties facing the conservative administration and articulated these grievances in a coherent ideological platform. Serapio Cruz, who led a loose coalition of military forces, published his list of grievances against Carrera. The "vandal Carrera" had imposed a system of absolutism, and Guatemala was being sold out to British greed. Other rebel leaders de-

100 nounced the unjust laws that emanated from the Carrera tyranny and Carrera's complicity with the foreign threat. In a letter to Guatemala's archbishop explaining his involvement with the rebellion, the renowned leader of the facciosos, Roberto Reyes, focused on the unfulfilled promises of the Carrera regime and its opportunistic economic agenda. Reyes charged that sharecroppers worked for entire weeks without being paid. People who had attempted to recover what they had lost were summarily executed and others were unjustly fired from jobs. The only promise fulfilled by Carrera was the restoration of the convents.[52]

Ultimately, Carrera was the problem for most of the liberal elites who joined up with the rebel groups. The "tyranny of the savage Carrera" was oppressing the people of Guatemala. While Europe in 1848 waves the banner of liberty "over the ruins of its kings," while the whole world marches toward "progress," "Guatemala retreats and suffers under the administration of a barbarian."[53] Yet when Carrera resigned in August and voluntarily left the country for a year, the various rebel groups could not unite to take over the country's fragile administration. Infighting and feuds among the insurgent leaders undid any long-term possibility of success. One cleric reported to the archbishop how troops were continually looting the towns, never paying heed to the orders of their elite liberal leaders.[54]

Acknowledging these two dimensions of the conflict in Guatemala's civil war (economic and moral despair among the population of the eastern highlands combined with an ongoing ideological challenge to Carrera from the disfranchised liberals), we may find still another source of tension emerging in this period. The historic struggle between indigenous communities and the encroaching ladino populations caught fire during the breach between the capital and the rural populations. Indians took advantage of the political crisis to push ladino elements out from their villages. The ladino town of Chamiquin completely disappeared in 1849. When, in February 1849, religious and political leaders went to Chamiquin to salvage church relics from the uprisings, they discovered the convent and the ladino houses burned to the ground. The Indians appeared to be "very content and the revolution was over."[55] In December 1848 Indians burned ladino houses in San Martín Jilotepeque. Two months later, Father Francisco Martínez went to Jilotepeque to talk with the Indians, to calm their spirits, and to encourage them to obey their priest. In response the Indians burned another ladino house to the ground that very night. Writing from Totonicapan in October 1848 Father José Matías Quiñones begged the archbishop to moderate the ruling Guatemalan administration's threats to resort to military action against the liberals of Los Altos who had separated once again from Guatemala. If these troops were to approach, Quiñones assured the archbishop, "the Indians in mass would attack the ladinos with their historic animosity, and the government's flag would wave over ruins in the century of civilization."[56]

What did Carrera perceive to be the key issues behind the revolts against his rule? One month before the Palencia revolt, Carrera continued to believe that the absence of parish ministers led to chaos and political anarchy. More ministers in the troubled departments would reestablish peace. Rafael Carrera wrote the archbishop in September 1847 and requested capable pastors for Jalapa and Sanarate, to help restore order to the "straying sheep," and suggested a pastoral visit to review the work. García Peláez termed these areas "dangerous posts" and offered to do what he could to send ministers of peace to these unhappy peoples.[57]

Yet the popular complaints that aired after the Palencia revolt focused not on the lack of ministers but on the self-serving Carrera regime. By February 1848 Carrera seems to have taken to heart his worst critics' message: that he was the problem. He contemplated resigning and leaving the country. Allegedly persuaded by various political and religious officials to the contrary, Carrera delayed his decision until August 1848, when he finally resigned and left for Mexico for a twelve-month exile. But with the factions unable to create any consensus and the war continuing, the caudillo returned in August 1849 with a self-assigned mandate to pacify the region.[58]

Writing to the archbishop from Mataquescuintla in late 1850, Carrera reflected on the reasons for the uprisings and returned to his earlier analysis: the people who lived scattered throughout the mountains had become demoralized without local authorities and pastors to work with them. For this reason, Carrera asserted, the government had to resort to rigorous methods of "extermination." Now that government forces had been successful in "pacification," civil and religious workers must come and heal the wounds caused by war. Once again, Carrera had returned to his original thesis on the cause of problems in eastern Guatemala and now called for an urgent response on part of the church to fulfill its mission in war-torn Guatemala.[59]

Within two weeks of Carrera's return, the government initiated a two-pronged strategy to pacify the rebellion: a military offensive closely followed by the spiritual balm of the Catholic clergy. The government explained that "when military operations begin in the areas of insurrection, priestly influence and suavity will be employed, so important among the people of the countryside." Padres were designated for Jutiapa, Jalapa, Sanarate, Guastatoya, and Mataquescuintla. In Carrera's own words, the priests "were the

102   basis of morality through their example and preaching. A priest will conquer
more assuredly with his advice than will a thousand bayonets."[60]

The archbishop responded positively but noted that Father Cambronero
left Jalapa under threat and no minister was currently in Sanarate and Guastatoya because of the scarcity of ministers and the high occurrence of assaults
in this area. Rafael Carrera wrote the archbishop to accentuate the need for
a clerical presence in these bellicose zones and pressed upon him the need of
a pastoral visit. In addition, Carrera offered financial support for parish
priests in these war-torn parishes.[61]

Carrera's strategy was highly successful. Father José Nicolás Arellano,
sent to Mataquescuintla, wrote the archbishop in December 1849, saying,
"I've been able to get the inhabitants of this town, who had been aimlessly
wandering in the mountains, to return to live in their houses." By September 1850 Arellano reported that arms were being turned in, and that
Mataquescuintla had been "conquered." The government newspaper, the
Gaceta, confirmed Arellano's conclusion and the validity of Carrera's strategy
in that the troops and priests had together brought peace.[62]

The insurgents' reaction to the priests' presence corroborated Arellano's
conclusion. Writing from Jalapa in November 1849 Father Andrés Pintelos
told the archbishop that since his arrival in a parish contested by the anti-
Carrera forces, he had been spied upon in order to justify his expulsion. Father Pintelos had received an official warm welcome from the head of the insurgents but had been warned to stay true to his priestly mission and avoid
any public political allegiances. The rebel leader cautioned Pintelos that "the
country's downfall had its origin in that the clerics [had] abandoned their
ministry and gotten involved in politics." With such distrust Pintelos moved
on to Pinula where he was well received. In Pinula Father Pintelos read a letter from Carrera telling them the caudillo had no interest in destroying them
but wanted only to protect them. After this reading Pintelos received an
order from the anti-Carrera insurgent leader to abandon the area. Pintelos reflected that he had done nothing more than fulfill his ministerial duties.
Javier González wrote of a similar experience in Sanarate. Well received by
the generals of the facciosos, he soon was the target of accusations that he was
"an agent of the Government and worked toward the disarmament of the
people." González reaffirmed his "political impartiality" and seemed confident of his position.[63]

Where there was abuse by government troops and by priests, Carrera's
strategy fell short. Commenting on abuses by both sides Father Pintelos said,
"I can patiently tolerate the abuses committed by the revolutionaries because

I consider their mission as a part of divine justice to destroy. But I cannot tolerate seeing government functionaries committing equal or greater vandalism." One mountain leader commented that their priest had taught them how to steal! The government complained to the archbishop that the curas were failing in Chiquimula to teach doctrine to the children because they were overly concerned with earning money.[64] Such clerics could not advance Carrera's effort to pacify the country.

The church's stance with regard to the civil war could not have been more contradictory. From the archbishop's perspective, the church was politically impartial. The church would do everything possible to bring an end to hostilities among its parishioners but would not take political sides. Yet this stance forced the church to a political option with consequences for its ministers. The church's representatives in the war-torn areas were identified with both the rebels and the government during these fluid political years. With Carrera in power, the clerics were identified with the government; with Carrera exiled to Mexico, clerics were suspected of supporting the rebels.

In a risky political move in June 1848 (almost a year after the rebellions began) and in response to Carrera's request, the archbishop issued a pastoral letter calling on the people in Santa Rosa, Jutiapa, Sansaria, and Jalapa to cease hostilities. "We are brothers and sisters: where do these rivalries and this hatred come from?" queried Archbishop García Peláez in his June pastoral letter. "Brotherly love and harmony are fundamental to society." Fearing rebuke from God, the archbishop called on parishioners in this war-ravaged area "to return" to the flock of Jesus Christ, to union and charity. Later, in October 1848, the archbishop rejected one priest's offer to mediate between warring groups. Priests sent to pacify the region, the archbishop reflected, were sent on "strictly peaceful missions with not the slightest intention of becoming involved in matters foreign to the priesthood." The archbishop confessed that he was growing weary trying to avoid any pretense of involvement in political activity.[65] But the archbishop's theological and political assumptions did little to affect popular and elite perceptions of the clergy in the war-torn areas.

The trials and tribulations of Fathers Francisco González Lobos and Juan Raull prove how difficult the archbishop's stance could be. Once again the famed guerrilla priest and ex-regular González Lobos was causing problems for the archbishop's besieged church. Now he was accused of fighting in battle on the side of the insurgents against Carrera's forces! Although testimony would clear González Lobos of this charge, his priestly ministry had once again become the source of conflict. Word had spread to the capital that

104   González Lobos had participated in the battle of Patzún in July 1848 where Carrera's weakened forces fought victoriously over the insurgents led by Serapio Cruz. Prisoners brought to testify before church authorities presented vague, conflicting testimony, often hearsay, about González Lobos. One prisoner swore he saw González Lobos enter the fight and encourage other soldiers to enter into battle; another saw the priest minister to the wounded only. Another witness saw González Lobos join Cruz's troops, remembered him carrying a gun, but also recalled the priest trying to head toward Carrera's troops, and officers detaining the priest. One prisoner heard the priest trying to lead troops but knew that the troops suspected him; another witness recalled seeing González Lobos with a small gun but remembered the priest trying to leave on horseback before he was captured by insurgent soldiers.[66]

González Lobos presented a well-thought-out defense, which not only proved his case but humiliated, and thus angered, the church authorities. While González Lobos was pastoring in Panajachel, Carrera had called on the Indian villages to attack the ladinos, and so González Lobos had to leave for fear of his life. Whereupon Cruz's forces captured and detained him until the battle of Patzum. González Lobos claimed that he worked with the wounded during the action and had carried no weapons. He never was present in the actual fighting but removed to a neighboring village. He only held weapons while soldiers lit their cigarettes. González Lobos did admit, though, that Cruz offered him the head of a division, but he turned it down. To support his testimony González Lobos presented his own witnesses who confirmed his defense; he presented a letter from Cruz (the insurgent leader) who reiterated that González Lobos had only been detained because of his past connection to Carrera; and he turned in an acknowledgment from the current Guatemalan president that no documents had been found linking the priest to Cruz.[67]

Church authorities concluded that most of the witnesses' testimony was hearsay, yet the priest's confession that he did bear arms went against clerical law and precedent. Also, church authorities chastised González Lobos for the "disrespectful language" he used in his defense. He was sentenced to nine days of spiritual exercises in a convent.[68]

Indeed, the ex-regular was not known for his deference. The archbishop and church authorities had no case against González Lobos, but their frustration with the priest was exhibited in their lengthening the judicial process against him. They were able to censor him by not providing him with the essential license to say mass and hear confession. González Lobos's penchant for conflict fundamentally challenged the hierarchy's understanding of the role of the priest in society. Borne out of his pastoral ministry, González Lobos had ended up in the heart of battle. From the point of view of church authorities, he had sought out conflict and compromised the institution.[69]

Father Juan Raull's capture and imprisonment was a much more bitter and testing experience for the archbishop. With Carrera's exile in August 1848 the Guatemalan government was soon led by the liberal elites. As part of their ascension, they were now in a position to express their suspicion about parish priests who had worked in the countryside to pacify the insurgents, their followers. Evidently some within the government thought that the priests might really be inciting the masses, not quelling them. Father José Nicolás Arellano wrote in October 1848 that word from the capital indicated that the government and public suspected his true intentions.[70]

On September 28, 1848, the cleric Juan Raull was arrested by government forces on the grounds that he was aiding the mountain insurgents. Evidence used to justify his capture was an intercepted letter in which Raull admitted to working with the insurgents. In this letter Raull showed no remorse and felt he had committed no crime. He intended to go home to his native Spain and watch events unfold. Raull knew he had been denounced as a "servile," the declared enemy of the liberals. In his mind he was "no one's enemy" since he did not belong to any party. Raull said, "I am only a friend of order and justice. I love my people, and, as for Guatemala, I assure you I profoundly care for Guatemala more so than I do for my native country." Raull's letter revealed his political bias, not unlike that of the archbishop's: "In all administrations, the people have been sacrificed. No positive good has come about, not even in the Conservative years when the Aycinenas dominated, nor when the Liberals reigned in the time of Morazán, nor during the long imperial rule of Carrera, in which the Conservatives and the Liberals took turns ruling."[71] Raull romanticized the mountain insurgents' political justification for rebellion. For him, they understood quite clearly what was happening in the city. The rebels knew no political party but had one opinion: to go against the capital city. But Raull admitted that even he was suspect by the mountain rebels, who had contemplated murdering him. Raull saw no end to the present conflict. The rebels were too fractured to succeed, and the government would only provoke unending conflict. Because of these threats Raull withdrew from both groups and made plans to return to Spain.

Raull admitted to accompanying the mountain insurgents for fear that "perverse men would manipulate these simple and ignorant people into causing unbearable sufferings upon the inhabitants of the city." He confessed to

106   leaving his parish in the capital city without the archbishop's approval but swore never to have touched any weapon. Due to Raull's solid constituency in the capital church of San Sebastian, the government granted him clemency in the hopes that other rebellious leaders would follow suit. Church authorities accepted his argument that for fear of his life he had abandoned his post without permission, and both political and religious cases against him were dropped.[72]

Both Father González Lobos and Father Raull had become involved in the civil war that ripped Guatemala apart. Both had acted out of a mixture of personal opportunism and a deep sense of morality. Either from circumstances or by design both had become key actors in Guatemala's political theater. Archbishop Francisco García Peláez had sought the safety of the middle road only to be dragged into the fray by his parish priests. Impartiality was an elusive goal. Yet the archbishop's desire for an end to the bloodshed was very real. Protection of the institution and concern for priests and parishioners had brought him to an indecisive stance during the civil war.

With Carrera's return and near total defeat of the mountain insurgency in 1849 and 1850, and fearing the caudillo's total success, El Salvador and Honduras invaded Guatemala in February 1851 in the hopes of terminating the conservative threat once and for all. In the battle of La Arada, however, Carrera and his outnumbered troops outmaneuvered the invaders and won a decisive victory. The net result of the foreign intervention was to integrate the various factions in Guatemala into a single movement against El Salvador and Honduras. What had been a divided country was now united.

The Republic Assured

Not until "foreigners" threatened Guatemala's integrity in 1851 and 1863 did Carrera and his clerical supporters construct a hegemony that triumphed over the factions in the civil war. Together Carrera and parish priests cultivated a growing nationalism in Guatemala's central and eastern highlands. Two wars, the constant threat of foreigners in Guatemala's eastern highlands, and the church's role in fomenting support for war engendered a nationalist spirit that emerged from the popular base of Guatemala's eastern region.

The fear of foreigners taking precious land away from the growing ladino population in Guatemala had sunk deep into the hearts of many who lived in the eastern portion of Guatemala's regions since the days of Gálvez. The liberal administration had forfeited more than half of Guatemala's arable land to a colonization project in the 1830s only to provoke the ire of the eastern inhabitants. Some of the many cries raised against the Carrera regime in the late 1840s included the fear of the Protestant foreigner coming to take the people's land and destroy their religion. With troops led by liberals, the allies of those who in Guatemala had given land away lined up on the Salvadoran and Honduran borders in 1851 poised to invade. Guatemala's eastern inhabitants responded to Carrera's call to defend its national integrity.[73]

The 1851 battle of Arada and the 1863 expedition against El Salvador's capital provide two different pictures of people preparing for war. The 1851 war counted on a smaller base of support. Through Carrera's strategic battle tactics, the ground war yielded victory to Carrera's troops over the forces of El Salvador and Honduras combined. Twelve years later, in 1863, a groundswell of support for the 1863 war demonstrated the real gains made under Carrera's regime and the growing sense of a popular nationalism in Guatemala. A brief analysis of the two wars and the nature of the troops committed to action will shed light on the development of a nationalist commitment among Guatemala's inhabitants.

In the 1851 conflict, Carrera found recruitment difficult and financial support from Guatemala City's economic leaders sparse. Deep divisions among the Guatemalan people still lingered after the four-year-long civil war, and now the caudillo was asking for support for another war? A disgusted Carrera requested more financial support for the expedition from the business leaders in Guatemala City. Measles was dropping thirty men a day, and he could not understand how the government could abandon its troops in such a critical situation. The capital folk, Carrera chided, were enjoying the luxury of town commodities while his soldiers suffered from want of food.[74]

In addition to weakening support from the capital, Carrera found it very difficult to raise troops from a broad sector of the Guatemalan society. The military leader of Chiquimula's division wrote Carrera asking for more troops from the capital and from the department of Jalapa. He found it odd that his troops from Chiquimula outnumbered all the troops combined from the other departments. Men from Zacapa did not respond to the call, and of those recruited 25 percent deserted. Carrera was so overwhelmed by the minimal support that he contemplated asking for Spanish troops from Havana to support his efforts. Persuaded that such an invitation would play into the hands of his enemies, he eventually gave up that idea.[75]

The circumstances were very different by 1863, according to field reports and witnesses. Forced recruitment was held to a minimum while volunteers poured in to aid Carrera in his fight against El Salvador and Honduras. The

108   mayor, judge, and Juan Solorzano, signing for "those who do not know how to write," contacted Carrera from Tecpan Guatemala. They declared themselves ready to join Carrera "to defend justice." Troops from Jalapa hurriedly left during the festivities of the town's patron saint "without knowing the purpose of their call" in order to support the war effort. Men from the department of Santa Rosa came forward without the government resorting to forced recruitment, prompting one official to exclaim that "these departments are the foundation of the republic."[76]

Field records indicating the basis of troop support outside the immediate capital city confirm that, in absolute numbers, Carrera's rural strength came from the Spanish-speaking highlands. Battalions and divisions were divided by regions, departments, cities, and haciendas. Table 7 and map 2 give us a breakdown by region of the troops that participated in the 1863 war against El Salvador. Medals distributed after the war confirm this preliminary finding. Records indicate that, of the 3,938 medals distributed to the troops, *all but 110* were distributed to soldiers from Guatemala's eastern highlands. Of the 3,938 medals distributed, 640 (17 percent) were given to the troops from Santa Rosa. Only the troops from Chiquimula received more (900 medals, or 23 percent).[77]

What factors prompted such an outpouring of support in 1863 compared to the stiff resistance in 1851? Clearly Carrera's military defeat of El Salvador and Honduras in 1851 protected the republic from external threats and led to a period of increased political and economic stability. Compared to the late 1840s and early 1850s, the passage from war to peace enabled Carrera's regime to restart the economy in a boom time built upon cochineal and the nascent coffee economy. Yet two other factors appear central: a large number of troops were drawn from areas where homogeneous indigenous communities were disappearing, and where clergy had been dedicated to resettling and pacifying the area since the civil war.

Field commanders made a clear distinction between ladino men capable of service to Carrera's army and to Indians. During the 1863 campaign two different letters queried the commander in chief whether the Indians were exempt from military service. Writing from Santa Rosa one commander noted that all the inhabitants of "Yxguatan, Tasico, and Guasapan" were Indians and in the past had served as pretty good soldiers. Another commander wondered if he could arm the Indians from Tecuaco and Nancin because of their past performance.[78] Although no reply to these questions has been discovered, the questions indicate the limit to which ladinos or creoles were willing to trust Indians with arms. What remains unanswered is the degree to which the Indians volunteered to serve or were forcibly recruited.

During this decade the church message emanating from the capital and filtering out to the countryside focused increasingly on commitment to Guatemala as the nation. An increasing sense of what it meant to be Guatemalan took hold in the Spanish-speaking highlands and lowlands. When the threat of war appeared, clerics in eastern Guatemala were more than ready to call parishioners to arms. By 1854 U.S. diplomat Henry Savage already understood that "those who evince the firmest adherence to Catholicism are the greatest zealots of the military sway." Chiquimula's corregidor

Table 7. Regional Guatemalan Troops for 1863 War

		No. of Troops	%
Region I	(Spanish Highlands)		
	Guatemala (Batallion N. 1)	330	
	Santa Rosa, Mataquescuintla	489	
	Amatitlan	305	
	Canales	367	
	Palencia, Calvario, Hacienda Nueva	469	
	Jalapa	177	
	Chiquimula, San Agustín	637	
	Sacatepequez	280	
	Jutiapa	118	
	Subtotal	3,172	81
Region II	(Lowlands)		
	Suchitepequez	93	
	Subtotal	93	3
Region III	(Indian Highlands)		
	Verapaz	277	
	Los Altos	359	
	Subtotal	636	16
Total		3,901	100

Source: See troop listing, August 14, 1863 (AGCA, exp. 53390–95, leg. 2443; and J. Luiz García, "Lista" (AGCA B.118, exp. 53216, leg. 2443. Given the sporadic nature of the reports, I compiled figures from the August report and supplemented them from September's report. The August record, taken from occupied territory in Quezaltepeque, El Salvador, notes that 361 Salvadoran troops from Cojutepeque and 413 from Quezaltepeque had joined Carrera's troops.

110   Vicente Cerna rallied priests in his vicinity to come to the defense of the republic and to convince parishioners of the imminent crisis.[79] Several priests responded positively, one writing that "he had already fulfilled this duty" before Cerna's letter arrived, "because the All Powerful honors those who defend Religion and their exalted President." Another cleric wrote Cerna say-

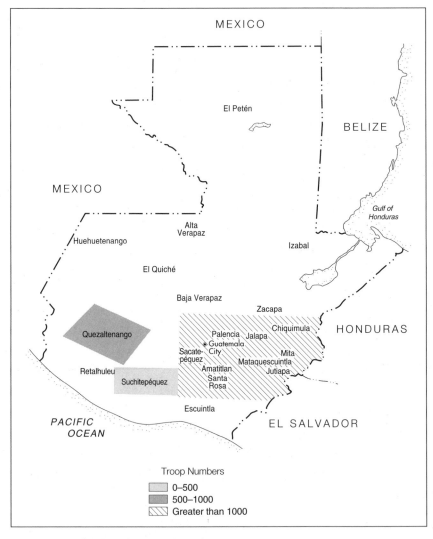

Map 2. Regional Guatemalan Troop Strength

ing that "the Lord of hosts will bless those venturing to conserve a just order,
the security and progress of the country *[patria]* and religion." One group,
writing from Chiquimula and describing themselves as "Guatemalans," offered their services to the caudillo, who had, they said, been chosen by divine
providence for what he had given to the republic. And when the Guatemalan
army attacked Santa Ana, they led with shouts, "Long live religion! Long live
the Bishop!"[80]

Subsequently, a defining sense of being "Guatemalan" developed over
and against foreigners in central and eastern Guatemala, especially "Honduran" and "Salvadoran." Fears among parishioners and government officials
of non-natives were increasing in this period. Parishioners writing from Am-
atitlán in 1856 asked the archbishop to send "a creole from our country
[Guatemala] because from time to time foreigners have hurt and mistreated
us. These foreigners are, speaking clearly, leeches of the people." Just prior to
the 1863 war, officials in Chiquimula worried that foreign priests holding
parishes in Zacapa and Chiquimula might cause problems. These officials
wondered if it might be better that these key pulpits were held by "religious
sons of this Republic since one was from El Salvador and another from Honduras."[81] Invoking cries once heard during Carrera's insurrection in the late
1830s, Guatemalan soldiers unleashed their fury on "foreigners" in El Salvador. At least once during battle in El Salvador, Carrera's troops evidently
executed a French doctor in the town of Cojutepeque. According to testimony from witnesses, Carrera's troops shouted "Long live the Bishop! Long
live Carrera! Death to White Men!" A senior aide to the French president
challenged Carrera's "religious fanaticism" for the death of their country-
man.[82]

Writing soon after the 1863 war, one cleric sought from Rafael Carrera a
letter of recommendation to return to Guatemala. The cleric had pastored in
Sonsonate, El Salvador, for more than a year for the "holy cause" that Carrera defended. Yet the Salvadorans paid the cleric nothing but "ingratitude."
The cleric explained his difficulty:

> Without even thanking me, they removed me from Sonsonate. It's
> true they did so because of my Guatemalan character. They assured
> me that the Bishop said that he wanted nothing other than "Sal-
> vadorans." This is the way they pay for Guatemala's hospitality.
>
> Thanks be to God! Serving my Savior (what I mainly strove to
> do) was to serve my country and this is not ingratitude. The proof
> is the brilliant reward given to its noble sons. I've done nothing in

the hopes of rewards. I am well paid, with the satisfaction of the achieved triumph![83]

After his victory over the liberal Salvadoran government and his triumphant return to Guatemala City, the caudillo received numerous letters praising him for being God's agent in protecting religion and defending the integrity of the republic. The municipality of Camapa thanked Carrera for protecting the sacred rights of religion, property, and liberty in Guatemala as an angel cares for political stability; and the municipality of Conguaco concluded theologically that God protected Guatemala and destroyed the Salvadoran government for having risen up against religion. The municipality and *común* of San Miguel Panan expressed their gratitude to Carrera for his triumph over El Salvador, which evidenced God's favor; the municipality of Asunción Mita said that the children of Guatemala thank the caudillo every day for his heroic actions; and those of Santa Rosa wished for God's continued favor toward the caudillo.[84] Carrera, in diplomatic fashion, deferred from accepting the accolades and attributed the victory to nothing more than divine providence. "We have been nothing more than simple instruments of God's Providence to protect our country: to God we owe it all; to Him be the glory."[85]

Many church people, especially from the female regular orders, made a special point of thanking the caudillo; a victory by the hostile liberal and anticlerical government in El Salvador would have meant their extinction. Sister Maria Mercedes, from the Convento de Nuestra Madre Santa Clara, told Carrera how she had prayed for God to send angels to protect him and the armies for the defense of religion; the prioress of the Convent of the Barefoot Carmelites thanked God for sending Carrera to reopen an almost closed church in the agonizing Republic of El Salvador. Bishop Aycinena told Carrera in a private note that the caudillo deserved to be called "Father of the Country" by all Guatemalans; Archbishop Francisco García Peláez remarked that divine providence had favored Guatemala's cause. It was Quezaltenango's priest Francisco Taracena who concluded that Guatemala's victory over El Salvador had assured Carrera a place in history. Taracena concluded that, in comparison with other governments, Carrera's administration had been consolidated on an extraordinary foundation.[86]

Carrera and the Church

In a confidential letter to the vicar general of the Catholic church written in April 1855, a priest narrated what he had witnessed on Carrera's hacienda. He told the gripping story of how Carrera had humiliated his fellow cleric Francisco Estevan López and threatened him with death in front of the whole municipality of Mazatenango. Carrera had long mistrusted López because of the cleric's ties to a separatist movement of white elites from the western highlands in Guatemala who had challenged Carrera unsuccessfully since 1839. Evidently, the municipality of Mazatenango, located in the Pacific lowlands, was not too familiar with the padre's background and had asked López to be part of a group riding out to welcome the recently arrived Carrera. When Carrera saw López in the reception committee, he remarked bitterly that he had been insulted.

Two days later, still bitten by López's presence, Carrera rode out to meet López where he called him "a traitor and a scoundrel" and said he should "be bound and cuffed and taken to Guatemala city." Carrera then shouted that "he was in charge" and the concordat between Rome and Guatemala had given him this authority not only over priests but also over the archbishop himself; that if he felt like it he could send any one of them to be whipped and jailed. Horrified and afraid, Father López left the hacienda, only to be called back the following day to meet with Carrera again. After much firm persuasion López agreed to the meeting, fearing the worst. This time, however, in front of the people, Carrera hugged López, begged his pardon for his earlier unkind actions and words, and asked López to accompany him to a neighboring town that very day.[87]

No single story captures better the complexities of the caudillo's relationship with the church during the second half of his regime. Alternately hostile and amicable, Carrera always kept the church guessing. Carrera needed the church as much as the church needed his support. During the 1850s and early 1860s Rafael Carrera consolidated his hold on power and moved much closer to the church. The church and the nation solidified a formal relationship, and Carrera now encouraged the return of the Jesuits to aid in the pacification of Guatemala's giddy multitudes. Yet no matter how close the dictator and clergy approached each other, Carrera still maintained the upper hand in the relationship and regularly demonstrated his command over priests such as López. A look at the institutional gains made by the church during the 1850s and 1860s and an examination of the struggle over capital investment in church buildings sheds light on this relationship.

Carrera's chastising of Father López laid bare the power struggle between the caudillo and the Catholic clergy. Far from being clay in the potter's hands, the military strongman remained the supreme power in Guatemala and was hardly subservient to clerical interests. The immediate years prior to

114   Carrera's confrontation with Father López proved pivotal ones for the church and for Carrera. Institutionally, the church was defining its relationship with the caudillo, as Carrera consolidated his political base.

Soon after the battle of Arada, Carrera began to reward the church for its strategic support in pacifying the country. Once resistant to the arrival of the feared Jesuits, Carrera's government now moved swiftly to open the way for their presence in Guatemala. On June 7, 1851, the government repealed the 1845 law that prohibited Jesuits from coming to Guatemala and welcomed their presence to fortify the church. By 1854 the archbishop was able to count on the government even to subsidize the Jesuit missions in Guatemala's western highlands.[88]

In October 1852 Carrera's government signed a concordat with Rome that assured the caudillo the privilege of patronage over the national church and guaranteed Rome the protection of its flock within the emerging nation. Two years later, Carrera would be sworn in as Guatemala's perpetual president. In both instances, García Peláez remained uncomfortable and unassured of the church's tranquillity. Responding in the early 1850s to the newly appointed papal representative in Mexico and Central America, Luis Clemente, García Peláez vetoed the idea of summoning a provincial council of the regional clerical leaders because of the "political circumstances of the country." Final maneuvering between Rome and Guatemala just barely secured the church's veto over any designation of church personnel made by Carrera.[89]

Even more revealing was the archbishop's equivocal stance on Carrera's perpetual presidency. Called to preside over the council deliberating the issue, the archbishop was placed in a difficult position given his hesitancy about the future of Carrera's political administration. In an unsigned letter to García Peláez, an adviser recommended that the archbishop, as president of the council, keep silent on the issue and do his best not to provoke discussion. The unnamed adviser warned García Peláez not to offend those "who believe that the issue does not warrant discussion." Rather, the archbishop should abstain from voting and say that he has arrived only to advise.[90]

From the demagogic pen of the anti-Catholic U.S. diplomat Henry Savage we learn that the archbishop evidently did not follow the advice of his anonymous counselor. Savage noted how the "perpetual presidency was slammed down the throat of Guatemalans" under the guise of popular power, and he perused "the uncanny silence" that dominated the meeting:

There was no altercation or debate, no amendment professed, a 115
deadly silence reigned, which the Archbishop was forced to break,
by repeatedly reminding the assemblege of the object of the meeting, which was to discuss the perpetuity of the Presidency, none
dared to open his lips. . . . And after they had rivetted on their own
necks the yoke of an illiterate Indian, they proceeded to the Cathedral, where tributing their genuflection to a wafer god, they returned thanks, for the boon obtained, the source of their future
prosperity.[91]

The church hierarchy had much to fear with the caudillo in power. Instead
of a church repressed and utilized by liberal elements in the spirit of Francisco Morazán the church now confronted a caudillo who worked for a for-
tified church, but one suitable to his political interests. It is ironic that the
church hierarchy feared a caudillo who envisioned a strengthened church as
part of a consolidated nation, not a weakened and decimated institution. Indeed, the caudillo was moving to exercise unquestionable control over the religious institution.

During negotiations over the concordat Guatemalan church authorities
clashed with Carrera over the control of *la fábrica*, the designated income for
capital improvement of church buildings. Each parish was required by ecclesiastical law to save a percentage of all tithes and offerings for la fábrica. In
the early part of 1852 Carrera's government decided that the departmental
magistrates would monitor the status of each parish fund designated for la
fábrica. The clergy immediately felt that their rights had been infringed, and
that the separation between the civil and religious spheres had collapsed.

State officials evidently began asking parish priests for information without notifying the archbishop of this new policy. Many departmental heads
went further, interpreting the policy to justify their control of the funds
themselves. Father José Mariano Galan, writing from Santa Rosa, warned the
archbishop of the transcendental nature of the event. The municipality of
Cuajiniquilapa had attempted to take the building funds away from their
priest.[92]

Archbishop García Peláez challenged the government's representative
Manuel José Pavón, saying that "this penetration of the Supreme Government" could not be tolerated. Pavón tried to calm the archbishop's fears, assuring him that the government had no plans to take the funds. Pavón did
however defend the state's legal right to inquire about the funds. Peace was

116   the goal of the state, and the upkeep of the church buildings was essential in securing order.[93]

Pavón tried to convince García Peláez of the consequential benefits of a close working relationship between the corregidor and the parish priest. The corregidor ensured that Indians married; that the people of the towns attended the church festivities; that children attended school; that people respected the festive days of the saints; and that priests were paid their dues. Pavón did admit that the government feared abuse on the part of some clerics who preferred to care for their parish houses instead of the church. "Some priests prefer to use parish income to acquire haciendas and other interests," and Pavón promised to put a halt to this waste.[94]

The archbishop's continued protests against government interference in church matters were backed by a thunderous protest among parish priests from Quiché, Quezaltenango, and Verapaz. The government evidently compromised. It promised not to interfere directly in church affairs but only to collect data from the parish priests. But the municipality of Acatenango broke the fragile cease-fire of words when it assumed the privilege of naming the majordomo of la fábrica, the person who would be in charge of all disbursements. Although Pavón agreed to right the specific wrong, his strong language in reply to the archbishop's complaint revealed the tensions existing between the church and the state. The corregidores were ultimately justified in taking the initiative to monitor the churches' building funds, he said, because the clergy were ineffectual. Pavón cited recent conflicts in Chimaltenango and Suchitepéquez and Retalhuleu where the buildings were falling apart. Clerics' postponement of action only infuriated the corregidores and parishioners.[95]

By 1854 corregidores were reporting to the capital on a regular basis on their concerted effort to repair churches. From Jutiapa the corregidor reported that sanctuaries in Jutiapa, Comapa, Jilotepeque, Jalpatagua, and Conguaco had been repaired and whitewashed. By 1867 major renovation of church facilities had been concluded. Indeed, during Carrera's regime, the church's physical infrastructure received the face-lift essential to its survival. For example, the convent of San Francisco was dedicated in Guatemala City in 1851; a convent was finished in Asunción Mita in 1867; and one of the country's best architectural structures was completed on the church in Retalhuleu in 1867. Church authorities had apparently acquiesced to governmental pressure, and under state direction churches and convents were restored and constructed across the nation.[96]

The conflict surrounding the church fund resurrected the uncertain relationship between church and state. Government representatives had crossed over into the sacred spheres of the religious just as had Morazán and his social reform policies. During the entire conservative regime, these two actors struggled to determine boundaries between the religious and the secular spheres. Religious workers and church officials consciously and unconsciously moved toward the modern concept of segregated spheres between the religious and the secular in order to protect their fragile institution while state officials continued to assume and work with de jure and de facto patronage rights.

Boundaries between religious and secular authorities altered in rural communities where corregidores and priests struggled to determine the limits of each other's power. In some cases corregidores accused priests of misusing community funds while priests charged corregidores with public immorality.[97] Some corregidores and priests worked together in a common cause to stop rebellion, while one corregidor mediated a conflict between a visiting regular missionary and an interim secular priest.[98] Corregidores were encouraged to work on improving relations with priests but to notify the government of any priestly misbehavior.[99]

Carrera's relationship with the church was based on power, and he understood that his authority was the greater one. His respect for the church did not equal subservience; rather, he saw the church as crucial to the pacification of the region. His humiliation of López in 1855 and his strong words reflected the power dynamic between Carrera and the church leadership. In his treatment of López the manic swing from menacing threat to warm camaraderie laid bare Carrera's recognition of the clergy's power. Carrera knew that he needed the church, and he could not jeopardize that relationship.

For this reason, Archbishop García Peláez feared Carrera's volatility. The archbishop did not fully trust Carrera and his political program. But equally, the high cleric could not bite the hand that fed him. Carrera had restored the church institutionally, even though at a certain cost to institutional autonomy. Yet the church's acquiescence to Carrera's rule, in the end, overidentified the religious institution with the military dictator.

Remember, Lorenzo Montúfar's myopic view of Carrera's thirty-year political dynasty reconstructed a history heavily influenced by the drama of the 1850s and 1860s in Guatemala. A consolidated dictatorship that supported the church blinded Montúfar to the real dynamic of power between Carrera and the clergy from the 1837 insurrection onward. If anything, Carrera's 1837 rebellion was molded by popular religious demands upon the liberal Gálvez administration.

118   Carrera was isolated from the clergy at his lowest point in December 1838 when Father González Lobos was utilized to pacify the military leader. Carrera's triumph, verified in his 1840 defeat of Morazán, set in motion a series of conflicts between the caudillo and the church hierarchy. Carrera demanded that the empty churches be pastored, and he protested Larrazábal's inability to do so. The church's hesitancy to bankroll his 1844 military expedition isolated the hierarchy once again, and the 1848 civil war threatened to rekindle the 1829 repression against the church.

Carrera's decisive triumph over the montañeses in 1851 was due, in the caudillo's mind, to the church's participation in his effort to pacify the bellicose areas. His government soon rewarded the church by welcoming Jesuits and encouraging a formal relationship with Rome. Yet the two powers were never reconciled ultimately. The archbishop maneuvered reservedly around the caudillo and Carrera taunted the clergy at times with his de facto and de jure veto power. Pressured by the political and social forces in Guatemala, García Peláez tactically supported the caudillo's perpetual presidency in order to protect his church. And Carrera returned the favor by strengthening the ecclesial infrastructure and guarding the churches' building funds. In all, both benefited from the strategic relationship.

Indeed, Carrera's government had withstood enormous challenges through three decades. A civil war, a cholera epidemic, and two wars with foreign governments had thoroughly tested Carrera's political acumen. What was the response? By the end of the 1863 war with El Salvador, Carrera's popularity soared. The caudillo built his strength upon two key factors: first, he acknowledged popular demands in the indigenous periphery and empowered the ethnic communities to recover their religious and political autonomy in support of the greater state. Popular religious concerns were given precedence in feuds over the location of the town cemetery, and the people slowly accepted clerical pleas to relocate the burial grounds. With the social opening provided by the triumphant caudillo's insurrection, many indigenous peoples reclaimed religious traditions cultivated secretly over three centuries. Many indigenous communities looked to Carrera as their ultimate authority and, hence, linked local concerns to a larger community through the persona of the caudillo. A protonationalism was thus seeded in the indigenous highlands.

Second, Carrera depended upon the Catholic church in the rebellious eastern highlands to pacify and to call to reason the armed insurgents who scorched Guatemala from 1847 through 1851. Carrera and many of his supporters had blindly alienated themselves from the very constituency that had

brought them to power. The explosive civil war left Guatemala with near an-   119
archic conditions for four years. Through some skillful ministry in the eastern highlands, Carrera reestablished and began the consolidation of the Republic of Guatemala. The government's support did not erode in the face of
the devastating 1857 cholera epidemic but proved resilient and sufficiently
forceful to withstand any challenge to its integrity.

With the continued rise of antiforeign sentiment in Guatemala, cultivated since the colonization projects of the 1830s and intensified with growing land pressures in the eastern part of Guatemala, many inhabitants rallied
eagerly to defend local and national interests when El Salvador threatened
them once again in 1863. Carrera's successful blitzkrieg replaced the liberal
Salvadoran government with a more favorable one and, in the process, guaranteed the continued revitalization of the Catholic church. Nationalist discourse spread throughout the professional and lay clergy as they thanked the
caudillo for preserving the nation and their religious communities. Indeed
Guatemala's Spanish highlands proved the backbone of Carrera's forces. Father Taracena correctly asserted that Carrera had forged a place in history for
himself but, more important, had successfully constituted the nation upon
an extraordinary basis. A multiethnic and multiclass alliance converged by
historical opportunity to coalesce a nation around the charisma of a caudillo
and the nationalist discourse of a rejuvenated church.

What Changed?

THE YEAR 1865 would not be forgotten within the church and in Guatemala. The prime spokesperson, Juan José de Aycinena, died at the age of seventy-two after a protracted infection in one of his legs. In and of itself, Aycinena's death on February 17, 1865, did not represent a cataclysmic event within Guatemala's Catholic church. Aycinena only gained the de jure status of bishop, within the Catholic church, and settled with his highest claim in Guatemala as rector of the San Carlos University.[1] As ideologue and theologian, however, Aycinena had left his mark on the republic by questioning the organic development of the federation. Aycinena had pressed forward with the theological notion that God had chosen Guatemala among its neighbors because of the country's historic protection of its religion. No other priest addressed these concerns more cogently and consistently during the celebrations of Guatemala's independence from Spain. Upon his death reports indicate that Carrera himself "humbly" received guests as the official "doorman" of the family. Little did Carrera know that he had less than two months to live.

According to Woodward, vascular dysentery felled the fifty-year-old Carrera on April 14, 1865. His dying on Good Friday seemed to confirm his unequaled role in saving Guatemala's church from certain doom. Jesuit leaders eulogized Carrera, and his body was laid to rest in a crypt in Guatemala's cathedral. Guatemala's conservative government did not collapse overnight with his death. Rather, the established government would rule for another five years before falling to the armed challenge of their liberal foes. The relatively easy political transition from Carrera to Vicente Cerna as president appeared to confirm a certain stability in Guatemala. Yet organized resistance to the political descendants of Carrera soon mounted.

By March 1869, Justo Rufino Barrios and Serapio Cruz had launched attacks on Guatemala from their bases in Chiapas. For more than a year, the raids yielded little success upon the conservative reins of power. So what was it that finally doomed the conservative regime led by Vicente Cerna? Evidence from the field indicates that, curiously, it was "technology" that enabled a few to overcome a brave many. Barrios's forces now commanded Winchester and Remington repeating rifles, which could aim and discharge a bullet every two seconds, whereas Cerna's forces, dependent upon the front end–loading guns, could shoot once per fifteen seconds, at best.[2]

The historian Paul Burgess makes the case that Barrios had no real popular backing. He had already been defeated in two prior attempts to overthrow the conservative government. But the addition of two hundred Remington rifles and fifteen Winchester repeating rifles made the decisive difference in the summer of 1871. One of the leaders of Barrios's insurgent forces wrote the U.S. diplomat Silas Hudson and confirmed that his "small numbers," aided by Winchesters and Remingtons, had overcome the government's larger forces. Although Hudson saw the government's defeat as a sign that it lacked popular backing, the opposition leader duly noted, "it is but just to state that the troops from Santa Rosa and Palencia fought bravely and well, but it was impossible to resist the superiority of our arms."[3] Given this superiority, Barrios forces defeated Cerna's loyal troops and occupied Guatemala City on June 30, 1871. Church leaders and parish priests did not miss the significance of the changing political landscape in Guatemala.

Liberal Politics and Religious Revolt

Within three months of Barrios's triumph, the liberal government issued decree after decree limiting the power of the church and forcibly expelling members of the regular orders. On September 3, 1871, the first decree expelled the Jesuits. On October 17, 1871, the government ordered the exile of Guatemala's archbishop. Within a short time, liberal measures mounted against the Catholic church in Guatemala, and the Catholic leadership found itself almost barren of spiritual aid from male and female religious orders. Thirty years of hard work at revitalizing the frail institution fell to swift and decisive measures of the liberal order. As Lloyd Mecham pointed out, Guatemala's Catholic church now experienced the liberal wrath that was gaining momentum in all of Latin America.[4]

The measures taken by the liberal elite in Guatemala City had extraordinary consequences in eastern Guatemala. A religious insurrection again appeared in response to the harsh political measures against the Catholic church. Concrete evidence and analysis of the turmoil in Santa Rosa and its surrounding area is lacking, but enough indirect evidence does suggest that the liberal government had to respond with armed engagement against the masses who had taken up arms against the overwhelming fire-power of the government. The "Remicheros" challenged the Barrios government sporadically for two years in response to the exile of the Jesuits and other admired regular orders. The name Remichero came from a combination of two popular words, *sheres* (an oaken club) and Remington. According to Burgess, most of the men fought with nothing more than machetes and wooden clubs. In the wake of a short-lived victory in Jalapa in January 1872, the people shouted "Long live the Remingtons of *shere*" and thus the shortened form of the expression, "Remicheros," was born.[5]

The Jesuit historian Rafael Pérez asserts that the liberal measures against the Jesuits, first in Quezaltenango, ignited the conflagration in eastern Guatemala in late August 1871. Once again, shouts of "Long live religion!" were heard in Santa Rosa, Jutiapa, and Chiquimula, and weapons were gathered to confront the liberal government. Paul Burgess notes that eastern Guatemala had "always been fanatically Catholic" and the news of the expulsion of the Jesuits "was like a spark in a powder magazine." One government document published on September 6, 1871, attempted to calm the warring spirits of eastern Guatemala, asserting that some are "taking advantage of fanaticism and ignorance of some of our brothers and sisters . . . circulating the rumor that our provisional government is trying to destroy the holy religion of our fathers. Instead of being known as 'ministers of God' they ought to be called 'Firebrands of Discord.'"[6]

Only one source indicates that the rebels gained the upper hand. Father Pérez claimed that the religious rebels actually arrived at the "doorsteps" of Guatemala City but, for fear of mass executions of the remaining Jesuits, withdrew from their vantage point. It is more likely that Barrios counterattacks proved too much for the rebels. In a series of military engagements Barrios quickly gained the upper hand. After a decisive battle in late September 1871, the rebels apparently did not threaten victory again. More important, the wars intensified the resolve of the liberal government to act quickly against the church, and it thus continued its programmed closing of regular orders and banished the archbishop.[7]

Barrios continued his military action against the religiously inspired up-

rising and even resorted to state terrorism in controlling the popular protest. 123
In June 1872 he ordered the expulsion of the renowned Capuchins, including Father Esteban de Adoáin "after the suppression of the Santa Rosa revolt." As the military gathered the members of the Capuchin order, Antiguans gathered in front of the monastery to protest their removal.
According to despatches from the U.S. minister in Guatemala, the military
opened fire on the crowd, killing three and wounding nine civilians. The Capuchins were forced to board a steam vessel headed for San Francisco, California. Father Adoáin returned to the Spanish convent in Bayonne, France,
evangelizing the Basque peoples until his death in 1880. As a sign that
progress had overcome religious backwardness, the Capuchin convent became Antigua's new train station. The last reports of rebel activity trickled to
a halt by December 1873.[8]

It is ironic that Barrios apparently sealed his own fate with his repressive
actions against the people and their popular religiosity in eastern Guatemala.
In another attempt to unify Central America by liberal design he invaded El
Salvador in the spring of 1885. To do so, he had to depend upon men and
equipment from eastern Guatemala. Although no one knows who actually
shot him, most historians agree that the stage was set for Barrios's death by
an initial rebellion of the battalion from Jalapa. Barrios resolved the initial
conflict concerning leadership of the Jalapan battalion by promising to lead
them himself into battle. As he led the charge near Chalchuapa, El Salvador,
he took a bullet to the heart. Initial reports indicated that a Salvadoran sniper
had picked off Barrios, but other reports and historical analysis of his death
raise the possibility that the liberal caudillo had been ambushed by one of the
Jalapan battalion in vengeance for Barrios's bloody repression of the
Remicheros of eastern Guatemala. Regardless of the origin of the assassin's
bullet, Barrios and his attempt to unify Central America fell short of the desired goal, and Guatemala—the religiously inspired vision of Carrera's 1837
insurrection—had withstood this particular liberal assault.[9]

What Changed?

On the anniversary of Independence, September 15, 1991, Guatemala's
archbishop Monseñor Prospero Penados del Barrio addressed the president
of the republic and other dignitaries and denounced the deterioration of the
human rights situation in Guatemala. He mentioned the alarming increase
in street crime and the unabated murders that plagued the capital. Archbishop Penados lamented the increasing poverty among the popular sectors

124   and called on all the branches of government to respond to the crisis that swamped Guatemala. He closed his sermon by praying to the Creator for blessings on the president, and for the well-being and peace essential "to the construction of a Guatemala, founded in Justice and Love."[10] Two months later editors of the two-year-old Guatemalan daily *Sigloveintiuno* initiated a campaign among Guatemalans, urging them "to transcend sectorial interests and embrace the vision and principles of our Nation." In the eyes of the paper's editors, the nation of Guatemala was fragmenting, a state of law did not exist, and a complete absence of solidarity and cooperation prevailed among and within all groups in Guatemala.[11]

One hundred and twenty years after the passing of the conservative regime church representatives and elite groups continued, through religious and political discourse, to reflect on and respond to the challenges facing the Guatemalan people. The archbishop's sermon created a powerful vision of a better Guatemala as he challenged the nation's representatives in much the same way as Bishop Aycinena did in his anniversary sermons. Yet there was as much historical discontinuity during the 1991 sermon: the archbishop did not develop any theological notion of Guatemala's election by God; he did not compare Guatemala to the biblical Israel; nor did he threaten his listeners with God's fateful wrath against sinful nations who abandoned the true religion. Aycinena had addressed a Catholic president whereas Penados preached to an Evangelical one. Aycinena warned of the dangers of too much liberty whereas Penados stressed the plight of the poor.

How does the historian account for the continuity and discontinuity between the two periods? A religious discourse, which sought to establish a distinctive relationship between the Guatemalan people and the Divine, emerged particularly during the Carrera years. Religion operated both at an institutional level and as a cultural force within these critical years, enabling different peoples to express deeply held convictions. From the insurrectionary movements in eastern Guatemala to the secret midnight masses in the indigenous highlands, religion informed political choices and provided meaning and coherence in turbulent situations. Several clerics participated with Carrera in the 1837 insurrection. Those parish priests who had worked within the eastern portions of Guatemala over a period of time were those priests more likely to join in arms with the insurgents. But since many rural priests feared Carrera's insurrectionary forces and distanced themselves from the masses, a high clergy–low clergy or capital-rural split does not properly capture the multifaceted response of clerics to the rebellious masses. Rather, parish priests who had served with the people of Santa Rosa, Jalapa, Jutiapa, and the Mitas were more likely to become involved.

By the end of December 1838 most, if not all, of the insurgent priests supporting Carrera had either been executed (Durán), jailed (Aqueche), or equivocated regarding their support of the caudillo (González Lobos). Although the professional representatives of institutional Catholicism were now estranged from the guerrilla leader, the religious commitment of the insurgents apparently did not wane. Carrera's troops through their victories in battle forced the government to reinstitute many of the former privileges granted the clergy, and the religious hierarchy soon shifted toward Carrera after Morazán's brutal repression of the priests in arms.

Carrera's relationship with church leaders evolved after his definitive triumph in 1840 over Morazán. Locking horns especially with the renowned vicar general Antonio Larrazábal, Carrera challenged the church's inability to fill key rural parishes in the east with competent ministers and, at his worst moment, implicated the church hierarchy in an egotistical plot to prevent the archbishop's return from Havana, Cuba. Open confrontation broke out in 1844 when Carrera banned all clergy from legislative appointments and prohibited the entry of the Jesuits who had come to rescue the ailing institution, while many of the clergy balked at economically supporting Carrera's armed ventures.

During this first decade of Carrera's rule a good deal of institutional confusion plagued the Catholic church as its leaders attempted to reverse the rate of decreasing numbers of priests. The appointment of Francisco de Paula García Peláez as archbishop in 1844 heralded a new chapter within the Guatemalan Catholic church. Through a series of pastoral visits to the rural parishes García Peláez infused the corporate body with a renewed sense of vitality and stopped the church's downward trend.

Yet the archbishop made two key historical decisions that adversely affected the long-term effectiveness of the church. Benefice appointments became a rare occurrence, as the archbishop for political reasons preferred interim appointments. In his telling correspondence to the papal representative in Mexico, García Peláez revealed his misgivings concerning the stability of the Carrera regime and told how he deliberately preferred the interim appointment over and against the beneficed one. The interim appointment gave the archbishop more short-term control over priests whereas the beneficed appointment opened up the possibilities of a long-term government appointment not to the liking of the religious hierarchy.

Archbishop García Peláez was an exceptional leader, was attuned to power struggles, and made many Machiavellian-like decisions that protected the integrity of the religious institution while forcing him to swallow his principled opinion. The archbishop's correspondence indicates that he min-

126   imized his involvement in the affirmation of Carrera as perpetual president, though it was clear to his advisers that he did not support such a decision. The archbishop had learned through the years to placate the caudillo whose volatile temper and quick, spirited political decisions left many dead. García Peláez had had enough experience with the caudillo's capricious sensitivities to learn how to work with Carrera's whims. Although not too religious personally Carrera perceived that he needed the church, politically, to pacify the rebellious easterners. Many times over, Carrera fumed that the lack of ministers impeded the subordination of the mountaineers. This colonial-style model had worked in the past, and the caudillo was convinced of its feasibility in the future.

With the end of the civil war in Guatemala in 1851, church representatives worked closely with Carrera and his new administration to send its ministers to the pacified eastern regions. Members of the regular clergy returned to aid in the spiritual battle and proved a key ingredient in the region's subjugation. Carrera and church leaders formalized their new relation through the concordat with Rome in 1852, and Carrera assumed de jure rights of patronage over clerical appointments.

The intense clerical turnover in rural parishes diminished, although the longevity of appointments never recovered from Morazán's initial repression in 1829. Complaints poured into the archbishop's office demanding more beneficed appointments, yet García Peláez continued his policy of making only interim ones. A constant tide of misgivings concerning the interim appointees appears to have steadily eroded the long-term impact of the Catholic church in crucial areas. Clearly, the centralization of clerical appointment in the capital city did not endear the religious institution to many who tired of seeing new faces in the church pulpit every Sunday.

A greater concentration of priests in the eastern highlands points to the long-term continuity of secular clergy who settled this commercial area in colonial times and explains why this concentration was relatively unaffected by Morazán's tidal wave of repression in the 1830s. The secular clergy were more available to the growing ladino population than were clergy in the highland periphery. Originally the fortress of the regular orders, the indigenous periphery experienced a drastic drop in the number of priests after Morazán's closure of most regular orders. With Carrera's multiethnic victory in 1840, Indians throughout the periphery returned to the mountains, abandoned many towns, and publicly returned to many preconquest religious traditions. Carrera was seen by many as a semidivine figure who had vindicated their interests over the encroaching creole and ladino landowners; many ladino houses were burned to the ground, and some priests were run out of town. Local religious leaders emerged, and they danced and prayed to the Sun God dressed in Catholic apparel while church leaders struggled to repress the newly energized indigenous faith.

Other indigenous groups protected their religious autonomy through the Catholic cofraternities, while some looked to the caudillo to rescue them from the financial duress of the sodality's obligations. Some cofraternities began to recover financially whereas others disappeared for lack of interest and funds. No regional or ethnic pattern has emerged to shed light on this dynamic, and further research is required as more records become available.

Religious discourse, especially sermons preached on the anniversary of independence from Spain, developed a sense of the nation of Guatemala among parishioners in the Spanish-speaking highlands. Building upon a covenant theology many of the clerics concluded that Guatemala had been chosen by God. To preserve this divine choice Guatemalans had to preserve their side of the bargain and protect the true religion from liberal assault. History appeared to confirm their theological reflections, as troops directed by Carrera repelled an invasion in 1851 and successfully removed the Salvadoran president in 1863 through a direct invasion of El Salvador. It is ironic that conservative Catholics were more effective in constructing a liberal-inspired sense of nation than were members of the Liberal party. Carrera, inspired by these clerical theologians, declared Guatemala to be a republic in March 1847, and the Constituent Assembly ratified his decision a year later on September 15, 1848.

Was this religious discourse in Guatemala unique among post-Independence Latin American nations? In one sense, this religious discourse paralleled that of other religions inventing a spiritual autonomy and national community. Weber stipulated that communities constantly reformulate their relationship to the Divine (see chapter 4). The largest Catholic community in the Americas also began a process of developing a spiritual autonomy. During the wars that eventually led to Mexico's independence, Miguel Hidalgo's battle cry lifted the Virgin of Guadalupe as a banner of loyalty among the peasants, proclaiming loyalty to Fernando VII.[12] The Mexican priest Mier appropriated the theological tradition that the Apostle Thomas had come to Mexico to evangelize the Indians and, thus, attempted to create a direct link of apostolic succession to the Mexican church, severing its spiritual link with Rome. In Argentina the caudillo Juan Manuel Rosas understood the power of the pulpit as he instructed the regular and secular clergy in their obligations toward the federalist cause. In a crude fashion Rosas pressured

128   the clergy to "expose the deceit of the Unitarians and strengthen the adhesion of the *porteños* to the Federal regime."[13]

In Guatemala, however, the religiously inspired discourse cleverly appealed to recent history as the basis of Guatemala's election and created a Catholic version of the "city on the hill." A covenant theology was invented that affirmed Guatemala's distinctiveness. Spiritual authority and national autonomy came directly from God. The clerics testified that Guatemala evidenced its distinction through its bloodless independence and thus its liberation differed from that of its Mexican neighbor. Catholicism had been protected in the articles of independence, and when liberal political powers detoured from this path, God was quick to punish the country with wars and pestilence. The 1850s and early 1860s were a decade of triumph for these clerics, as their numbers increased, finances stabilized, and outside threats diminished.

This nationalism grew in the fertile ground tilled by the increasing, almost xenophobic, antiforeigner sentiment growing in Guatemala's eastern highlands. Cultivated by the misguided liberal policies of the 1830s, colonization projects ranging from Guatemala's eastern port throughout eastern regions of the country exacerbated social tensions in the region. In addition, the acute perception that Salvadorans and Hondurans were "foreigners" grew, after Morazán's troops warred in Guatemala in the late 1830s and Salvadoran troops invaded Guatemalan soil in 1844 and 1851.

The relative stability and economic growth of the 1850s strengthened the national infrastructure and linked disparate parts of the country with the capital. Roads, bridges, and ports were built, and these improved the church's ability to communicate with rural priests. Thus, an expanding national integration combined with an antiforeigner sentiment to create a strong sense of identification with "Guatemala."[14]

But what of the majority indigenous population in the western highlands of Guatemala? How did they link up with the nascent state? Most of the indigenous groups saw in Carrera someone who would vindicate their grievances. Carrera could mobilize Indians to clear out all the ladinos, if he so desired, and sometimes did so unhesitatingly (as González Lobos testified). Indians addressed land disputes and complaints about overbearing priests directly to the caudillo. Their admiration for and loyalty toward the caudillo linked them with a territory that far exceeded their own social space. This bond linked the multiethnic indigenous peoples with Carrera and his vision for a religiously inspired and independent republic.

Robert Carmack in his analysis of Momostenango detailed how Carrera

patronized the Indians. He entrusted a limited amount of autonomy to them
until their actions threatened his regime. Carrera's power with the Indians,
however, emanated not only from a colonial-style relationship, as Carmack
has argued, but also from one based in the preconquest traditions. For the
indigenous peoples Carrera was a divine figure who had redeemed them
from their conquerors. The divinelike accolades heaped upon Carrera during
the insurrection and subsequent battles emerge out of a long man-god tradition described by Serge Gruzinski. Carrera's hold upon the people reached a
mythic quality in the indigenous highlands. Like many who swore that Za-
pata would return one day on his white steed, numerous reports coming out
of the indigenous highlands indicate that a good portion of the people
awaited the caudillo's return even after he had been dead for several years.[15]
Reports even circulated that one liberal military leader invoked the dead
caudillo's name in order to attract the indigenous peoples into his military
ranks in the 1870 liberal rebellion.[16]

Carrera's popular support from the indigenous population did not just
originate exclusively from his ethnic identity or his godlike prowess. Rather,
the caudillo astutely responded to specific demands from the highland communities and, in many instances, acceded to those claims. One popular con-
cession arose out of fights over the town's cemetery. Liberal politicians,
adopting the new European health standards in the 1830s, passed measures
requiring the relocation of town cemeteries to the outskirts of the town. This
new law provoked immediate uprisings in a number of villages, especially between Indian and ladino inhabitants, and added more fuel to the fire simmering beneath the liberal administration. Carrera's 1839 victory granted
control of the town cemetery to local villages, and in many instances cemeteries were moved back to the church.

Village priests were caught between loyalty to parishioners, who begged
them to protect their cemeteries as a locus of tradition and meaning, and
obedience to liberal government officials, who interpreted any hesitation as
sedition. When various epidemics swept Guatemala, bodies poorly buried
protruded from the grasp of the grave (usually the church floor) and caused
fetid smells to plague the village priest. These foul odors meant contamination according to the doctrine of miasmas, and priests begged town officials,
corregidores, and church leaders to move the cemeteries. When clerics attempted to persuade officials to move the burial grounds, many people resorted to interment in family plots or in unmarked graves in the hills. Many
of the larger cemeteries were eventually relocated by the 1857 cholera epidemic, though in some instances the church patio continued to serve as the

130   final resting place of many. Cemetery revolts were confined for the most part to the periphery.

During the cholera epidemics in both 1837 and 1857, outsiders were suspected of poisoning the village water. The Gálvez government suffered the most from such accusations by priests working in the Mitas region. Yet several priests themselves were the target of such accusations and were forced to flee villages. Epidemics exposed multiple layers of conflict: tensions among competing ethnic groups exploded, opposing epistemologies collided, and economic pressures ripped through the government's inept handling of the crisis. What is striking about the two epidemics was Carrera's ability to withstand the challenge whereas Gálvez's political defeat was initiated by the first appearance of cholera.

The cemetery revolts, accusations springing from cholera epidemics, and liberal measures against the Catholic church, all point to the broader process of secularization described by Durkheim and Weber. The emerging secular state during the Gálvez administration in Guatemala assumed control over marriage, death, and burial. Although institutional religion lost its power, religion as a cultural force continued to intrude into the secular domain, such as the cemetery revolts, setting limits to state power. The secular state, implemented by Gálvez, overstepped its bounds; social chaos and confusion resulted when the secular state destroyed the sacred core of society; and thus, as Durkheim proposed, anomie ensued. Carrera's government, far more in tune with the popular religiosity of his people, recognized and worked within these limits. Yet Carrera was never the Byzantine ruler whose policies eclipsed the dawning of modernization. Rather, the state under his leadership continued to be secularized and to secularize, but at a more moderate pace. Proof of his success lies in the fact that, by the 1857 cholera epidemic, many cemeteries had been successfully relocated.[17]

History did not sustain the Catholic clergy's covenant theology. Faced with a radical shift in social and political relations resulting from the independence from the Spanish monarchy and faced also with a fundamental challenge to their institutional integrity coming from liberal elites, clerics sought a way out of the box canyon. As political events unfolded and power struggles gave victory to Carrera and his followers, elite clerics saw providence at work in history. Guatemala was different from other countries, the religious leaders assumed, and would always be different if the people protected their true religion. Although clerics enjoyed the temporary reprieve from liberal policies, many knew that relations had fundamentally shifted between the church and the world they knew. Writing from the highland periphery, Quezaltenango's parish priest Fernando Antonio Davila complained in 1847 about some priests who continued to be seduced by avarice and greed. Davila concluded:

> these priests have eyes but they don't see, nor are they capable of discerning that in this age of reforms it would be completely absurd to continue these abuses. . . . It is of utmost importance to work for the intimate conviction that the numerous circumstances which sustained the colonial regime have changed or completely disappeared. In that epoch, the government wanted the people to submit to their priests since civil power obtained its authority from this compliance. Now, this means of governance is scorned, and two other means have been substituted: the contemporary one [Carrera's method], the power of the indigenous masses, used limitlessly, willfully and capriciously; or one assured by bayonets.[18]

Six years after Carrera's death, the tables turned once again against religious workers, just as Davila had predicted. Catholic priests and religious workers suffered another season of institutional repression when the liberal regime headed by Justo Rufino Barrios in 1871 completed the secularization of the state initiated by Francisco Morazán in 1829. In another strange twist of events, the Barrios administration invited Presbyterian missionaries from the United States to come and infuse Guatemalans with an alternative religious orientation hostile to Catholicism. Although the Presbyterian church remained small in numbers, its presence initiated a new period in Guatemalan society. By the 1990s, a Pentecostal fervor was spreading throughout urban and rural sectors, indigenous as well as ladino, challenging Catholicism at every turn. In one true sense the Pentecostal fervor emphasized autonomy, deemphasized Catholic tradition, and focused on biblical authority. It thus inverted religious hierarchy, accentuated the commonality of men and women, and tapped into the popular religiosity common to the autonomous sodalities, indigenous rituals, and religious protest prominent in nineteenth-century Guatemala.[19]

What is to be made of Carrera's accomplishments? The historical legacies of the Carrera years are populist and antidemocratic. Indians still fill the ranks of the armed services, and military strongmen come and go. Sadly so, the many peoples of Guatemala have endured various seasons of violence wrought by different powers during the last twelve decades, and with no real end in sight. By the 1990s, the "imagined community" of Guatemala is col-

132   lapsing under the weight of repression and institutional violence. Even the geopolitical territory of Guatemala was still in flux as President Serrano finally recognized the independence of Belice in 1991. Guatemalans are now faced with the peculiar task of building a nation upon many nations. But corruption, the search for unbridled power, and the clash of internal and external interests subvert every noble attempt to build such an edifice.[20]

The archbishop's 1991 Independence sermon was born out of a new religiosity influencing the Latin American Catholic church for the past two decades, a tendency now known as Liberation Theology. A revived laity, an increasing emphasis on biblical authority, and a renewed vitality in worship invigorates the Guatemalan Catholic church, as also in El Salvador, Nicaragua, and Brazil. This internal reformation threatens many sectors of Guatemalan society and results in increased repression and the assassination of priests, nuns, and lay workers. But the church leaders carry on and courageously respond to the challenge of the day nonetheless. If history teaches anything, people from all ranks of society—religiously or politically inspired—have visions of what a community can become. The Guatemalan nation is a peculiar one, born out of liberal failure and conservative success, led by military strongmen, but tempered by its dependence on an export-oriented economy. It cannot be foretold whether the nation will survive, or join another attempt to federate with a Central American nation, or fragment into several ones. What can be predicted is that people will constantly struggle to imagine and create a community through discourse and ritual. It will be the historians' task to make sense of these representations that remain as testament to the peoples' search for meaning and community.

Notes

Unless otherwise noted, all translations are my own.

Note on the Archival Sources

Two archives figure prominently in this work, the Archivo General de Centro América (Guatemala City, Guatemala) and the Archivo Histórico Arquidiocesano "Francisco de Paula García Peláez" (Guatemala City, Guatemala). The referencing system of the first archive, Archivo General de Centro América (AGCA), which depends on three sets of letters and numbers, is quite confusing to the novice. Those familiar with this rich collection of colonial and national documents and its peculiar history understand that I have recorded all numbers found on the different types of documents. For example, "AGCA B Leg 28567 Exp 183" expresses most, if not all, relevant information listed on each document. The letter "B" represents the material from the national period; "leg." or "legajo" equals the principal file while "exp." stands for "expediente" or the particular document. At times "B" is not followed by a number, and "leg." and "exp." can switch order, depending on the source cited. I have merely followed the listing in the ever evolving AGCA card catalogue.

The second archive, Archivo Histórico Arquidiocesano "Francisco de Paula García Peláez," is abbreviated AHAG (traditionally AEG, Archivo Eclesiástico de Guatemala). Respecting the wishes of the current directors, I use an abbreviation more akin to the title of the institution. Since I enjoyed supervised access to the archives, I noticed the "thumbprint" of at least two, and potentially three archivists.

I have created the following formula for documents. Most bound and unbound correspondence and printed ephemera are shelved in boxes within the AHAG. I designate each cited source according to the box in which it is found (For example, box T2.123). To further refine the search, I include a second series of labels. In one half of the archive, church letters and documents are bound according to the church's regional districts (vicariates). Thus, I list such references (AHAG no. 189, box T4.65).

The major portion of this archive, however, contains loose-leaf letters marked and sorted by year and boxed. I designate this correspondence by the year of the box in which the letter is placed. For example, [AHAG 1845.30.14, box T2.89] indicates the loose-leaf number 14 of document 30 bound in the group of letters dated 1844 in box T2.89. Since some key documents were written in one year and "hidden" in another, researchers must pay attention to both the AHAG number and the box number.

134   Chapter 1. Piety, Power, and Politics

1. Francisco González Lobos, *Contestación* [al Serrano], May 29, 1844, in Archivo Histórico Arquidiocesano Francisco de Paula García Peláez, Guatemala City (hereafter cited as AHAG), box T2.56. See also the unnumbered note above, at the beginning of the notes.

2. Francisco Malespin, *Carta que dirige al Sr. General Presidente del Estado del Salvador, al Sr. Presbítero Francisco González Lobos,* Guatemala, May 24, 1844 (AHAG, box T2.56); Antonio Letono to Francisco González Lobos, Guatemala, 1846 (AHAG 1846.5.3, box T2.91); González Lobos, *Contestación* [al Malespin], Jutiapa, May 29, 1844 (AHAG, box T2.56); Manuel Serrano, *Carta del Sr. Vicario del exército salvadoreño al Sr. Cura de Jalapa Francisco Gonzalez Lobos,* Jutiapa, May 24, 1844 (AHAG, box T2.56).

3. Juan José de Aycinena y Piñol, *Aniversario XL de la Independencia de Guatemala. Discurso religioso pronunciado en la Santa Iglesia Catedral el 16 de septiembre de 1861,* 9–10.

4. Rafael Carrera, *Memorias del General Carrera, 1837 a 1840,* 15; Alejandro Marure, *Memoria sobre la insurrección de Sta. Rosa y Matesquescuintla en Centro-America, comparada con la que estalló en Francia, el año de 1790, en los departamentos de la Vendée.*

5. It would be an understatement to say that academic debate has been prolific concerning the "definition" of the words *Indian* and *ladino.* The anthropologist Carol Smith provides one current historiographical analysis of the debate in her edited work *Guatemalan Indians and the State, 1540–1988,* 26–27 nn. 1–4. She argues for a cultural understanding of ethnic differences with respect to questions of political and economic power. The debate also surfaces in *De la etnia a la nación* (Guatemala: AVANCSO, 1996). In this collection of essays Richard N. Adams argues that ethnic identities emerge out of an identification with or an understanding of a common past. See Richard Adams, "Comunidad y cultura en el proceso étnico-estado," 47–71.

6. Henry Dunn, *Guatimala: or, The Republic of Central America, in 1827–8: being sketches and memorandums made during a twelve-months' residence,* 94–95.

7. Adriaan C. van Oss, *Catholic Colonialism: A Parish History of Guatemala, 1524–1821,* xv, 13. See also Agustín Estrada Monroy, *Datos para la historia de la iglesia en Guatemala,* 1:44. See also Enrique Dussel et al., *América Central,* vol. 6 of *Historia general de la iglesia en América Latina;* Hans-Jürgen Prien, *La historia del cristianismo en América Latina,* 197–253; Luis Diez de Arriba, *Historia de la iglesia católica en Guatemala. Período colonial,* vol. 1.

8. Inga Clendinnen, *Ambivalent Conquests: Maya and Spaniard in Yucatan, 1517–1570.* For a history of the colonial Catholic church in Guatemala, see van Oss, *Catholic Colonialism.*

9. Vicente Hernández to Francisco García Peláez, Santa Catarina Ixtahuacán, July 26, 1849 (AHAG 1849.135.7, box T2.99).

10. Murdo Macleod, *Spanish Central America: A Socioeconomic History, 1520–1720,* 228–31; van Oss, *Catholic Colonialism,* 45–49; Christopher H. Lutz and W. George Lovell, "Core and Periphery in Colonial Guatemala," in Smith, *Guatemalan Indians and the State,* 35–37; Ralph Lee Woodward Jr., *Central America, A Nation Divided,* 23. The word *regular* comes from the Latin *regula,* meaning rule, while the word *secular* comes from *sæculum,* meaning world or worldly. According to church historians these terms became more or less fixed within Roman Catholicism by the twelfth and thirteenth centuries. See F. L. Cross, ed., *The Oxford Dictionary of the Christian Church,* 1147, 1236; Kenneth Scott Latourette, *A History of Christianity,* 336, 441–42.

11. Macleod, *Spanish Central America,* 385.

12. Ibid., 380–82; Ralph Lee Woodward Jr., *Class Privilege and Economic Development: The*

Consulado de Comercio of Guatemala, 1793–1871; Edelberto Torres Rivas, *History and Society in* 135 *Central America;* Robert S. Smith, "Indigo Production and Trade in Colonial Guatemala," *Hispanic American Historical Review* 34 (May 1959): 181–211.

13. Woodward, *Central America,* 94–97. The Central American federation was formally known as the United Provinces of Central America.

14. Jorge Luis Arriola, *Gálvez en la encrucijada. Ensayo crítico en torno al humanismo político de un gobernante;* J. Lloyd Mecham, *Church and State in Latin America: A History of Politico-Ecclesiastical Relations,* 372–73.

15. William J. Griffith, *Empires in the Wilderness: Foreign Colonization and Development in Guatemala, 1834–1844.*

16. Pedro Tobar Cruz, *Los montañeses;* Juan Carlos Solórzano, "Rafael Carrera. Reacción conservadora o revolución campesina? Guatemala, 1837–1873," *Anuario de Estudios Centroamericanos* 13 (1987): 13–35; H. M. B. Ingersoll, "The War of the Mountains: A Study of Reactionary Peasant Insurgency in Guatemala, 1837–1873."

17. Clemente Marroquín Rojas, *Francisco Morazán y Rafael Carrera* (Guatemala: Editorial José de Piñeda Ibarra, 1971).

18. Pedro Tobar Cruz, *Los montañeses. La facción de los lucíos, y otros acontecimientos históricos de 1846 a 1851* (hereafter cited as *Los montañeses. La facción*).

19. Ralph Lee Woodward Jr., *Rafael Carrera and the Emergence of the Republic of Guatemala, 1821–1871,* 331.

20. Solórzano, "Rafael Carrera," 27; Ingersoll, "War of the Mountains," 337–42.

21. Torres Rivas, *History and Society in Central America;* Richard Adams, *Crucifixion by Power: Essays on Guatemalan National Social Structure, 1944–1966.*

22. Lorenzo Montúfar, *Reseña histórica de Centro América,* vol. 2. See also Alejandro Marure, *Efeméridas de los hechos notables acaecidos en la República de Centroamérica desde el año de 1821 hasta el de 1842.*

23. Ingersoll, "War of the Mountains"; Keith Miceli, "Rafael Carrera: Defender and Promoter of Peasant Interests in Guatemala, 1837–1848," *The Americas* 31 (July 1974–April 1975): 72–95; Gustavo Palma Murga, "Algunas relaciones entre la iglesia y los grupos particulares durante el período de 1860 a 1870. Su incidencia en el movimiento liberal de 1871"; Solórzano, "Rafael Carrera"; Ralph Lee Woodward Jr., "Liberalismo, conservadurismo, y la actitud de los campesinos de la montaña hacia el gobierno de Guatemala, 1821–1850," *Anales de la Academia de Geografía e Historia de Guatemala* 56 (January–December 1982): 195–210; E. Bradford Burns, *The Poverty of Progress: Latin America in the Nineteenth Century,* 97–106.

24. Julio Cambranes, "El derrocamiento de la dictadura conservadora," *Estudios* 6 (1975): 31; Julio Pinto Soria, *Centroamérica de la colonia al estado nacional (1800–1840),* 233. Prior to Cambranes and Pinto Soria, Antonio Batres Jáuregui significantly revised Montúfar's historical analysis and offered a more sympathetic analysis of the Carrera years. Building on Batres's work, Luis Beltranena Sinibaldi credited Carrera with the founding of the Guatemalan Republic. See Antonio Batres Jáuregui, *La América Central ante la historia 1821–1921. Memorias de un siglo,* vol. 2, and Luis Beltranena Sinibaldi, *Fundación de la República de Guatemala.*

25. Ingersoll, "War of the Mountains," 77–82; Woodward, *Central America,* 102, and *Rafael Carrera,* 68; Solórzano, "Rafael Carrera," 15; Palma Murga, "Algunas relaciones entre la iglesia y los grupos particulares," ch. 3.

26. Mary Holleran, *Church and State in Guatemala,* 128–46; Hubert J. Miller, *La iglesia católica y el estado en Guatemala, 1871–1885,* trans. Jorge Lujan Muñoz (Guatemala: Universidad de Guatemala, 1976); David Lee Chandler, *Juan José de Aycinena, idealista, conservador de*

136 *la Guatemala del siglo XIX.* Ricardo Bendaña Perdomo in *La iglesia en Guatemala. Síntesis histórico del catolicismo,* 62, overlooks the contribution of the Carrera years to the issue of "nationalism" and asserts that only in the pre-Carrera years does a nascent nationalism emerge among creoles.

27. Estrada Monroy, *Datos para la historia,* vols. 1–3.

28. Dussel et al., *América Central;* Estrada Monroy, *Datos para la historia.*

29. Pinto Soria, *Centroamérica de la colonia;* Severo Martínez Peláez, *La patria del criollo. Ensayo de interpretación de la realidad colonial guatemalteca;* Steven Paul Palmer, "A Liberal Discipline: Inventing Nations in Guatemala and Costa Rica, 1870–1900," 3, 57.

30. Woodward, *Central America,* 119.

31. Woodward, *Rafael Carrera,* 52–53, 59, 80, 257–61, 317.

32. Solórzano, "Rafael Carrera," 10.

33. Lowell Gudmundson and Héctor Lindo-Fuentes, *Central America, 1821–1871: Liberalism Before Liberal Reform,* 90, 108.

34. Carol A. Smith, "Origins of the National Question in Guatemala: A Hypothesis," in Smith, *Guatemalan Indians and the State,* 93.

35. Richard E. Palmer, *Hermeneutics,* 148.

36. Zygmunt Bauman, *Hermeneutics and Social Science;* Clifford Geertz, *The Interpretation of Cultures;* Robert Wuthnow, *Meaning and Moral Order: Explorations in Cultural Analysis.*

37. Geertz, *Interpretation of Cultures,* 1–30. See also Karl Marx and Friedrich Engels, *On Religion;* Emile Durkheim, *The Elementary Forms of the Religious Life;* Max Weber, *The Sociology of Religion;* Paul Ricouer, "The Task of Hermeneutics," in *Philosophy Today* 17: 112–29; Victor Turner, *Dramas, Fields, and Metaphors: Symbolic Action in Human Society.* I am especially indebted to Robert Wuthnow for his interpretative framework provided in *Meaning and Moral Order,* 18–65.

38. Wuthnow, *Meaning and Moral Order,* 57.

39. Roger Chartier, *Cultural History: Between Practices and Representations,* 4.

40. Eric Hobsbawm and Terence Ranger, eds., *The Invention of Tradition,* 1; Eric Hobsbawm, *Nations and Nationalism Since 1780: Programme, Myth, Reality.*

41. Hobsbawm and Ranger, *Invention of Tradition,* 13.

42. Cited in Hobsbawm, *Nations and Nationalism,* 10.

43. Benedict Anderson, *Imagined Communities: Reflections on the Origin and Spread of Nationalism,* 15.

44. Ibid., 16.

45. Ibid.

46. Florencia E. Mallon, "Nationalist and Antistate Coalitions in the War of the Pacific: Junín and Cajamarca, 1879–1902," 233. Mónica Quijada argued that a "homogenization" of the notion of "nation" evolved over nineteenth-century Latin America. See the provocative essay "Qué nación? Dinámicas y dicotomías de la nación en el imaginario hispanoamericano del siglo XIX," 49–51.

47. Caroline Ford, *Creating the Nation in Provincial France: Religion and Political Identity in Brittany,* 3–8, 221–27.

48. Hobsbawm, *Nations and Nationalism,* 12. Hobsbawm wisely concluded that one neglected dimension of the study of nationalism is that "national consciousness develops unevenly among the social groupings and *regions* of a country."

49. Anderson, *Imagined Communities,* 40.

50. N. J. Demerath III and Rhys H. Williams, "Secularization Assessed: The Abridging of

Faith in a New England City," *Journal for the Scientific Study of Religion* 31 (June 1992): 137
189–206.

Chapter 2. The Catholic Church Regroups

1. Rafael Carrera, *Rafael Carrera teniente general y general en gefe del exercito del estado de Guatemala, a sus conciudadanos,* December 12, 1840 (AHAG, box T4.58).

2. For example, see references to such letters in Rafael Carrera to Antonio Larrazábal, Guatemala, June 9, 1840 (AHAG no. 19, box T4.62); Carrera to Larrazábal, Guatemala, June 13, 1842 (Archivo General de Centro América [hereafter referred to as AGCA], B.83.2, exp. 25172, leg. 1114). See also the unnumbered note above, at the beginning of the notes.

3. Antonio Larrazábal, *Memoria documentada, que al Illmo. Sr. Arzobispo Coadjutor de esta Santa Iglesia, Dr. Francisco Garcia Peláez . . . ,* nos. 4–5; Holleran, *Church and State in Guatemala,* 235–36; van Oss, *Catholic Colonialism,* 187; R. Bendaña, "Guatemala," in Dussel et al., *América Central,* 250; Luis Diez de Arriba, *Historia de la iglesia católica en Guatemala,* 2:65. Bendaña's analysis of Larrazábal's *Memoria* asserted that 453 priests served the archdiocese of Guatemala in 1805, whereas only 186 were left in 1844. And van Oss reported 453 in 1805 and 119 in 1872. Actually, these authors assume (mistakenly) the same unit of analysis. By 1844 El Salvador's church is independent of Guatemala's. The unit of analysis in 1805 is all of Central America, that is, the archdiocese of Guatemala. By the mid-1850s Nicaragua, El Salvador, and Costa Rica have independent dioceses. By *priests* we shall refer only to priests serving parishes in what came to be the Republic of Guatemala. This of course will exclude those in the bureaucracy and the cloistered regular orders.

4. Mecham, *Church and State in Latin America.*

5. Estrada Monroy, *Datos para la historia,* 2:426–84.

6. Van Oss, *Catholic Colonialism,* 186–87; Estrada Monroy, *Datos para la historia,* 2:521–25.

7. Van Oss, *Catholic Colonialism,* 59–60. For a detailed look at the nature of the examinations in eighteenth-century Mexico, see William Taylor, *Magistrates of the Sacred: Priests and Parishioners in Eighteenth-Century Mexico,* 99.

8. For example, D. T. Batres to Secretary General, Guatemala, July 8, 1831 (AGCA B.83.13, exp. 24945, leg. 1113).

9. Ibid.

10. Antonio Larrazábal to Ramón Casáus y Torres, Guatemala, April 29, 1841 (no. 60, box T3.56).

11. Francisco Morazán to José Antonio Alcayaga, Guatemala, April 22, 1829 (AHAG 1829.63, box T1.93).

12. See Antonio Larrazábal to Carrera, Guatemala [1841] (AHAG 1849.260, box T2.97); Larrazábal, *Memoria,* no. 3. The first document states that only seven were ordained from 1829 through 1841; the second document lists the priests who died from July 1829 through February 1844. If one includes interim priests, the number who had died reaches forty-one. They mostly died of old age: in 1829 the average age of a beneficed priest was forty-five and he had served as a priest for an average of twelve years. The eldest was ninety years old, the youngest was twenty-seven. At least five priests died in the Carrera insurrection, but no record indicates how many died during the 1837 cholera epidemic. See "Lista de los 136 curatos" (AHAG 1829.32, box T1.93). The pattern set during the liberal period continued under the conservatives: from 1844 to 1854 eighty-four priests died whereas only forty-seven were ordained.

138   Clearly the church had slowed but not stopped the process of diminishing its personnel by the latter 1840s and early 1850s. See Francisco García Peláez to Leandro Navor, Guatemala, September 12, 1854 (AHAG no. 557, box T7.66).

13. Van Oss, *Catholic Colonialism,* 174–75.

14. García Peláez, "Católogo General [for apostolic delegate Luis Clemente]," Guatemala, 1852 (AHAG 1852.40.35, box T2.105).

15. García Peláez to Luis Clemente, Guatemala, July 24, 1852 (AHAG 1852.202, box T2.107).

16. García Peláez, "Concurso 1861," Guatemala, April 22, 1861 (AHAG 1861.175.1, box T3.84).

17. Ibid.

18. Van Oss, *Catholic Colonialism,* 126–52.

19. Ibid., 140.

20. Monroy, *Datos para la historia,* 2:527. See also Shannon Hernandez, "Charity, the State, and Social Order in Nineteenth-Century Guatemala, 1778–1881" (Master's thesis, University of Texas at Austin, 1992).

21. Antonio Larrazábal to Ramón Casáus y Torres, Guatemala, April 29, 1841 (no. 60, box T3.56).

22. Van Oss, *Catholic Colonialism,* 160.

23. García Peláez to Luis Clemente, Guatemala, July 24, 1852 (AHAG 1852.202, box T2.107).

24. García Peláez to Clergy, Guatemala, 1849 (AHAG 1849, box T4.89), Guatemala, 1862 (AHAG 1862.305, box T3.79), and Guatemala, 1862 (AHAG 1863.29, box T3.79). To compile the database for analysis we created a roster for each parish based on these three sources, which spanned the period from 1819 through 1862. It was possible to correct some mistakes where the two records overlapped, but otherwise it was impossible to verify the record of each parish. We have thus taken at face value those records submitted by the parish priests. Since each priest was responsible for a certain financial quota to the archbishop's office, depending on the time and parish he served, there was a certain financial incentive not to exaggerate one's stay in a parish. Additional data for the capital and parishes in eastern Guatemala came from the marvelous microfilm collection of baptismal and marriage records available through the Church of Latter Day Saints of Jesus Christ. My special gratitude to José Chaclán, archivist at the AHAG and historian for Guatemala's University of San Carlos, for his unyielding energy and painstaking interest in compiling this information. Without his assistance, it would have been an impossible task.

25. I have excluded figures from the vicar general and from parishes in Guatemala City in my computation of the median stay of priests in the Spanish highlands. With this decision I have purposefully decided to analyze the strength of the Catholic church in the countryside, away from the elite circles of the capital city. Those sought-after parishes in Guatemala City experienced a consistently high turnover and significantly altered the median stay of those parishes outside Guatemala City.

26. *Libro de Defuncciones* (AHAG).

27. Pedro Cortés y Larraz, *Descripción geográfico-moral de la diocesis de Goathemala . . . ,* 1:43.

28. Van Oss, *Catholic Colonialism,* 173.

29. Jacinto Soto to García Peláez, Don García, September 1858 (AHAG 1856.82.31, box T2.117).

30. Municipality of Cuajiniquilapa to García Peláez, Cuajiniquilapa, April 24, 1854   139
(AHAG 1854.86); Alcaldes to García Peláez, Sacualpa, September 16, 1847 (AHAG 1854.92,
both in box T7.66).

31. Municipality to García Peláez, Petapa, 1862 (AHAG 1855.113, box T2.114); Municipality to García Peláez, Tejutla, October 1856 (AHAG 1856.341, box T2.118).

32. Angel Sierra to García Peláez, San Pedro Carchá, July 22, 1858 (AHAG 1858.220); García Peláez to Sierra, Guatemala, July 26, 1858 (AHAG 1858.220; both in box T3.97).

33. Justo Milla to García Peláez, Cuajiniquilapa, [October 1853] (AHAG 1853.81, box
T7.66).

34. For example, see García Peláez to Carrera, Guatemala, September 17, 1847 (AHAG
1847.3.8, box T2.92). Chapter 3 examines in more detail the role of Carrera and clergy in the
eastern mountains.

35. See Cuartas Episcopales, unnumbered box now in center aisles of AHAG. See also
*Libro 2. de ingresos de la renta decimal, con arreglo á el acuerdo de el Mui Ilustre y Venerable Ca-
bildo de esta Sta. Iglesia Metropolitana . . .* , Guatemala, 1848–1859 (AHAG, box T5.137). See
Douglass Sullivan-González, "Piety, Power, and Politics: The Role of Religion in the Formation of the Guatemalan Nation-State, 1839–1871" (Ph.D. diss., University of Texas at Austin,
1994), app. 5, for a listing of these numbers. See also *Resolución modificando el cobro del diezmo*
. . .

36. Sr. Juan Obispo de Arendal to García Peláez, Chimaltenango, March 22, 1861 (AHAG
1860.33.1, box T6.62).

Chapter 3. Popular Protest and Religious Commotions

1. Rosendo García de Salas to Francisco García Peláez, Totonicapan, September 1, 1855
(AHAG 1855.249, box T2.116). See also P. José Valenzuela, "Decreto," *Boletín Oficial* 35, April
15, 1834, 249–50; José M. Quiñones to García Peláez, Totonicapan, December 24, 1847 (no.
363, box T6.58).

2. John L. Stephens, *Incidents of Travel in Central America, Chiapas and Yucatan,* 2:371–72.

3. Pedro A. Gutierrez to Provincial Vicariate of Sololá, Santa Clara la Laguna, November
13, 1868 (AHAG 1868.470.1, box T4.79).

4. Pedro T. Valenzuela, "Decreto," *Boletín Oficial* 41, August 22, 1834, 308.

5. Pedro Vox to Diego Batres, Momostenango, January 23, 1834 (AHAG 1834.33, box T87).

6. Salvador Narraez to Provisor, Quiché, September 19, 1836 (AHAG 1836.154, box T1.82).

7. Second Alcalde to Political Chief of Chimaltenango, San Martin, June 21, 1839 (AGCA
B.119.1, leg. 2503, exp. 55716).

8. Individuals to Municipality of Gomera, San Pedro Chipilapa, September 1837 (AGCA
B.119.2, exp. 57016, leg. 2521), fol. 1; José M. Cobar to General Secretary of State of
Guatemala, Guatemala, October 14, 1837 (ibid.), fol. 5.

9. A. Carlos Rojo to Larrazábal, Santa Maria Cahabón, December 10, 1839 (AHAG 1839,
box T4.63).

10. Antonio Carrillo to Municipality, Escuintla, March 1840 (AGCA B.119.3, exp. 58967,
leg. 2504), fol. 3.

11. Guillermo Pons, "Informe," Zacapa, December 15, 1852 (AHAG Visita Pastoral
1852.137, box T6.60).

140   12. Linda Schele and David Freidel, *A Forest of Kings: The Untold Story of the Ancient Maya,* 45.

13. Stephens, *Incidents of Travel,* 1:74.

14. João José Reis, *A morte é uma festa. Ritos fúnebres e revolta popular no Brasil do século XIX,* 73.

15. Ibid., 73–78.

16. Ibid., 16.

17. Antonio Chinchilla to García Peláez, Ostuncalco, March 27, 1848 (AHAG no. 266, box T6.59).

18. Larrazábal to Venancio Gomez, Guatemala, December 1, 1840 (AHAG no. 192, box T4.63).

19. Baltasar Baldwini to García Peláez, Cahabón (AHAG Visita Pastoral 1846.115, box T6.58); Baltasar Baldwini, "Los pueblos indígenas de Cahabón y Lanquin en el departamento de Verapaz. Año de 1847," in *Anales de la Sociedad de Geografía e Historia de Guatemala* 57 (January–December 1983): 76.

20. Pedro Muñoz to García Peláez, Zacapulas, January 15, 1848 (AHAG Visita Pastoral 1848.54, box T6.59).

21. José Mariano Herrarte to García Peláez, Tejutla, March 11, 1848 (AHAG Visita Pastoral 1848.183, box T6.59).

22. Ramón Solis to Municipality, Chimaltenango, June 26, 1839 (AGCA B.119.1, leg. 2503, exp. 55716); Manuel Sij, Rabinal, November 17, 1840 (AHAG no. 192, box T4.63); T. M Argueta to Corregidor de Totonicapan Momostenango, February 23, 1847 (AGCA B, exp. 29, leg. 28537). During the 1848 pastoral visit to Santa Catarina Ixtahuacán, parishioners requested that the archbishop approve returning the interment of bodies to the church cemetery. See Antonio Domingo to García Peláez, Ixtahuacán, March 1848 (AHAG Visita Pastoral 1848.207, box T6.59).

23. Francisco Lemus to Provisor Gobernador, Huehuetenango, August 12, 1837 (AHAG 1837.171, box T1.84).

24. Ibid.

25. Eugenio Cordova to Curia Metropolitana, Lanquin, October 12, 1837 (AHAG 1837.212, box T1.84).

26. José M. Figueroa to the President, Momostenango, [1847] (AGCA B, exp. 29, leg. 28537), fol. 1; quotation from Ygnacio Cordova to Minister of Interior, Totonicapan, March 4, 1847 (AGCA B, exp. 29, leg. 28537), fol. 4.

27. José Antonio Aguilar to García Peláez, Cajolá, March 31, 1848 (AHAG no. 314, box T6.59).

28. Bernardo Piñol to García Peláez, Quezaltenango, April 18, 1850 (AHAG no. 192, box T7.67).

29. Larrazábal, *Memoria.*

30. Eugenio Cordova to the Curia, Lanquin, October 12, 1837 (AHAG 1837.212, box T1.84).

31. J. J. Sabino de Leon to García Peláez, Cajolá, October 27, 1848 (AHAG no. 397, box T7.64).

32. Fray José Maria Figeroa to García Peláez, Momostenango, January 11, 1848 (AHAG Visita Pastoral nos. 47–48, box T6.59).

33. Nancy M. Farriss, *Maya Society Under Colonial Rule: The Collective Enterprise of Survival,* 323.

34. José Maria Valdez to García Peláez, San Pedro Carchá, January 5, 1846 (AHAG Visita   141
Pastoral 1846.90, box T6.58).

35. See Sabino de Leon, "Informe," Cubulco, February 17, 1846 (AHAG Visita Pastoral
1846.149, box T6.58). For a brief description of the Mexican Councils, see Enrique Dussel, *Introducción general a la historia de la iglesia en América Latina,* 488–96. Farriss noted that priests
who permitted this religious autonomy among the indigenous leaders were considered by
some bishops to be derelict in their duty. Yet most priests openly allowed indigenous choirmasters to conduct the funerals. Clerics in nineteenth-century Guatemala, on the other hand,
did not exude this permissive attitude and certainly did not discriminate between the wealthy
and the poor when it came to collecting fees. See Farriss, *Maya Society,* 517–18, n. 9.

36. José María Ortiz to García Peláez, "Tactic," April 13, 1852 (AHAG 1852.71.16–18, box
T2.105).

37. Antonio Adolfo Perez, "Informe," San Pedro Carchá, March 1, 1864 (AHAG Visita
Pastoral 1860.34A.25).

38. José M. Muñoz to García Peláez, Huehuetenango, January 12, 1866 (AHAG 1866.23,
box T4.74); Román Gordillo to Sr. Juan Felix de Jesus Zepeda, Chimaltenango, October 24,
1860 (AHAG Visita Pastoral 1860.29.9, box T2.62); El Común y indios de Momostenango,
Momostenango, October 1870 (AGCA B, leg. 28627, exp. 402).

39. Fernando Aguado to García Peláez, Retalhuleu, August 6, 1857 (AHAG 1861.287.1);
Pedro González Batres to the Archbishop, San Cristobal Totonicapan, 1869 (AHAG
1852.147.52, box T2.106); Pedro Abella to Sr. Corregidor de Verapaz, San Pedro Carchá, March
27, 1862 (AGCA B, leg. 28587, exp. 24), fol. 13.

40. Felix Castañeda to Sr. Ministro de Gobernación del Supremo Gobierno, Huehuetenango, November 29, 1859 (AGCA B, leg. 28579, exp. 232), fol. 2; M. Fuentes Franco to Felix
Castañeda, Comandancia de los Altos (AGCA B, leg. 28579, exp. 232), fol. 2. Missing judicial
records in the AGCA prevent any further investigation of this fascinating religious event. It is
to be hoped that more careful organization and protection of nineteenth-century records will
shed greater light on the story. The last record mentioned an armed expedition sent to capture the boy, but no formal follow-up has been discovered. Also see Serge Gruzinski, *Man-
God in the Mexican Highlands.*

41. Vicente Cerna to Sr. Ministro de Gobernación del Supremo Gobierno, Chiquimula,
July 23, 1851 (AGCA B, leg. 28553, exp. 110). As in the case of the man-god from Santa Eulalia,
further documentation is not available in the AGCA because of judicial records' being mis-
placed or lost.

42. Vicente Hernández, "Informe," Santa Catarina Ixtahuacán, December 21, 1847
(AHAG Visita Pastoral 1847.261, 265, box T6.58).

43. Governor and Común of Santa Catarina Ixtahuacán to Archbishop, Santa Catarina Ix-
tahuacán, October 22, 1853 (AHAG no. 219, box T7.67); Hernández to García Peláez, Santa
Catarina Ixtahuacán, October 30, 1853 (AHAG no. 221, box T7.67), and January 20, 1854
(AHAG 1854.27, box T2.111).

44. Hernández to García Peláez, Santa Catarina Ixtahuacán, October 30, 1853 (AHAG no.
221, box T7.67), and January 20, 1854 (AHAG 1854.27, box T2.111).

45. Hernández to García Peláez, Santa Catarina Ixtahuacán, April 20, 1853 (AHAG no.
210, box T7.67).

46. Hernández to García Peláez, Santa Catarina Ixtahuacán, July 30, 1853 (AHAG no.
214–15, box T7.67).

142   47. For Valenzuela's comments on Hernández's work, see Pedro Valenzuela to García Peláez, Guatemala, January 2, 1854 (AHAG 1854.1, box T2.111).

48. Ibid.

49. Hernández to García Peláez, Santa Catarina Ixtahuacán, July 30, 1853 (AHAG no. 215, box T7.67).

50. The archbishop announced each pastoral visit with a letter outlining the intentions of his pilgrimage. In each visit he focused on an analysis of the cofradías. For example, see García Peláez to Clergy of Verapaz, Guatemala, October 17, 1845 (AHAG no. 11, box T6.58).

51. León Aloazar to García Peláez, Cuyotenango, January 11, 1862 (AHAG Visita Pastoral 1862.351–61, box T3.63); Manuel Lopez to Vic. Provincial de Quezaltenango, Olintepeque, July 1, 1869 (AHAG 1869.277.5, box T4.85); José Maria Navarro, *Estado actual de esta parroquia de Concepción de Villa Nueva, formado por el presbítero Jose Maria Navarro su cura encargado en 1864,* 17; Bernardo Solano, "Informe," Chimaltenango, 1860 (AHAG Visita Pastoral 1860.29.14, box T6.62); Juan Sabino Linares, "Informe," Cuilco, March 4, 1848 (AHAG Visita Pastoral 1848.166, box T6.59); Blas Florentino Vleasco, Cuilco, October 15, 1861 (AHAG 1861.191, box T3.84).

52. Francisco de Rueda to García Peláez, San Pedro Sacatepequez, March 16, 1848 (AHAG Visita Pastoral 1848.250, box T6.59); José Ma. Orellana to García Peláez, San Pedro Sacatepequez, 1861 (AHAG 1861.189.2, box T3.84); [Razón de cofradías e hermandades], Coban, 1831 (AHAG 1831.126, box T1.92); Vicente Ferver Chivillers to García Peláez, Coban, May 30, 1856 (AHAG 1856.85.15, box T2.117); Venancio Gálvez, "Estado de los cofradías," Ravinal, October 30, 1841 (AHAG no. 223, box T4.63); Antonio Adolfo Perez to García Peláez, Rabinal, January 1864 (AHAG 1860, box T6.62); Inocente Cordon to García Peláez, Jalpatagua, February 1858 (AHAG Visita Pastoral 1852.287, box T6.60); José Güell y Busquets to García Peláez, Conguaco, May 23, 1864 (AHAG 1864.164, box T3.69). David McCreery, in *Rural Guatemala, 1760–1840* (Stanford: Stanford University Press, 1994), overstates the case when he argues that cofradias in nineteenth-century Guatemala were at the brink of collapse.

53. Estevan Lorenzana to Larrazábal, Coban, October 9, 1838 (AHAG, box T4.63); Chinchilla, "Informe," Ostuncalco, March 27, 1848 (AHAG Visita Pastoral 1848.269–70, box T6.59); José María Figueroa to García Peláez, Momostenango, "Informe," January 11, 1848 (AHAG Visita Pastoral 1848.16–17, 48, box T6.59); Cayetano Serra, "Informe," Huehuetenango, February 19, 1848 (AHAG Visita Pastoral 1848.140, box T6.59).

54. Juan Raull to García Peláez, Totonicapan, September 19, 1853 (AHAG no. 113, box T7.67); Raymundo Fourcado to Fernando Gonzalez, San Jacinto, December 9, 1865 (AHAG 1866.542.9, box T4.72); José Maria T. Gutierrez to Justo Gavarette, Asunción Mita, November 6, 1850 (AHAG 1849.257.23, box T2.7); José Inocente Cordon to García Peláez, San Cristobal Acasaguastlan, November 1860 (AHAG no. 221, box T3.63); Joaquin de Valle to García Peláez, Conguaco, September 9, 1855 (AHAG 1855.260, box T2.116).

55. J. Sabino de Leon to García Peláez, Mataquescuintla, July 6, 1847 (AHAG 1847.78.5, box T2.92).

56. "Decreto," Guatemala, May 9, 1847 (AHAG 1861.187, box T3.83); A. Tolares to Sabino de Leon, Santa Rosa, April 24, 1847 (AHAG 1847.78.4, box T2.92).

57. Sabino de Leon to García Peláez, Mataquescuintla, July 6, 1847 (AHAG 1847.78.5, box T2.92).

58. José Inocente Cordon to García Peláez, San Cristobal Acasaguastlán, November 1860 (AHAG 1860.221, box T3.63); J. Maria Mijangos to García Peláez, Acatenango, April 21, 1856

(AHAG 1857.113.6, box T2.121); García Peláez to J. Maria Mijangos, Guatemala, April 13, 1856   143
(AHAG 1857.113.11, box T2.121).

59. José María Cuyil and Gaspar Rabinal to Sr. Corregidor, Tecpan Guatemala, July 1860
(AHAG 1848.203.22, box T2.93).

60. J. C. Lorenzana to Supreme Government, Chimaltenango, July 17, 1860 (AHAG
1848.203.23, box T2.93). The Catholic hierarchy responded by affirming the government's
right to limit the number of fiesta days. See Beteta to Sr. Ministro, Guatemala, July 31, 1860
(AHAG 1860.203.23–24, box T2.93).

61. See Sullivan-González, "Piety, Power, and Politics," table 11, p. 115.

62. Charles E. Rosenberg, *The Cholera Years: The United States in 1832, 1849, and 1866*, 2–3.

63. "Diary of a Young Man, July 18, 1832" (Manuscript Division, New York Historical Society), quoted in Rosenberg, *The Cholera Years*, 3.

64. M. J. Palacios to Provisor, Guatemala, September 22, 1837 (AHAG 1837.199.1); M. de
Leon to Provisor, Guatemala, April 4, 1837 (AHAG 1837.199.3); Salasar to Prov. Cap.,
Guatemala, 1837 (AHAG 1837.199.5); Salazar to Vic. Capitular, Guatemala, May 18, 1837
(AHAG 1837.104); Feliciano García to Prov. Gov. del Arzobispado, Panajachel, June 24, 1837
(AHAG 1837.132); M. Alvarado to Antonio Letona, Zunil, July 29, 1837 (AHAG 1837.153; all
in box T1.84).

65. Pedro A. Gutierrez to Provincial Vicariate, Santa Clara la Laguna, November 13, 1868
(AHAG 1868.470.1, box T4.79); Rosendo García de Salas to García Peláez, Totonicapan, September 1, 1855 (AHAG 1855.249, box T2.116).

66. Tobar Cruz, *Los montañeses*, 51–52, n. 2.

67. José Maria Aguero to Antonio Letona, La Laguna, June 30, 1837 (AHAG 1837.134, box
T1.84); Municipalidad de San Luis Xilotepeque to Antonio Larrazábal, San Luis Xilotepeque,
March 10, 1838 (AHAG 1838.45, box T4.65); Ysidro Menéndez to Prov. Governador,
Quimango, May 28, 1838 (AHAG 1838.59.3, box T1.84); Francisco Lemus to Prov. Gov., Santa
Maria Chiquimula, August 12, 1837 (AHAG 1837.171, box T1.84); Salasar to Prov. Gov.,
Guatemala, May 31, 1837 (AHAG 1837.110, box T1.84); Eugenio Cordova to Curia Metropol-
itana, Lanquin, October 12, 1837 (AHAG 1837.212, box T1.84).

68. Municipalidad de San Luis Xilotepeque to Antonio Larrazábal, San Luis Xilotepeque,
March 10, 1838 (AHAG 1838.45, box T4.65).

69. José María Ycasa to García Peláez, Chiquimulilla, July 28, 1857 (AHAG 1860.15.33, box
T3.90); José Antonio Díaz to García Peláez, Mataquescuintla, September 13, 1857 (AHAG
1855.39.8, box T2.114); Felipe de Jesús Betancourt to García Peláez, Guatemala, November 8,
1857 (AHAG 1860.123.76, box T3.89). In his time-honored *Datos para la historia de la iglesia
en Guatemala*, Estrada Monroy incorrectly reports that the priest and the governor were both
murdered in the riot following the cholera outbreak. Only the governor was killed. See
Estrada Monroy, *Datos para la historia*, 2:772.

70. José María Ycasa to García Peláez, Chiquimulilla, July 28, 1857 (AHAG 1860.15.33, box
T3.90); Ycasa to García Peláez, Sonsonate, September 10, 1857 (AHAG 1857.323, box T2.123).
According to Ralph Lee Woodward Jr. economic factors must also account for the varied results of the 1837 and 1857 cholera epidemics. See Woodward, *Rafael Carrera*, ch. 17, for a detailed look at the Guatemalan economy during the Carrera years.

71. Sebastian Váldez to García Peláez, Jutiapa, February 2, 1857 (AHAG 1858.57, box
T3.99).

72. J. Ma. Mollinero to García Peláez, Escuintla, December 29, 1856 (AHAG 1856.340,
box T2.118).

144   73. Padre Buenaventura de Cogollos Vega, *Los capuchinos en Guatemala,* 21.

74. In an analysis of Guatemala, the U.S. diplomat Beverly Clark stated that Santa Rosa was comprised of thirty thousand people, with very few Indians. See Beverly Clark, Guatemala City, September 29, 1859, in U.S. Department of State, *Despatches from United States Ministers to Guatemala, 1824–1906* (microfilm).

75. Gumersindo de Estello, *Historia y empresas apostólicas del siervo de Dios P. Esteban de Adoáin,* 257.

76. See chapter 4 on the religious discourse emanating from the capital.

77. De Estello, *Historia y empresas apostólicas,* 257. This history was compiled through several letters written to the headquarters of the Capuchins in Spain and analyzed by de Estella later on. Personal reflections of the Capuchin Ignacio de Cambrils, who accompanied Adoáin in his pilgrimage, provide the basis of the most cited document concerning the Capuchins in Guatemala: Ignacio de Cambrils, *Cronicón de la misión de pp. capuchinos en Centro América o fundación y propagación de la religión capuchina en la América Central,* 79–80.

78. Ildefonso de Ciáurriz, *Vida del siervo de Dios P. Fr. Esteban de Adoáin, capuchino misionero apostólico en América y España,* 270–71; P. Lazaro de Aspurz, *Esteban de Adoáin llevó el evangelio de la paz a siete naciones. Restauró la Orden capuchina en España* (Pamplona, Spain: Ediciones Navasal, 1980), 161.

79. De Cambrils, *Cronicón,* 80. The five who did not put down their weapons were never identified. See also Esteban de Adoáin to Garcia Peláez, Tempisque, March 17, 1858 (AHAG 1858.101, box T3.98), and from Guatemala, April 1859 (AHAG 1859.101, box T3.91). These last two letters from Adoáin suggest that a significant portion of the population acquiesced in legitimizing their marriages and receiving communion. After the Capuchins' religious mission to Guatemala's eastern region, no correspondence from clerics during the late 1850s and 1860s noted any further hostility toward the clergy.

80. Rafael Pérez, *La compañia de Jesús en Colombia y Centro-América* . . . , pt. 2, 21–22. Church records indicate that the parish income of Santa Rosa doubled 100 percent within the year of the Capuchin visit. For example, the capital improvement fund *(fondo de fábrica)* increased from some 229 pesos during 1857 to 510 pesos in 1860. This capital improvement fund represented 4 percent of the yearly income of the church and was dedicated to the church's structural maintenance. Manual Uriarte, "Estado de los ingresos y egresos habidos en el fondo de la Parroquia de Sta. Rosa," March 24, 1862 (AGCA B, leg. 28587, exp. 019), fol. 8.

Chapter 4. The Covenant

1. Stephens, *Incidents of Travel,* 1:230, 232.

2. The earliest mention of celebration comes from Asamblea Nacional Constituyente, "Decreto de 26 Agosto que dispone la festividad el dia 15," Guatemala, [1823] (AGCA B.78.25, exp. 16934, leg. 727). Numerous references to the September 15 celebration can be found in the Guatemalan AGCA, AHAG, and CB archives. Annual governmental requests to the Catholic leadership for religious services commemorating Independence preceded the celebrations by between two and four weeks. For example, see Pedro N. Ariagga to Francisco García Peláez, Guatemala, August 12, 1850 (AHAG 1850.121, box T2.100). Thanks to the hard work and professional interest of Carmen Valenzuela de Garay, archivist of the César Brañas library, an updated list of September 15 sermons and speeches is available for the researcher.

See Arturo Taracena Flores, "Oradores oficiales en las celebraciones de la independencia desde el año de 1831" (photocopy; CB 41052), for a listing that dates from 1831 to 1934. 145

3. Gobierno de Guatemala, "Circular," Guatemala [1829] (AGCA B.87.1, exp. 28851, leg. 1189). Records indicate that celebrations took place sporadically in most departments during the 1830s. However, it is not possible to determine which departments celebrated and which did not. In 1835 Chiquimula and San Marcos responded affirmatively, and in 1836 Escuintla officials called for similar demonstrations. See "Circular a los Gefes Departamentales," Guatemala, August 28, 1835 (AGCA B.87.1, exp. 28997, leg. 1191); "Carranza a las Municipalidades," Guatemala, September 10, 1836 (AGCA B.119.3, exp. 58617, leg. 2541).

4. J. A. Alcayaga to Secretario General, Guatemala, September 13, 1829 (AGCA B.94.1, exp. 32417, leg. 1396).

5. Taracena Flores, "Oradores oficiales."

6. "Quince de septiembre," *Gaceta Oficial* 2, September 25, 1845, p. 67; "15 de septiembre de 1842," *Gaceta Oficial,* September 17, 1842, p. 267. On Carrera, see Pedro de Aycinena to García Peláez, Guatemala, September 13, 1854 (AHAG 1854.214, box T2.112); Manuel Echeverría to García Peláez, Guatemala, September 13, 1855 (AHAG 1855.267, box T2.116). See also Miguel Arrazola, "Discurso."

7. Chiquimula's corregidor Esteban Lanquin advised governmental authorities that he had received twelve copies of the 1841 anniversary speech and had circulated it. See Esteban Lanquin to Ministro General del Supremo Gobierno del Estado, Chiquimula, October 10, 1841 (AGCA B.119.2, exp. 57696, leg. 2529). Copies of Aycinena's 1862 sermon were circulated to all church clerics in 1862. See García Peláez to Church Clerics, Guatemala, October 27, 1862 (AHAG 1862.365, box T3.77).

8. Taracena Flores, "Oradores oficiales." The Taracena Flores Collection, located at the Benson Latin American Collection at the University of Texas, contains the greatest number of these speeches. Guatemala's University of San Carlos's César Brañas Collection has the second-largest collection.

9. José Matías Quiñones, *Al soldado ilustre de la patria . . . en el Aniversario de Nuestra Gloriosa Independencia;* Simon Vasconcelos, "[Discurso] 15 de Septiembre," *Boletín Oficial,* September 15, 1835, p. 876; José Francisco Barrundia, *Discurso pronunciado el día 15 de septiembre de 1836,* 1; Pedro Molina, *Discurso acerca de la utilidad de la Independencia de Centro-América,* 1; Un Militar, *Observaciones sobre el discurso pronunciado por el Bachiller José D. Milla, en el Aniversario de la Independencia de Centro-América,* 3. For other Independence speeches delivered during the 1830s, see José Barrundia, "Al nacimiento de la Patria en el 15 de septiembre," in *El Centro-Americano. Extraordinario,* September 15, 1833, pp. 199–206; Mariano Gálvez, "[Discurso, 15 septiembre 1832]," *Boletín extraordinario. Segunda parte,* September 30, 1832.

10. Quiñones preached in Los Altos, the general area surrounding Guatemala's Quezaltenango, Totonicapan, and Sololá, which temporarily split from Guatemala to join the Central American federation in the late 1830s and early 1840s. Quiñones claimed to represent the Quiché Indians who had been "humiliated" in the sixteenth century by Spanish conquest but now had become a sovereign state of the Central American union. See José Matías Quiñones, *Sermon predicado en la parroquia de Totonicapan . . .* (CB 3091), 1. See also Pedro C. Bustamante, "[Discurso, 15 septiembre 1832]," *Boletín extraordinario. Segunda parte,* September 30, 1832 (CB 1505).

11. Gudmundson and Fuentes, *Central America,* 108. See also Pedro José Valenzuela, "Discurso sobre la igualdad de clases y diferencias de aptitudes," *Boletín Oficial,* September 1, 1831, pp. 127–40; Molina, *Discurso acerca de la utilidad,* 3–5.

146   12. Juan José de Aycinena, *Discurso pronunciado en la casa del Supremo Gobierno del Estado de Guatemala. El Quince de Setiembre Aniversario XIX. De su Independencia del Gobierno Español* (hereafter cited as *Discurso 1840*).

13. Juan José de Aycinena, *Discurso que en la fiesta de acción de grácias celebrada en la Catedral de Guatemala el 15 de septiembre de 1837,* [5–10] (hereafter cited as *Discurso 1837*). This disgust with the popular religiosity of the nonwhite Guatemalans ran deep and for a long time within elite discourse. Vicente Molina retorted in 1842 that "fanaticism had made the people more addicted to religious ceremonies than to moral principles." See Vicente Molina, *Discurso pronunciado el 15 de septiembre de 1845 vigesimo cuarto Aniversario de la Independencia de Guatemala en el salon del supremo poder ejecutivo,* 6. See also Andres Andreu, *[Discurso pronunciado el 15 de septiembre de 1839],* 5.

14. Aycinena, *Discurso 1840,* [10]. See also Manuel Echeverría, *Discurso que el 15 de septiembre de 1844, Aniversario XXIII de la Independencia de Centro-América . . . ,* [4]. Aycinena's reversal earned him the scorn of his liberal colleagues. Much liberal historiography views this switch as a conservative scheme to co-opt the ignorant and pliable Carrera. I will demonstrate that any alliance the church made with Carrera was undertaken with trepidation and not with patronizing arrogance.

15. Juan José de Aycinena, *Discurso pronunciado el 15 de setiembre de 1850, XXIX Aniversario de la Independencia de Guatemala,* 12 (hereafter cited as *Discurso 1850*); José Nicolás Arellano, *Sermón predicado el 15 de septiembre de 1845, vigesimo cuarto Aniversario de nuestra Independencia del Gobierno Español en la Santa Iglesia Catedral de Guatemala,* 6–7 (hereafter cited as *Sermón 1845*); Basilio Zeceña, *Sermón que en la función de grácias celebrada el día 1 de enero de 1844 en la Sta. Iglesia Catedral antes las Supremas Autoridades del Estado Guatamalteco,* 4, 11 (hereafter cited as *Sermón 1844*).

16. Aycinena, *Discurso 1840,* 4. See also Juan José de Aycinena, *Discurso pronunciado el 15 de setiembre de 1848, XXVII Aniversario de la Independencia de Guatemala,* 11; Bernardo Piñol, *Discurso que en la solemne acción de grácias . . . ,* 5; José Antonio Urrutia, *Exhortación dirigida al pueblo de Guatemala en el llano del incienso. . . . En la fusilación de Feliciano Masariegos. El dia 3 de mayo de 1849,* [5]. Even the civil war in the United States was interpreted as divine punishment for straying from divine law. See Juan José de Aycinena, *Sermón predicado en la festividad del primer aniversario de la dedicación solemne del Templo Catedral de la Archdiócesis de Santiago de Guatemala.*

17. This 1843 anniversary sermon by García Peláez was quoted by Montúfar in *Reseña histórica,* 4:177. No copy of this sermon has been located in any of the researched archives.

18. Aycinena, *Discurso 1850,* 9.

19. Aycinena, *Discurso 1840,* 3. See also Arellano, *Sermón 1845,* 8; Aycinena, *Discurso 1850,* 4, 9, 12; Juan José de Aycinena, *Discurso pronunciado el 15 de setiembre de 1853, XXXII Aniversario de la Independencia de Guatemala,* 4 (hereafter cited as *Discurso 1853*); Juan José de Aycinena, *Aniversario XXXVIII de la Independencia de Guatemala. Discurso religioso pronunciado en la Santa Iglesia Catedral el 16 de septiembre de 1859,* 14 (hereafter cited as *Discurso 1859*); Manuel Francisco Velez, *Discurso político-religioso pronunciado en la S.I. Catedral el 15 de setiembre de 1869. XLVIII Aniversario de nuestra Independencia de la Monarquia Española,* 15–16 (hereafter cited as *Discurso 1869*). France's "fall from grace" and ensuing social chaos was illustrative of a society's straying from the straight and narrow. In the first Independence sermon, Castilla remarked that France, once made up of pious people, now found itself divided into parties and bathed in blood. See José María Castilla, *Al heróico pueblo de Guatemala,* 8; José Mariano Dominguez, *Bernado Domingues padre del presbítero . . . ,* 5.

20. Castilla, *Al heróico pueblo*, 6.

21. Estrada Monroy, *Datos para la historia*, 2:277–78. Within the numerous sermons printed during the first half of the nineteenth century, none could be found attributed to Castilla save the 1821 sermon. Recently arrived in the country in 1838, John Stephens encountered the Reverend Castilla and confirmed the cleric's prominence and his elite education. Castilla was on his way to Havana to negotiate for the archbishop's return from exile in Cuba. See Stephens, *Incidents of Travel*, 1:49.

22. Friar Luis Escoto, *Sermón que en la acción de grácias que el comercio de la ciudad de Guatemala tributó a Maria Santísima . . . ,* [7].

23. Sicilia y Montoya, "Oración eucaristica que pronunció el Sr. Dr. D. Sicilia y Montoya . . . ," 13.

24. Francisco Ramón Casáus y Torres to Antonio Larrazábal, Havana, Cuba, November 8, 1839 (AHAG no. 41, box T3.56).

25. Manuel Zacarías Velasquez, *Discurso político-religioso pronunciado en la Santa Iglesia Catedral de Guatemala el día 15 de septiembre de 1844 . . . ,* 1 (hereafter cited as *Discurso 1844*).

26. Juan José de Aycinena, *El toro amarillo*, and *Respuesta*, 1–4.

27. Lorenzo Montúfar asserts that Juan José de Aycinena authored the October 1842 statement of Guatemala's president Mariano Rivera Paz that God's continued blessing of Guatemala was evident in the September 15, 1842, execution of Morazán. Although there is cause for suspicion in much of Montúfar's criticism of Aycinena (due to Montúfar's unyielding obsession with this elite leader), I am inclined to agree, since the theological assumptions of Rivera Paz's statement closely mirror Aycinena's views. See Montúfar, *Reseña histórica*, 4:16.

28. Aycinena, *Discurso 1850*, 6; *XXXVII Aniversario de la Independencia de Guatemala*, 5; *XLII Aniversario de la Independencia de Guatemala*, 6, 10; Francisco de Paula García Peláez, *Discurso pronunciado el 15 de septiembre de 1856 XXXV Aniversario de la Independencia de Guatemala*, 2 (hereafter cited as *Discurso 1856*).

29. For a descriptive biography of Juan José de Aycinena, see Chandler, *Juan José de Aycinena*.

30. Juan José de Aycinena, *Aniversario XXXVII de la Independencia de Guatemala. Discurso religioso pronunciado en la Santa Iglesia Catedral el 16 de septiembre de 1858*, 12 (hereafter cited as *Discurso 1858*). Additionally, consult Aycinena, *Discurso 1837*, [6], and *Discurso 1850*, 7; Juan José de Aycinena, *Sermón que en la fiesta anual que celebra el I. Colegio de Abogados el dia 18 de octubre de 1857*, 6.

31. Aycinena, *Discurso 1858*, 7; Juan José de Aycinena, *Aniversario XLII de la Independencia de Guatemala. Discurso religioso pronunciado en la Santa Iglesia Catedral el 15 de setiembre de 1864*, 9–10 (hereafter cited as *Discurso 1864*). Additionally, consult Juan José de Aycinena, *Sermón predicado el 24 de agosto de 1862. Trecentesimo aniversario de la reforma de carmelitas descalzas en la Iglesia de Santa Teresa de esta ciudad conventual de la misma orden*, 5. See also Bernardo Piñol, *Sermón que el día 29 de mayo de 1839 . . . ,* 3–4, 7; Tomás Suaso, *Sermón predicado el quince de septiembre . . . ,* 1.

32. Francisco de Paula García Peláez, *Discurso 1856*, 2, 4.

33. Zeceña, *Sermón 1844*, 11; Garcia Peláez, *Discurso 1856*, 2; Piñol, *Sermón 1839*, 9. Guatemalan clerics held to this one theological assumption more than most. Friar Juan de Jesus Zepeda surpassed most of his colleagues by treating this theological affirmation with great agility: "God allows ephemeral triumphs of evil in order to punish those who offend him and to test His chosen ones in the crucible of adversity." Juan de Jesus Zepeda, *Descripción del Templo de San Francisco de Guatemala*, 11.

148   34. Weber, *Sociology of Religion*, 16.

35. Sydney E. Ahlstrom, ed., *Theology in America: The Major Protestant Voices from Puritanism to Neo-Orthodoxy*, 24–33.

36. Winthrop, cited in Alan Simpson, "The Covenanted Community," 19–20.

37. Leonard Thompson, *The Political Mythology of Apartheid*, 170.

38. Aycinena, *Discurso 1858*, 14.

39. Garcia Peláez, *Discurso 1856*, 2. Also see Aycinena, *Discurso 1853*, 5–6, and *Discurso 1858*, 4, 7.

40. *Facsimile del Acta de Independencia de Centro América. Firmada en la ciudad de Guatemala el 15 de septiembre de 1821.*

41. Juan José de Aycinena, *Discurso religioso pronunciado en la S.M.I. de Santiago de Guatemala, el 15 de septiembre de 1855. Aniversario XXXIV de Independencia*, 3–4 (hereafter cited as *Discurso 1855*).

42. "En el día de la patria," *Siglo Veintiuno*, September 15, 1991, p. 10. *Siglo Veintiuno's* editorial page challenged head-on the lingering notion that independence from Spain cost nothing, by highlighting the resistance and sacrifice of many Indians and creoles who either died in armed resistance (Manuel Tot in Verapaz) or were jailed. This troubling assertion must have originated in the stark contrast with neighboring Mexico's bloody insurrection that stimulated a caste war led by Miguel Hidalgo.

43. Castilla, *Al heróico pueblo*, 6.

44. Aycinena, *Discurso 1837*, 5; Basilio Zeceña, *Discurso pronunciado en la Catedral de Guatemala . . .* , 15; José Mariano Herrarte, *Sermón predicado el quince de setiembre . . .* , 3; Molina, *Discurso acerca de la utilidad*, 2. See also Aycinena, *Discurso 1850*, 3.

45. Zacarías Velasquez, *Discurso 1844*, 8. His printed text referred to the clerics Ruiz, Miguelena, and Soto.

46. The friars were held in jail until 1819, when Fernando VII issued a general pardon. For further information on the conspiracy of Belén, see J. E. Arellano, "Nicaragua," in Dussel et al., *América Central*, 225.

47. Miguel Muñoz to Francisco García Peláez, Guatemala, December 15, 1858 (AHAG 1858.360, box T2.124).

48. According to Estrada Monroy, Guatemala's archbishop Casáus y Torres was hand-picked to respond to Hidalgo's *Grito de Dolores*. Casáus y Torres wrote the *Cartilla de párrocos* that was printed and circulated in Mexico and Central America. See Estrada Monroy, *Datos para la historia*, 2:223–37. Also, Alejandro Marure published a perceptive tract in 1838 reminding his compatriots of what happened to European colonists in Santo Domingo (Haiti), who were killed indiscriminately by the ex-slaves in their revolt. Marure's words reflected a constant fear among white Guatemalans as he warned of a possible caste war that could end "in our complete destruction." See Marure, *Memoria sobre la insurrección*, 21–22.

49. Aycinena, *Discurso 1864*, 5–11. Additionally, consult Juan José de Aycinena, *Aniversario XL [sic XLI] de la Independencia de Guatemala. Discurso religioso pronunciado en la Santa Iglesia Catedral el 15 de septiembre de 1862*, 4 (hereafter cited as *Discurso 1862*); Aycinena, *Discurso 1850*, 3, and *Discurso 1858*, 7, 11; Juan José de Aycinena, *Aniversario XXXIX de la Independencia de Guatemala. Discurso religioso pronunciado en la Santa Iglesia Catedral el 15 de setiembre de 1860*, 9.

50. Antonio Larrazábal, "Funerales celebradas en la Santa Iglesia Catedral," *Gaceta de Guatemala*, March 21, 1851, p. 3; Rafael Carrera to the People of Guatemala, Chiquimula, Feb-

ruary 5, 1851 (AHAG, box T6.61); Francisco García Peláez, *Nos el Doctor D. Francisco de Paula* 149
García Peláez . . . (Guatemala, January 4, 1851). In the archbishop's call for prayer, he reiterated that the spirit of rebellion and discord were God's way of making the people atone for their sins. See also García Peláez, *Discurso 1856,* 8. In Aycinena, *Discurso 1853,* 8, Aycinena affirmed God's watchful care over Guatemala at the very moment invaders tried to conquer Guatemala.

51. Juan José de Aycinena, *Oración fúnebre que pronunció en la S.I.M. de Guatemala el dia 14 de enero de 1857* . . . , 3.

52. Pérez, *La compañia de Jesús,* 30; de Cambrils, *Cronicón,* 69–72.

53. García Peláez, cited in De Cambrils, *Cronicón,* 78.

54. Sor Maria Clara to Carrera, Capuchin Convent in Guatemala, December 3, 1863 (AGCA B.118.6, exp. 53312, leg. 2443), fol. 4; Aycinena to Carrera, Guatemala, November 17, 1863 (AGCA B.118.6, exp. 53278, leg. 2443), fol. 15; García Peláez to Carrera, Guatemala, November 16, 1863 (AGCA B.118.6, exp. 53278, leg. 2443), fol. 14. There is more on this incident in chapter 5.

55. Aycinena, *Discurso 1850,* 13–14.

56. Aycinena, *Discurso 1862,* 4–18; Velez, *Discurso 1869,* 9. See also Aycinena, *Discurso 1853,* 5; *Discurso 1850,* 4, 13–14; *Discurso 1855,* 5–8; and *Discurso 1859,* 5.

57. Antonio Larrazábal to General Secretary of Supreme Government, Guatemala, November 25, 1843 (AHAG 1843.142, box T3.61). See Frederick Crowe's own biographical account of his venture in Guatemala in the 1840s, *The Gospel in Central America. . . . A History of the Baptist Mission in British Honduras and of the Introduction of the Bible Into the Spanish American Republic of Guatemala.*

58. Aycinena, *Discurso 1850,* 5–6; Prudencio Puertas, *Discurso político-religioso pronunciado en la Sta. Iglesia Catedral el 15 de setiembre de 1854, XXXIII Aniversario de la Independencia de Guatemala,* 8 (hereafter cited as *Discurso 1854*); Angel María Arroyo, *Discurso político-religioso pronunciado en la Sta. Iglesia Catedral Metropolitana el día 15 de septiembre de 1871 en celebración del Aniversario L de la Independencia nacional,* 9. Additionally, consult Juan José de Aycinena, *Sermón predicado en la S.I. Metropolitana de Guatemala el día 1 de enero de 1864,* 3–4; Aycinena, *Discurso 1862,* 5–6; Aycinena, *El toro amarillo,* 39.

59. Aycinena, *Discurso 1850,* 12; Velez, *Discurso 1869,* 14; Zeceña, *Sermón 1844,* 4; Puertas, *Discurso 1854,* 8–9; Bernardo Piñol, *Discurso pronunciado en la Santa Iglesia Catedral el 15 de setiembre de 1849 en el vigesimo octavo Aniversario de la Independencia,* [4–5]. See also Arellano, *Sermón 1845,* 7–8; Juan José de Aycinena, *Sermón predicado en la S.I.M. de Guatemala el dia 1. de enero de 1862 en la función que se celebra con asistencia de todas las autoridades,* 6–7.

60. Aycinena, *Discurso 1862,* 16, 18.

61. Juan José de Aycinena, *Demostración del derecho de propiedad que en la plazuela llamada "Del Sagrado" tiene la Santa Iglesia Metropolitana de Guatemala,* 18. This legal treatise, written in 1850 by Aycinena, concludes with an 1865 challenge by Archbishop García Peláez to Guatemalan officials who once again contested ecclesiastical ownership. When church officials sought to sell the plaza in order to finance the building of the cathedral's bell towers, municipal officials blocked the sale, arguing that they were the rightful owners of the small plaza despite the unusual circumstances of its having been seized during the liberal anticlerical measures of the 1820s.

62. Un Militar, *Observaciones,* 1. Like Milla, clerical and nonclerical discourse often focused on the Spanish conquest. In 1841 Basilio Porras minimized the historical blame falling

150   on Spanish descendants of the conquistadors in nineteenth-century Guatemala. On the contrary these descendants, exclaimed Porras, deserved credit for independence from Spain. By the late 1860s Christopher Columbus was described as a messenger of God. See Basilio Porras, *Discurso de ley pronunciado en el salón de sesiones de la Asamblea Constituyente el 15 de septiembre de 1841*, 2; José Antonio Urrutia, *Aniversario XLVII de la Independencia de Guatemala. Discurso religioso pronunciado en la Santa Iglesia Catedral el 15 de septiembre de 1868*, 6–7. See José Milla, *Esplicación de algunos de los conceptos contenidos en el discurso pronunciado en el salon del Supremo Gobierno del Estado de Guatemala, el dia 15 de septiembre de 1846, Aniversario XXV de la Independencia Nacional*, for Milla's response to the charges.

  63. Puertas, *Discurso 1854*, 9–10.

  64. Unos Salvadoreños, *Observaciones al discurso pronunciado por el presbítero Don Prudencio Puertas en la catedral de Guatemala el 15 de Setiembre de 1854*, 4. Intermittent challenges to the Guatemalan and Salvadoran Catholic church came from critics in El Salvador. See Manuel Suarez, *Aniversario XL de la Independencia de Centro-America. Discurso pronunciado en el salon del Supremo Poder Ejecutivo de la Republica del Salvador . . .*

  65. Carlos María Obispo de Chiapas to García Peláez, San Cristobal de las Casas, Mexico, June 13, 1857 (AHAG 1857.191, box T2.122). Only once did Aycinena clarify his understanding of God's relationship to the Spanish Crown, given his assertion that God established a covenant with independent Guatemala. In his last Independence sermon, Aycinena declared that the "people of Guatemala having been Catholic for three centuries had a covenant with Jesus Christ, son of God and savior of the world, and emancipating themselves from political domination, did not disown their old covenant, but wanted to enjoy full liberty and give to God a new testament of fidelity, promising and vowing to be Catholic in the successive centuries" (*Discurso 1864*, 12).

  66. Antonio Larrazábal, *Ejercicio devoto a Señor San José, en acción de gracias por su protección á Goatemala . . . , El Gobierno del Estado en decreto de 22 del corriente . . .*, and *Siendo muy justo que el venerable clero solemnice con su asistencia la acción de grácias . . .*

  67. Durán to Larrazábal, Guatemala, March 24, 1840 (AGCA B.86.5, exp. 83573, leg. 3605); Antonio Larrazábal, *Antonio Larrazábal, penitenciario de esta Santa Iglesia Metropolitana . . .* In the latter document Larrazábal writes that the Constituent Assembly declared in August 1840 that March 19, 1840, would be commemorated each year. On evidence supporting annual celebrations of March 19, 1840, see Pedro de Aycinena to Bishop of Camaco, Guatemala, March 17, 1864 (AHAG 1864.88, box T3.71).

  68. B. Cividanes to Ministro de Relaciones, Chimaltenango, March 13, 1843 (AGCA B.119.1, exp. 56078, leg. 2505); Ramón Godoy to Ministro de Relaciones, Escuintla, September 4, 1843 (AGCA B.119.2, exp. 57912, leg. 2532); Juan José de Aycinena to Ministro de Hacienda y Guerra, Escuintla, February 23, 1843 (AGCA B.119.3, exp. 59204, leg. 2545). The conclusion that these festivities were limited to the capital is based on the dearth of materials suggesting otherwise. Many records do exist showing that celebrations of the anniversary of Independence occurred outside the capital, but nothing similar for March 19.

  69. "Acuerdos del Gobierno de Guatemala del Año 1851," Guatemala, March 14, 1851 (AGCA, Acuerdos); Ministerio de Gobernación, Justicia y Negocios Eclesiásticos to Sres. Corregidores de los Departamentos, Guatemala, March 9, 1852 (AGCA, B, leg. 28556, exp. 77), fol. 1.

  70. On the celebration of the 1851 battle of Arada, see Pavón to Srs. Corregidores, Guatemala, January 9, 1852 (AGCA, B.78.25, exp. 17013, leg. 729), fol. 1; on the 1864 victory

festivities, see *Relación de las fiestas con que se celebró en los días 29 y 30 de noviembre, 1 y 2 de diciembre, el regreso a la capital del Exmo. Señor Presidente y de las fuerzas espedicionarias;* and *Relación de la fiesta que el colegio seminario dió al Excmo. Sr. Presidente de Guatemala, Don Rafael Carrera, y a su ejército espedicionario, el 9 de marzo de 1864.*

71. Bernardo Piñol, *Sermón predicado por el Sr. Dr. Dn. Bernardo Piñol cura de los Remedios de esta ciudad . . . ;* Francisco García Peláez, *Nos el Dr. Don Francisco de Paula García Peláez . . . ;* "Función religiosa," *Gaceta de Guatemala* 5, June 28, 1850, p. 2; Juan José de Aycinena, *Oración pronunciada en la S.I.M. de Santiago de Guatemala, por le Maestre-Escuela Dr. P. Juan José Aycinena, el 30 de junio de 1850 . . .* Also see Pius IX, *Alocución de nuestro Santísimo Padre . . . ; Noticia de las funciones con que se celebró la definición dogmática de la Imaculada Concepción de la Santísima Virgen María . . . en los días 20, 21, 22, 23 de julio de 1855* (Guatemala: Imprenta de la Luna, 1855).

72. Henry Savage to L. Marchy (secretary of state), Guatemala, May 31, 1853, in U.S. Department of State, *Despatches.*

73. Quoted in Pedro Antonio Escalante Arce, *Brasseur de Bourbourg. Esbozo biográfico,* 54.

74. On the cholera epidemic and resulting celebration thanking the Virgin Mary, see Fernando Aguado to García Peláez, Retalhuleu, November 28, 1857 (AHAG 1857.430, box T2.123); Manuel Echeverra to García Peláez, Guatemala, December 7, 1857 (AHAG 1857.448, box T2.123); José Barrutia y Croquer, *Al venerable clero y demás fieles de este arzobispado . . . ,* 2–3. Curious historians and Guatemalan enthusiasts must be pondering why no mention of the renowned Black Christ of Esquipulas exists in this analysis of nineteenth-century Guatemalan religion. In the first place, almost no significant comments about the Black Christ occur in the examined archives of the Catholic church nineteenth-century correspondence. Research on the Black Christ, which was constructed in 1594 and located in the strategic eastern border town of Esquipulas, revealed that the icon became popular around the turn of the twentieth century. Father Juan Paz Solorzano, parish priest of Esquipulas, recorded miracles attributed to the Black Christ, and the majority occurred in the first decade of the twentieth century. Religious historians will note the convergent popularity of Mary apparitions in late nineteenth- and early twentieth-century Europe. At this point, we must conclude that popular religiosity of the shrine of Esquipulas did not exist during the Carrera years, contrary to what Carl Kendall asserts in "The Politics of Pilgrimage: The Black Christ of Esquipulas," 155. See Juan Paz Solorzano, *Historia del Señor crucificado de Esquipulas,* 81; David Blacbourn, *Marpingen: Apparitions of the Virgin Mary in Nineteenth-Century Germany.*

75. Hobsbawm, *Nations and Nationalism,* 48.

76. Turner, *Dramas, Fields, and Metaphors,* 38–42.

77. Juan Arévalo, *Juicio Criminal,* Guatemala, September 19, 1837 (AGCA B.90.1, exp. 30894, leg. 1269).

78. Yndalecio Perdomo to General Minister of Supreme Government, Chiquimula, September 26, 1840 (AGCA B.119.2, exp. 57365, leg. 2526); José Maria Mondragon to Corregidor del Departamento de Escuintla, Escuintla, September 1855 (AGCA B, leg. 28567, exp. 183), fol. 4; García Peláez to Manuel Echeverría, Guatemala, September 24, 1855 (AGCA B, leg. 28567, exp. 183), fol. 3.

79. Yanuario Xiron to García Peláez, Chiquimula, September 15, 1865 (AHAG 1865.353, box T4.71).

80. José Maria Barrutia, Juan José de Aycinena, Bernardo Piñol, Julian Alfaro, and Prudencio Puertas to García Peláez, Guatemala, 1857 (AHAG 1857.100, box T2.121).

152   81. Juan La Canal to Ministro de Gobernación de Justicia, y Negocios Eclesiasticos, Escuintla, September 17, 1869 (AGCA B, leg. 28618, exp. 141), fol. 2.

82. Juan E. Valdez to J. M. Barrutia, Salamá, October 11, 1862 (AHAG 1862.376, box T3.77).

83. Cordillera, "15 septiembre," October 27, 1862 (AHAG 1862.365, box T3.77). One cannot help but wonder if the alcalde and community friend feigned ignorance as a resistance strategy or if indeed they could not fathom the larger community in question in the elite political struggles.

84. García Peláez to Clergy of Verapaz, Guatemala, October 17, 1845 (AHAG no. 11, box T6.58).

85. Francisco Puente to Antonio Letona, Cotzal, February 28, 1842 (AHAG no. 321, box T5.57).

86. José Antonio Urrutia, "Informe," Santa María Cahabón, December 1845 (AHAG no. 119, box T6.58).

87. Ibid. The perception that Cahabón had fewer priests prior to the murder is technically correct, but the record shows that from 1819 to 1829 five different priests served the parish, and eleven served from 1829 to 1845. See García Peláez to Srs. Vicario Provinciales, Guatemala, May 14, 1849 (AHAG, box T3.80).

88. Sr. Juan Obispo de Arendal to García Peláez, Guatemala, March 22, 1861 (AHAG 1860.33.1, box T6.62).

89. Vicente Hernandez to García Peláez, Sta. Catarina Yxtahuacan, January 20, 1854 (AHAG 1854.27, box T2.111); José Ma. Trinidad Gutierrez to Bernardo Piñol y Aycinena, San Juan Ostuncalco, August 31, 1869 (AHAG 505.44, box T4.89).

90. García Peláez, Santa Maria Cahabón, January 15, 1846 (AHAG no. 110, box T6.58).

91. Baltasar Baldwini to García Peláez, Cahabón, August 4, 1849 (AHAG 1849.159, box T2.99). See also José Antonio Urrutia to García Peláez, Santa Maria Cahabón, January 1846 (AHAG nos. 123–24, T6.58).

92. Baltasar Baldwini to Yrungaray, Cahabón, September 21, 1847, published in *Anales de la Academia de Geografia e Historia de Guatemala* 57 (January–December 1983): 58–59.

93. Juan José de Aycinena, "Informe," *Gaceta Oficial* 2.33–34 (1846): 132, column A.

Chapter 5. Carrera, the Church, and Nation Formation

1. Quoted in Tobar Cruz, *Los montañeses,* 51–52, n. 2. The full text, printed in Tobar Cruz's monograph, is apparently the only copy available to historians. The original document is not available, having been lost or assigned a new document number.

2. José Maria Aguero to Antonio Letona, La Laguna, June 30, 1837 (AHAG 1837.134, box T1.84); Municipalidad de San Luis Xilotepeque to Antonio Larrazábal, San Luis Xilotepeque, March 10, 1838 (AHAG no. 45, box T4.65). See chapter 3 for a closer look at the 1837 and 1857 cholera epidemics and at the general accusations made against priests in both disasters.

3. "Necrologia," in *El Tiempo* (Guatemala), September 11, 1839 (AGCA); Carrera, *Memorias,* 83. Woodward in *Rafael Carrera* cites six priests who were killed, four of whom were confirmed in this research.

4. Ingersoll, "War of the Mountains," 77–82.

5. Antonio Larrazábal, *Exhortación cristiano que el vicario capitular . . .* , 6, 15. Ingersoll,   153
"War of the Mountains," 185–87; Carrera, *Memorias*, 71–74.

6. Larrazábal, *Exhortación cristiano*, 6; Antonio Velasquez to Provisor, Antigua, Guatemala, March 19, 1838 (AHAG no. 235, box T4.61); Florencio Arriasa to Pedro Bustamante, Sansaria, March 5, 1838 (AHAG 1838.24, box T1.84); Pablo José Casasola to Antonio Larrazábal, Gualan, June 15, 1838 (AHAG no. 189, box T4.65); Juaquin Arellano to Larrazábal, Zacapa, September 21, 1839 (AHAG no. 217–22, box T4.65); Juaquin Arellano to Larrazábal, Salamá, March 16, 1839 (AHAG no. 201, box T4.65); Carlos Salazar, "Califico," 21 July 1837 (AHAG no. 295 T3.55).

7. We cannot obtain a profile of the insurrectionary departments at this time. Listings from these key parishes were never submitted in 1849; the civil war engulfed these areas at the very time the archbishop called on priests to submit rosters of priests who had served parishes between 1820 and 1849. A second roster created in 1862 provides an incomplete picture of Guatemala's eastern highland parishes dating from 1837 to 1862. See Sullivan-González, "Piety, Power and Politics," appendix, for a roster of clergy serving Guatemalan parishes, 1819–1868.

8. Marure, *Memoria sobre la insurreción;* Stephens, *Incidents of Travel,* 1:62; Montúfar, *Reseña histórica,* 2:343.

9. Ignacio Gómez, *Discurso pronunciado en la solemne clausura de las sesiones de la lejislatura de Guatemala . . .* , 2; Antonio Larrazábal, *El pueblo de la capital de Guatemala a sus hermanos los demás pueblos de Centro-América.*

10. Solórzano, "Rafael Carrera," 10, 15. Solórzano is indebted to Jaime Torres's theoretical insights on the role of religion in peasant movements, in *Liberalismo y rebeldía campesina, 1820–1823* (Barcelona: Ed. Ariel, 1976), 20–22.

11. Carrera, *Memorias,* 15. In a handwritten note dated January 3, 1838, Carrera had emphasized the same: "Que haya religión en ntra. America, y salga los ereges" (May there be religion in our America, and may all the heretics leave). See Carrera to the People of Mataquescuintla, Guatemala, January 3, 1838, in U.S. Department of State, *Despatches.* Rafael Carrera also called his army the "defender of religion" since God had miraculously supplied his army's military needs. See Rafael Carrera, *Pronunciamiento del General Rafael Carrera y del ejercito defensor de la Constitución del Estado de Guatemala.*

12. Carrera to the Salvadorans, Jutiapa, September 20, 1839 (printed circular; CB 3105); Stephens, *Incidents of Travel,* 1:232.

13. Montúfar, *Reseña histórica,* 3:299.

14. In his analysis of Carrera, Woodward saw that it took more than a decade for the alliance between Carrera and the conservative elite to be firmly established. See Woodward, *Rafael Carrera,* 124.

15. Estrada Monroy, *Datos para la historia,* 2:545–82.

16. Stephens, *Incidents of Travel,* 1:307–8.

17. Carrera, *Religion.* See also Antonio Larrazábal, *Edicto, con el breve pontificio relativo á la disminución del número de dias festivos.*

18. [Antonio Larrazábal to Carrera,] Guatemala, [1840] (AHAG 1849.260, box T2.97).

19. José Francisco Ortiz to Antonio Larrazábal, Guatemala, January 13, 1841 (AHAG no. 295); Larrazábal to Ortiz, Guatemala, January 16, 1841 (AHAG no. 296; both in box T4.62).

20. Mariano Rivera Paz, *Decreto 191,* Guatemala, March 19, 1844 (AHAG, box T2.54).

21. Francisco García Peláez to Manuel España et al., Guatemala, July 2, 1844 (AHAG

154   1844.58.9); Manuel España to García Peláez, [1844] (AHAG 1844.58.11); Juan José Vega to García Peláez, [1844] (AHAG 1844.58.12); Sebastian Valdez to García Peláez, Escuintla, 1844 (AHAG 1844.58.16; all in box T2.86).

    22. José A. Azmitia, *Decreto 66,* Guatemala, July 2, 1844 (AHAG 1844.74.8); Manuel F. Pavón to García Peláez, Guatemala, July 2, 1844 (AHAG 1844.74.2); José M. Quiñones to García Peláez, Totonicapan, July 4, 1844 (AHAG 1844.74.10); José Pablo Casarola to Jayme Gomila, Gualan, June 21, 1844 (AHAG 1844.59.10; all in box T2.86).

    23. José Maria Castilla to García Peláez, Guatemala, July 2, 1844 (AHAG 1844.74.4, box T2.86). Castilla's letter mentions the called meeting and advises that he will not be able to attend.

    24. José Antonio Alvarado to García Peláez, Guatemala, July 9, 1844 (AHAG 1844.74.22, box T2.86).

    25. Manuel F. Pavón to García Peláez, Guatemala, September 12, 1844 (AHAG 1844.74.64), and September 13, 1844 (AHAG 1844.74.66; both in box T2.86). A majority of priests not contributing were from the western highlands and had direct links with the failed separation of Los Altos.

    26. Manuel F. Pavón to García Peláez, Guatemala, September 26, 1844 (AHAG 1844.74.67, box T2.86); Ingersoll, "War of the Mountains," 282.

    27. Vicente Casado to García Peláez, Guatemala, March 7, 1845 (AHAG 1845.30.10); García Peláez to Sebastian Valdez, March 1845 (AHAG 1845.30.12); García Peláez to Vicarios, Guatemala, March 1845 (AHAG 1845.30.14). See also José Mariano Mendez to Antonio Letona, Guatemala, July 28, 1845 (AHAG 1845.30.156; all in box T2.89).

    28. Estrada Monroy, *Datos para la historia,* 2:593–94; Guatemala, Comisión de Negocios Eclesiásticos, *Dictamen que la comisión de negocios eclesiásticos presentó . . . ,* and *Documentos relativos al establecimiento de la Compania de Jesus en la Republica de Guatemala.*

    29. Rafael Carrera, *Rafael Carrera teniente general, y general en gefe del exercito del Estado de Guatemala,* March 17, 1945 (AHAG, box T2.56).

    30. Crowe, *Gospel in Central America,* 156.

    31. Ibid., 162; Stephens, *Incidents of Travel,* 1:226. Three ecclesiastical trials against González Lobos provide the basis of our interpretation of the guerrilla priest. The first judgment involved his participation in Carrera's insurrection; the second church trial focused on his role in the death of an indigenous community leader in San Pedro Pinula in 1844; the final judgment came out of his equivocal role in Guatemala's civil war in the late 1840s. Although not comprehensive these records provide a glimpse into the personality and philosophy of a priest who identified with the insurrectionary masses and challenged the authority of the Catholic church.

    32. Carlos Alfonso Alvarez-Lobos Villatoro, "Doctor Francisco González Lobos," in *Revista de la academia guatemalteca de estudios genealógicos, heráldicos e históricos,* no. 8 (1983), 193–94. A copy of González Lobos's ordination paper to the sacred diaconate of the Franciscan order is located in AHAG 1828.180, box T1.100.

    33. Francisco González Lobos to Provisor General, Guatemala, January 1837 (AHAG 1837.9.1, box T1.81). This particular correspondence enables us to deduce that González Lobos was originally from Tabasco, Mexico, since he went to be with his ailing mother. How and why he went to Guatemala in 1822 to begin his ministry with the Franciscans is unclear. After fifteen months in Mexico he felt more at home in Guatemala and returned toward the end of 1836.

34. Promotor Fiscal, "Francisco González Lobos," Guatemala, September 1838 (AHAG 155
1838.108.4, box T1.83). See also the clerical listing of 1849 and 1862. The record is not clear on
González Lobos's pilgrimage from January 1837 (when he was assigned to Patulul) until August 1838 (when he was assigned to Jalapa).

35. Promotor Fiscal, "Francisco González Lobos," September 7, 1838 (AHAG 1838.108.1,
box T1.83).

36. Francisco González Lobos, *Antigueños;* Antonio Letona [Promotor Fiscal], "Francisco
González Lobos," Guatemala, September 1838 (AHAG 1838.108.9–12, box T1.83).

37. Antonio Larrazábal to González Lobos, Guatemala, 1838 (AHAG 1838.108.7–8, box
T1.83).

38. Ibid.

39. Francisco Morazán to Antonio Larrazábal, [1838] (AHAG 1838.108.13A); Larrazábal to
Morazán, Guatemala, [1838] (AHAG 1838.108.13B); Agustin Gúzman to Larrazábal, [1838]
(AHAG 1838.108.18; all in box T1.83).

40. González Lobos to Larrazábal, Santa Rosa, 28 January 1839 (AHAG 1838.108.21–22);
Francisco González Lobos, "A los gefes oficiales y soldados del General Rafael Carrera,"
Mataquescuintla, November 6, 1838 (AHAG 1838.108.20; both in box T1.83).

41. Promotor Fiscal to Francisco González Lobos, Guatemala, February 10, 1839 (AHAG
1838.108.25, box T1.83).

42. González Lobos to Larrazábal, Guatemala, 1838 (AHAG 1838.108.24, box T1.83).

43. Santos Carrera to Senior Minister of Supreme Government, Guatemala, June 14, 1841
(AHAG no. 23, box T4.62).

44. Común y principales to Provisor Vicario Capitular, San Pedro Pinula, February 1842
(AHAG 1842.13.1); Antonio Larrazábal, "Oficio," Guatemala, February 11, 1842 (AHAG
1842.13.7; both in box T2.83).

45. Antonio Larrazábal, "Oficio," Guatemala, February 1842 (AHAG 1842.13.1, box
T2.83). The following description of this matter is all from this document.

46. Francisco González Lobos and M. Figueroa, *Boletín Oficial del Exercito,* Guatemala,
June 12, 1844 (AHAG 1844.58.6); Francisco González Lobos to García Peláez, Guatemala, 1844
(AHAG 1844.58.3); García Peláez to González Lobos, Guatemala, May 27, 1844 (AHAG
1844.58.4; all in box T2.86).

47. García Peláez to González Lobos, Guatemala, July 5, 1844 (AHAG 1844.48.2);
González Lobos to García Peláez, Guatemala, [1844] (AHAG 1844.58.18; both in box T2.86).

48. Tobar Cruz, *Los montañeses. La facción,* 123–36.

49. Ibid. See also Woodward's excellent narrative of events leading to the uprising in Palencia in October 1847, in Woodward, *Rafael Carrera,* 193–94.

50. Ministerio de Gobernación, *Decreto Num. 1,* Guatemala, September 3, 1848 (AHAG
T2.56).

51. Francisco Carias to the Guardian of the Recolects, General Headquarters of the Plebeian Army, 1848 (AHAG 1848.228.3, box T2.93); José Nicolás Arellano to José Maria Barrutia, Mataquescuintla, January 24, 1848 (AHAG 1848.12, box T2.97).

52. Serapio Cruz, *A los guatemaltecos;* Los Lucios, *Manifestación del ejercito de los pueblos a
los Chiquimultecos;* Roberto Reyes to García Peláez, La Montaña de Jalapa, December 2, 1849
(AHAG 1849.244, box T2.97).

53. [Los Lucíos,] *A los pueblos de Guatemala.*

156   54. Juan Raull to Mariano Padilla, Carrizal, September 1848 (AHAG 1848.150.13, box T2.96).

55. Pedro Abella to the Bishop, Coban, May 16, 1864 (AHAG 1864.57.6, box T3.70).

56. Ciriaco Antonio Giron to García Peláez, Santa Catarina Mita, December 5, 1848 (AHAG no. 644); Francisco Martinez to García Peláez, Santa Catarina Mita, February 26, 1849 (AHAG. no. 654; both in box T7.66). José Matías Quiñones to García Peláez, Totonicapan, October 2, 1848 (AHAG no. 33, box T7.67). Carrera's ability to empower Indians always threatened the liberal elites of Los Altos. Everyone knew Carrera could count on the western highland Indians as a reliable constituency. See Manuel Maria Zeceña to José María Barrutia, San Salvador, February 22, 1849 (AHAG 1849.4.74, box T2.98).

57. García Peláez to Carrera, Guatemala, September 17, 1847 (AHAG 1847.3.8, box T2.92).

58. Rafael Carrera, *Rafael Carrera* (Guatemala, February 4, 1848), cited in Tobar Cruz, *Los montañeses. La facción*, 147–48; Carrera to the Assembly, Guatemala, August 15, 1848, in ibid., 212.

59. Carrera to García Peláez, Cuartel General de Mataquescuintla, September 23, 1850 (AHAG 1850.154, box T2.100).

60. Pedro Arriaga to García Peláez, Guatemala, November 2, 1849 (AHAG no. 219, box T7.66); Pedro Arriaga to García Peláez, Guatemala, August 30, 1849 (AHAG 1849.178); Carrera to García Peláez, Guatemala, October 29, 1849 (AHAG 1849.219, box T7.66).

61. García Peláez to Minister of Government, Guatemala, August 31, 1849 (AHAG 1849.178.2; both in box T2.99); Carrera to García Peláez, Guatemala, September 10, 1849 (AHAG 1849.188, box T2.99).

62. José Nicolás Arellano to García Peláez, Mataquescuintla, December 26, 1849 (AHAG no. 225, box T7.66), Santa Rosa, September 4, 1850 (AHAG 1850.134, box T2.100), and Mataquescuintla, September 10, 1850 (AHAG 1850.144, box T2.100); "Pacificación," *Gaceta de Guatemala*, September 13, 1850, p. 3.

63. Andrés Pintelos to García Peláez, Jalapa, November 6, 1849 (AHAG 1849.247); Javier González to García Peláez, Sanarate, December 10, 1849 (AHAG 1849.243; both in box T2.97).

64. Andrés Pintelos to García Peláez, Jalapa, February 28, 1850 (AHAG 1850.25, box T2.102); Andrés Pintelos to José Antonio Ortiz, Mataquescuintla, July 15, 1850 (AHAG 1850.96, box T2.102); Pedro Arriaga to García Peláez, Guatemala, September 9, 1850 (AHAG 1850.142, box T2.100).

65. Francisco García Peláez, *A nuestros amados diocesanos los fieles del distrito de las parroquias de Santa Rosa, Jutiapa, Sansaria y Jalapa, salud en Nuestro Señor Jesu-Christo;* García Peláez to Manuel Cepeda, Guatemala, October 1, 1848 (AHAG 1848.167.5, box T2.93).

66. Francisco García Peláez, "Para esclarecer," Guatemala, January 10, 1849 (AHAG 1849.12.23); Francisco García Peláez, "Mediante," Guatemala, February 19, 1849 (AHAG 1849.12.18; both in box T2.98).

67. José Maria Barrutia, Guatemala, September 24, 1849 (AHAG 1849.12.36); Serapio Cruz to Francisco González Lobos, Palencia, February 9, 1849 (AHAG 1849.12.14); M. Paredes, "Certifico," Guatemala, [1849] (AHAG 1849.12.11); González Lobos to García Peláez, Tuxtla, Mexico, July 21, 1848 (AHAG 1849.12.5); González Lobos to García Peláez, Guatemala, October 13, 1849 (AHAG 1849.12.42), and October 18, 1849 (AHAG 1849.12.44; all in box T2.98). In this correspondence González Lobos made it known to the archbishop that Carrera's brother Santos was partly responsible for the difficulty. González Lobos charged that

Santos Carrera, in order to save his son who had fought with the insurgents, persuaded Rafael 157
Carrera that González Lobos had encouraged the people of Jalapa to fight Carrera's government. Evidently, as the letterhead indicates, González Lobos joined Rafael Carrera for a brief
time in Mexico and evidently patched up his questioned relationship with the caudillo.

68. José M. Barrutia, Guatemala, November 12, 1849 (AHAG 1849.12.48); Friar Juan
Zepeda, Franciscan convent, November 25, 1849 (AHAG 1849.12.50; both in box T2.98).

69. González Lobos to García Peláez, Guatemala, September 21, 1849 (AHAG 1849.12.37,
box T2.98).

70. José Nicolás Arellano to José María Barrutia, Mataquescuintla, October 31, 1848
(AHAG 1848.177, box T2.93).

71. M. Dardon to García Peláez, Guatemala, September 29, 1848 (AHAG 1848.150.8); Juan
Raull to Mariano Padilla, Carrizal, September 1848 (AHAG 1848.150.13; both in box T2.96).

72. Juan Raull to García Peláez, Guatemala, October 24, 1848 (AHAG 1848.150.44), and
October 31, 1848 (AHAG 1848.150.53); García Peláez to Raull, Guatemala, November 4, 1848
(AHAG 1848.150.54); Naredo Monterey to García Peláez, Guatemala, December 1, 1848
(AHAG 1848.150.58); Salazar to García Peláez, Guatemala, December 4, 1848 (AHAG
1848.150.53; all in box T2.96).

73. Griffith, *Empires in the Wilderness.*

74. Carrera to Treasury Minister of Supreme Government, Sta. Catarina Mita, January 18,
1851 (AGCA B.118.5, exp. 52401, leg. 2439), fol. 1.

75. Vicente Cerna to Comandante General, Chiquimula, January 5, 1851 (AGCA B.118.5,
exp. 52344, leg. 2439), and December 16, 1850 (AGCA B.118.5, exp. 52287, leg. 2439); Cascara
to Carrera, Guatemala, December 12, 1850 (AGCA B.118.5, exp. 52273, leg. 2439), and December 14, 1850 (AGCA B.118.5, exp. 52280, leg. 2439).

76. J. Maria de Leon et al. to Carrera, Tecpan Guatemala, 1863 (AGCA B.118.6, exp. 52658,
leg. 2440); J. Victor Zavala to Major General of the Army of the Republic, Jutiapa, December 26, 1862 (AGCA B.118.6, exp. 52626, leg. 2440); Luis Arrivillaga to Carrera, Santa Rosa,
January 23, 1863 (AGCA B.118.6, exp. 52657, leg. 2440). The only report to mention forced recruitment and subsequent resentment originated in Mataquescuintla. See J. D. Morales to
Carrera, Santa Rosa, January 1863 (AGCA B.118.6, exp. 52732, leg. 2440).

77. [Francisco Gavarette,] October 1864 (AGCA B.118.6, exp. 5314, leg. 2443).

78. Antonio Solares to Carrera, Santa Rosa, February 8, 1863 (AGCA B.118.6, exp. 58691,
leg. 2440); J. Domingo Morales to Carrera, Santa Rosa, February 14, 1863 (AGCA B.118.6,
exp. 52732, leg. 2440).

79. Henry Savage to Marcy (secretary of state), Guatemala, November 10, 1854, in U.S.
Department of State, *Despatches;* Zamario Xiron to Vicente Cerna, Chiquimula, January 30,
1863 (AGCA B, leg. 28591, exp. 030), fol 2.

80. Pedro Figueredo to Vicente Cerna, Esquipulas, February 4, 1863 (AGCA B, leg. 28591,
exp. 030), fol. 7; Vicente Frias to Cerna, Quezaltepeque, February 3, 1863 (AGCA B, leg.
28591, exp. 030), fol. 5; Abelardo Arreolo et al. to Carrera, Chiquimula, February 12, 1863
(AGCA B.118.6, exp. 52717, leg. 2440). See also Gerardo Barrios, *Manifiesto del Capitan General Don Gerardo Barrios, Presidente de la Republica de El Salvador a sus conciudadanos* (New
York: Imprenta de S. Hallet, 1864), 25.

81. Sebastian Peres et al. to García Peláez, San Cristobal Palin de Amatitlan, April 1856
(AHAG 1856.116, box T2.119); Juan B. Peralta et al. to Carrera, Chiquimula, December 7, 1862
(AGCA B.118.6, exp. 52614, leg. 2440).

158   82. *El Coronel Galinier al Presidente Carrera;* "Le coloniel d'Etat major, primer aide de Comp. de Sou Excellence le Présidut de la Republique, San Salvador," 1863 (AGCA B.118.6, exp. 53107, leg. 2442).

83. Manuel Maria Silva to Carrera, Leon, Nicaragua, January 24, 1864 (AGCA B.118.6, exp. 53332, leg. 2443).

84. José Sotero Ortiz to Carrera, Camapa, 1863 (AGCA B.118.6, exp. 53380, leg. 2443); Bruno Garcia to Carrera, Conguaco, 1863 (AGCA B.118.6, exp. 53376, leg. 2443); Municipalidad y común del pueblo de San Miguel Panan to Carrera, San Miguel Panan, April 6, 1864 (AGCA B.118.6, exp. 53345, leg. 2443); José Maria Chinchia to Carrera, Asunción Mita, 1863 (AGCA B.118.6, exp. 53379, leg. 2443); Municipalidad de Santa Rosa to Carrera, Santa Rosa, November 21, 1863 (AGCA B.118.6, exp. 53278, leg. 2443), fol. 27.

85. Carrera quoted in Pérez, *La compañia de Jesús,* 41.

86. Sor Maria Mercedes del Corazon to Carrera, Convento de Nuestra Madre Santa Clara, December 2, 1863 (AGCA B.118.6, exp. 53312, leg. 2943), fol. 1; Priora Sor Maria Asunción del Niño Jesus, Convento de Nuestra Señora de Belén, Guatemala, December 4, 1863 (AGCA B.118.6, exp. 53312, leg. 2443), fol. 6; Juan José de Aycinena to Carrera, Guatemala, November 15, 1863 (AGCA B.118.6, exp. 53278, leg. 2443), fol. 15; García Peláez to Carrera, Guatemala, November 16, 1863 (AGCA B.118.6, exp. 53278, leg. 2443), fol. 14; Francisco Taracena to Carrera, Quezaltenango, December 2, 1863 (AGCA B.118.6, exp. 53312, leg. 2443), fol. 2.

87. [Confidential] Fernando Aguado to José María Barrutia, Regalhuleu, 27 April 1855 (AHAG 1855.115A, box T2.114).

88. Pedro N. Arriaga, "Decreto Num. 99," Guatemala, November 5, 1851 (AHAG 1851.199, box T2.103); *Acuerdos del Gobierno,* March 4, 1854 (AGCA, *Acuerdos*).

89. García Peláez to Luis Clemente, Guatemala, 1852 (AHAG 1852.40.35, box T2.105); Pope Pius IX to García Peláez, Rome, October 3, 1853 (AHAG 1853.98.4, box T2.108).

90. Anonymous to García Peláez, [Guatemala,] [1854] (AHAG 1866.319, box T4.75). This letter was misfiled among correspondence dating from 1866, yet the discussion centers on the perpetual presidency of Carrera, an issue that dates it to October 1854.

91. Henry Savage to Marcy (secretary of state), Guatemala, November 10, 1854, in U.S. Department of State, *Despatches.*

92. José Mariano Galan to García Peláez, Santa Rosa, March 25, 1852 (AHAG 1852.71.2, box T2.105).

93. García Peláez to Ministro de Gobernación, Justicia y Asuntos Eclesiasticos, Guatemala, March 27, 1852 (AHAG 1852.71.3, box T2.105).

94. Manuel J. Pavón to García Peláez, Guatemala, April 14, 1852 (AHAG 1852.71.4, box T2.105).

95. García Peláez to Sr. Ministro de Gobernación, Guatemala, April 19, 1852 (AHAG 1852.71.8); Andres Goicolea to García Peláez, Sta. Cruz Quiché, April 11, 1852 (AHAG 1852.71.10); Bernardo Piñol to García Peláez, Quezaltenango, [1852] (AHAG 1852.71.12); Vicario de Verapaz to García Peláez, Verapaz, [1852] (AHAG 1852.71.20); Manuel J. Pavón to García Peláez, Guatemala, June 11, 1852 (AHAG 1852.71.27; all in box T2.105).

96. Leandro Nabos to Sr. Ministro de Gobernación, Jutiapa, May 1, 1854 (AHAG 1854, box T2.111); Zepeda, *Descripción del Templo de San Francisco de Guatemala;* Juan Barrutia to Secretario de Obispo, Asunción Mita, June 11, 1867 (AHAG 1861.8.24, box T3.81); Guillermo Pons to Obispo de Caristo, Retalhuleu, January 18, 1867 (AHAG 1861.187.81, box T3.84).

97. Juan E. Valdez to Sr. Ministro de Gobernación, Justicia y Negocios Eclesiasticos,

Salamá, April 21, 1866 (AGCA B, exp. 252, leg. 28606); Luis Arrivillaga to Sr. Ministro de   159
Santa Rosa, Santa Rosa, March 13, 1862 (AGCA B, leg. 28588, exp. 76), fol. 1; Bernardo Piñol
to Sr. Ministro de Gobernación, Justicia y Negocios Eclesiasticos, Guatemala, July 29, 1869
(AGCA B, leg. 28617, exp. 107), fol. 1.

   98. Solares, "Por cuanto," Santa Rosa, May 14, 1857 (AGCA B, leg. 28572, exp. 95), fol. 18;
Vicente Cerna to Ministro del Gobierno, Chiquimula, December 12, 1862 (AGCA B, leg.
28587, exp. 54), fol. 3.

   99. [Gobierno de Guatemala], "Puntos de instrucción para los corregidores de los distritos de Jutiapa, Jalapa, y Santa Rosa," Guatemala, July 1850 (AHAG 1850.iii, box T2.102).

Chapter 6. What Changed?

   1. "Apuntes biográficos del Illmo. Sr. Dr. P. Juan José de Aycinena, Obispo titular de Trajanópolis," *Gaceta de Guatemala* (March–April 1865); F. Hernández de Leon, *El libro de las
efeméridas. Capitulos de la historia de la América Central,* 1:286. Aycinena was appointed bishop
of Trajanópolis *in partibus infidelium* (literally, in infidel lands) in 1859. See *Gaceta de
Guatemala,* March 21, 1859, quoted in Woodward, *Rafael Carrera,* 546, n. 60.

   2. My thanks to John W. Whitten III for his expertise on nineteenth-century weapons.

   3. Paul Burgess, *Justo Rufino Barrios,* 70–74; Charles E. Mordaunt (chief of staff of General Granados's insurgent forces) to Silas A. Hudson, Joyabaj, May 26, 1871, in U.S. Department of State, *Despatches;* Hudson to Hamilton Fish (secretary of state), Guatemala, June 3,
1871 (ibid.). Woodward indicates that Indians from western Guatemala were moved in part to
protest new restrictions on the sale of liquor and tobacco, while Cerna allowed certain coffee
companies to encroach upon Indian lands. See Woodward, *Rafael Carrera,* 345–46.

   4. Hugh Miller, *La iglesia católica y el estado en Guatemala, 1871–1885,* in Mechan, *Church
and State in Latin America,* 375–79.

   5. Burgess, *Justo Rufino Barrios,* 102.

   6. Pérez, *La compañia de Jesús,* 192; Tobar Cruz, *Los montañeses,* 433; Burgess, *Justo Rufino
Barrios,* 93–95; broadside, September 5, 1871, cited in ibid., 99.

   7. Pérez, *La compañia de Jesús,* 192–93; Burgess, *Justo Rufino Barrios,* 101.

   8. Silas A. Hudson to Hamilton Fisk (secretary of state), Guatemala, June 12, 1872, in U.S.
Department of State, *Despatches;* Eliadio Prado, *La orden franciscana,* 408–9; de Cambrils,
Cronicón, 229–30, 238; "Al Publico," Rinconcito, March 2, 1873 (AHAG 1873.164.2, box
T4.99); Manuel Estupinian to Prov. Gob. del Arzobispo, Asunción Mita, December 1873
(AHAG 1873.731, box T5.98).

   9. Burgess, *Justo Rufino Barrios,* 281–82; Luis Beltranena Sinibaldi, *La tragedia de
Chalchuapa,* 2–4, 8–10, 13–14. Luis Beltranena evaluates firsthand testimony and published reports appearing three years later in *El Patriota,* August 2, 1891, to account for the diverse ac-
counts of Barrios's death. He leans toward the explanation that the Jalapan corporal Onofre
Ovando and eight other Jalapans took positions to ambush Barrios and, in the subsequent
confusion, reintegrated back into the regiment.

   10. Prospero Penados del Barrio, "Mensaje para conmemorar el ciento setenta Aniversario
de Independencia de Guatemala," in *Sigloveintiuno,* September 18, 1991, p. 7.

   11. "Por una nación justa, digna y solidaria," *Sigloveintiuno,* November 21, 1991, p. 10.

   12. Taylor, *Magistrates of the Sacred,* 294. Taylor suggests that Indians in rebellion refused

160   to heed Hidalgo's orders not to sack the estates of one Spanish administrator, because the Virgin of Guadalupe had given them permission. One Mexican priest preached in 1822 that "if the country of Anáhuac breathes freely, we owe it all to the Virgin of Tepeyac" (ibid., 251). On the origin of the Virgin of Guadalupe, see ibid., 282; and Stafford Poole, *Our Lady of Guadalupe: The Origins and Sources of a Mexican National Symbol, 1531–1797*, 151.

   13. David Charles Borbridge, "The Return of the Jesuits to Chile, 1836–1866," 22; David A. Brading, *The First America: The Spanish Monarchy, Creole Patriots, and the Liberal State, 1492–1867*, 583–84.

   14. See Beverly Clarke, Guatemala, September 29, 1859, in U.S. Department of State, *Despatches;* Woodward, *Rafael Carrera*, 351–70.

   15. Robert M. Carmack, "State and Community in Nineteenth-Century Guatemala: The Momostenango Case," in *Guatemalan Indians and the State, 1540 to 1988*, 188–20; Gruzinski, *Man-God*, 187.

   16. *Algunas reflexiones sobre la última sedición (artículos publicados en los números 37, 38, y 39 de la Semana)*, 7.

   17. N. J. Demerath III and Rhys H. Williams, *A Bridging of Faiths: Religion and Politics in a New England City. Studies in Church and State;* Rodney Stark and William Bainbridge, *The Future of Religion;* Durkheim, *Elementary Forms of the Religious Life.* See also Rosenberg, *The Cholera Years*, 5. Rosenberg noted a shift in ministerial explanations of the 1832 and 1849 cholera epidemics in the United States. In the former, cholera was a consequence of sin; in the latter, a result of remediable faults in sanitation. Although such a shift did not occur in explaining the cholera epidemics in Guatemala, one did occur concerning the impact of the cemetery's location. Notably by 1857 limited dissent concerning the location of the cemetery occurs among Guatemala's population.

   18. Fernando Antonio Davila, Quezaltenango, July 2, 1847 (AHAG no. 457, box T7.64).

   19. Heinrich W. Schäfer, "Identidad de iglesia entre represión y liberación. La Iglesia Presbiteriana en Guatemala" (manuscript submitted for publication, Studies from the World Alliance of Reformed Churches, 1988); David Stoll, *Is Latin America Turning Protestant? The Politics of Evangelical Growth.*

   20. Robert M. Carmack, ed., *Harvest of Violence: The Maya Indian and the Guatemalan Crisis;* Jim Handy, *Gift of the Devil: History of Guatemala;* Rigoberta Menchu, *I, Rigoberta Menchu: An Indian Woman in Guatemala.*

September 15, 1821	Central American independence from Spain
January 5, 1822	Central American territories unite with Mexico
July 1, 1823	Central America secedes from Mexico
1824	United Provinces of Central America Constitution adopted
1826–1829	Civil war over control of federation
1829	Liberals win control of federation through leadership of Francisco Morazán
1829–1831	Archbishop exiled; most regular orders closed; church tithe *(diezmo)* suspended

1831	Mariano Gálvez assumes presidency of state of Guatemala
1836	Colonization projects initiated on Atlantic coast
1837	Cholera epidemic
June 9, 1837	Insurrection begins in eastern departments led by Rafael Carrera
1838	Father Antonio Larrazábal appointed vicar general of Guatemalan Catholic church
January 31, 1838	Troops loyal to Rafael Carrera enter Guatemala City; Gálvez resigns presidency
April 1838	Morazán begins counteroffensive
September 1838	Carrera loses key battle in Villa Nueva; Father Durán captured and Father González Lobos seen directing Carrera's troops
December 1838	Treaty of Rinconcito
April 14, 1839	Carrera retakes Guatemala City
June 1839	Liberal measures against Catholic church rescinded

March 1840	Morazán defeated in last-ditch effort to retake Guatemala City
September 15, 1842	Morazán executed in Costa Rica
February 1844	El Salvador invades Guatemalan territory but leaves after negotiated settlement
March 1844	Francisco de Paula García Peláez appointed coadjutor to archbishop
September 1844	Troops rampage in Guatemala City

162

December 1844	Rafael Carrera appointed president
March 1845	Jesuits prevented from disembarking in Port St. Tomás
July 1845	Jesuits return to Belgium
September 1846	Francisco de Paula García Peláez becomes Guatemala's twenty-fifth archbishop
March 21, 1847	Rafael Carrera declares Guatemala an independent republic
October 1847	Violence erupts in eastern Guatemala, and initiates four-year-long civil war
August 1848	Rafael Carrera exiles himself to Mexico
August 1849	Rafael Carrera returns to Guatemala and directs war against rebellion
February 2, 1851	Salvadoran and Honduran troops battle Carrera's outnumbered soldiers at La Arada. Carrera's victory concludes Guatemala's civil war and consolidates Guatemalan nation
June 1851	Jesuits authorized to return to Guatemala
October 7, 1852	Concordat signed with Rome
October 21, 1854	Carrera assumes presidency for life
July 1856	Guatemala sends troops to battle William Walker's filibusters in Nicaragua
1857	Cholera epidemic
1857	Capuchin missions to eastern Guatemala
November 1863	Carrera victorious over El Salvador and Honduras
April 14, 1865	Rafael Carrera dies from vascular dysentery; Vicente Cerna takes presidency
January 25, 1867	Francisco de Paula García Peláez dies; Father Bernardo Piñol assumes leadership of Guatemalan Catholic church
June 30, 1871	Justo Rufino Barrios, at head of rebel troops, assumes control of Guatemala and ends conservative rule
August 1871	Jesuits expelled from Quezaltenango; eastern Guatemala, centered around Santa Rosa, erupts in violent protest against liberal regime
October 17, 1871	Archbishop Piñol exiled from Guatemala, presaging expulsion of most regular orders and suspension of tithe
June 1872	Capuchins expelled from Guatemala
December 1873	Religious insurrection quelled in eastern Guatemala
April 2, 1885	Justo Rufino Barrios shot by sniper, probably from Jalapan battalion

Bibliography

ARCHIVAL SOURCES

Guatemala

AGCA. *See* Archivo General de Centro América (AGCA).
AHAG. *See* Archivo Histórico Arquidiocesano Francisco de Paula García Peláez (AHAG).
Archivo General de Centro América (AGCA). Guatemala City, Guatemala.
Archivo Histórico Arquidiocesano Francisco de Paula García Peláez (AHAG). Guatemala City, Guatemala. Other scholars refer to the AHAG by its popular designation, Archivo Eclesiástico de Guatemala (AEG).
Biblioteca César Brañas (CB). Guatemala City, Guatemala.
Biblioteca de la Académia de Geografía e Historia. Guatemala City, Guatemala.
CB. *See* Biblioteca César Brañas (CB).
Centro de Investigaciones Regionales de Mesoamérica. Antigua, Guatemala.

United States

Benson Latin American Collection (BLAC). University of Texas at Austin. Austin, Texas.
Church of Latter Day Saints of Jesus Christ. Salt Lake City, Utah. Microfilm collection.
Kenneth Spencer Research Library. University of Kansas. Lawrence, Kansas.
Latin American Library. Tulane University. New Orleans, Louisiana.

PRIMARY SOURCES

Algunas reflexiones sobre la última sedición. (Artículos publicados en los números 37, 38, y 39 de la Semana). Guatemala: Imprenta de la Paz, 1870.
Andreu, Andrés. *Discurso pronunciado el 15 de septiembre de 1842. Aniversario XXI de Centro América*. Guatemala: Imprenta de la Paz, 1842.
———. [*Discurso pronunciado el 15 de septiembre de 1839*]. Guatemala, 1839. BLAC.
———. *Oración pronunciada en el salon del supremo gobierno el 13 marzo de 1849, en honra de la memoria de los senores Dr. Mariano Rivera Paz y L.D. Gregorio Orantes, por el Dr. D. Andres Andreu, diputado á la Asamblea Constituyente de la República de Guatemala*. Guatemala: Imprenta de la Paz, 1849.
Arellano, José Nicolás. *Sermón predicado el 15 de septiembre de 1845, vigesimo cuarto Aniversario de nuestra Independencia del Gobierno Español en la Santa Iglesia Catedral de Guatemala*. Guatemala: Imprenta de la Paz, 1845.

164   Arrazola, Miguel. "Discurso." In *Relación de las fiestas con que se celebró en la Antigua Guatemala el XXX Aniversario de la Independencia y la inauguración del Palacio Municipal en la parte reedificada en el presente año*. Guatemala: Imprenta de la Paz, 1851.

Arroyo, Angel María. *Discurso político-religioso pronunciado en la Sta. Iglesia Catedral Metropolitana el día 15 de septiembre de 1871 en celebración del Aniversario L de la Independencia nacional*. Guatemala: Imprenta de la Luna, [1871].

Aycinena y Piñol, Juan José de. *Aniversario XXXVII de la Independencia de Guatemala. Discurso religioso pronunciado en la Santa Iglesia Catedral el 16 de septiembre de 1858*. Guatemala: Imprenta de la Paz, 1858.

————. *Aniversario XXXVIII de la Independencia de Guatemala. Discurso religioso pronunciado en la Santa Iglesia Catedral el 16 de septiembre de 1859*. Guatemala: Imprenta de la Paz, 1859.

————. *Aniversario XXXIX de la Independencia de Guatemala. Discurso religioso pronunciado en la Santa Iglesia Catedral el 16 de setiembre de 1860*. Guatemala: Imprenta de la Paz, 1860.

————. *Aniversario XL de la Independencia de Guatemala. Discurso religioso pronunciado en la Santa Iglesia Catedral el 16 de septiembre de 1861*. Guatemala: Imprenta de la Paz, 1861.

————. *Aniversario XL [sic XLI] de la Independencia de Guatemala. Discurso religioso pronunciado en la Santa Iglesia Catedral el 16 de septiembre de 1862*. Guatemala: Imprenta de la Paz, 1862.

————. *Aniversario XLII [sic XLIII] de la Independencia de Guatemala. Discurso religioso pronunciado en la Santa Iglesia Catedral el 16 de setiembre de 1864*. Guatemala: Imprenta de la Paz, 1864.

————. *Demostración del derecho de propiedad que en la plazuela llamada "Del Sagrado" tiene la Santa Iglesia Metropolitana de Guatemala*. Guatemala: Imprenta de la Paz, 1865.

————. *Discurso pronunciado el 15 de setiembre de 1848, XXVII Aniversario de la Independencia de Guatemala*. Guatemala: Imprenta de la Paz, 1848.

————. *Discurso pronunciado el 15 de sepiembre de 1850, XXIX Aniversario de la Independencia de Guatemala*. Guatemala: Imprenta de la Paz, 1850.

————. *Discurso pronunciado el 15 de setiembre de 1853, XXXII Aniversario de la Independencia de Guatemala*. Guatemala: Imprenta de la Paz, 1853.

————. *Discurso pronunciado en la casa del Supremo Gobierno del Estado de Guatemala. El Quince de Setiembre Aniversario XIX. De su Independencia del Gobierno Español*. Guatemala: Imprenta del Gobierno, [1840].

————. *Discurso que en la fiesta de acción de grácias celebrada en la Catedral de Guatemala el 15 de setiembre de 1837*. Guatemala: Imprenta del Gobierno, 1837.

————. *Discurso religioso pronunciado en la S.M.I. de Santiago de Guatemala, el 15 de septiembre de 1855. Aniversario XXXIV de Independencia*. Guatemala: Imprenta de la Paz, 1855.

————. "Oración Funebre." En *Relación de las exequias que se hicieron al señor canónigo Dr. D. José María de Castilla, en la iglesia de S. Juan de Dios, el 28 de Julio de 1848*. Guatemala: Imprenta de la Paz, 1848.

————. *Oración fúnebre que pronunció en la S.I.M. de Guatemala el dia 14 de enero de 1857, en las exequias solemnes por el descanso de los SS. Generales D. Mariano Paredes y D. Joaquin Solares, y demás gefe, oficiales y soldados muertos en la campaña de Nicaragua*. Guatemala: Imprenta de la Paz, 1857.

———. *Oración pronunciada en la S.I.M. de Santiago de Guatemala, por le Maestre-Escuela Dr. P. Juan José Aycinena, el 30 de junio de 1850, en la fiesta de acción de gracias, que por disposición del Ilustrísimo Señor Arzobispo Dr. D. Francisco García Peláez, se celebró, con motivo de la plausible noticia de haber regresado á Roma el 12 de abril último N. Smo. P. El Sr. Pio IX.* Guatemala: Imprenta de la Aurora, 1850. 165

———. *Respuesta.* Guatemala: Imprenta de la A. de Estudios, 1839.

———. *Sermón predicado el 24 de agosto de 1862. Trecentesimo aniversario de la reforma de carmelitas descalzas en la Iglesia de Santa Teresa de esta ciudad conventual de la misma orden.* Guatemala: Imprenta de la Paz, 1862.

———. *Sermón predicado en la festividad del primer aniversario de la dedicación solemne del Templo Catedral de la Archdiócesis de Santiago de Guatemala.* Guatemala: Imprenta de la Paz, 1861.

———. *Sermón predicado en la S.I.M. de Guatemala el dia 1 de enero de 1862 en la función que se celebra con asistencia de todas las autoridades.* Guatemala: Imprenta de la Paz, 1862.

———. *Sermón predicado en la S.I. Metropolitana de Guatemala el día 1 de enero de 1864.* Guatemala: Imprenta de la Paz, 1864.

———. *Sermón que en la fiesta anual que celebra el I. Colegio de Abogados el dia 18 de octubre de 1857.* Guatemala: Imprenta de Luna, 1857.

———. *El toro amarillo.* Biblioteca de Cultura Popular 20 de Octubre, vol. 54. Guatemala: Editorial José de Pineda Ibarra, [1832–1834] 1980.

Baldwini, Baltasar. "Los pueblos indígenas de Cahabón y Lanquin en el departamento de Verapaz. Año de 1847." In *Anales de la Sociedad de Geografia e Historia de Guatemala* 57 (January–December 1983): 76.

Barrios, Gerardo. *Manifiesto del Capitan General Don Gerardo Barrios, Presidente de la Republica de El Salvador a sus conciudadanos.* New York: Imprenta de S. Hallet, 1864.

Barrundia, José. "Al nacimiento de la Patria en el 15 de septiembre." *El Centro-Americano. Extraordinario,* September 15, 1833, pp. 199–206.

Barrundia, José Francisco. *Discurso pronunciado el día 15 de septiembre de 1836.* Guatemala, 1836.

Barrutia y Croquer, José. *Al venerable clero y demás fieles de este arzobispado y de la diocesis de Chiapa, salud en Nuestro Señor Jesucristo.* Guatemala, April 17, 1860.

Bustamante, Pedro C. "[Discurso. 15 septiembre 1832]." *Boletín extraordinario. Segunda parte,* September 30, 1832. CB 1505.

Carrera, Rafael. *Memorias del General Carrera, 1837 a 1840.* Edited by Ignacio Solis. Guatemala: Tipografía Sánchez y de Guise, 1906.

———. *Pronunciamiento del General Rafael Carrera y del ejercito defensor de la Constitución del Estado de Guatemala.* Guatemala: Imprenta de la N. Academia de Estudios, 1839.

———. *Rafael Carrera teniente general y general en gefe del exercito del estado de Guatemala, a sus conciudadnos.* Guatemala: Imprenta del Exército, December 12, 1840. AHAG, box T4.58.

———. *Rafael Carrera teniente general, y general en gefe del exercito del Estado de Guatemala.* Guatemala, March 17, 1845. AHAG, box T2.56.

———. *Rafael Carrera, teniente jeneral, presidente de la República de Guatemala, y jeneral en jefe del ejército; a sus habitantes.* Guatemala, 1848.

166   ———. *Religion.* Guatemala: Imprenta del Exercito, 1840. AHAG no. 12, box T4.58.

Castilla, José María. *Al heróico pueblo de Guatemala.* Guatemala: Imprenta de la Libertad, 1821.

Cortés y Larraz, Pedro. *Descripción geográfica-moral de la Diocesis de Goathemala hecha por su arzobispo, el Illmo. Sor. Don Pedro Cortés y Larraz del consejo de S.M. en el tiempo que la visito y fue desde el día 3 de noviembre de 1768 hasta el día 1 de julio de 1769; desde el día 22 de noviembre de 1769 hasta el día 9 de febrero de 1770; y desde el día 6 de junio de 1770 hasta el día 29 de agosto del dho. 1770.* Vols. 1–2. Guatemala: Sociedad de Geografía e Historia de Guatemala. Tipografía Nacional, 1958 [1770].

[Crowe, Frederick]. *The Gospel in Central America; Containing a Sketch of the Country, Physical and Geographical—Historical and Political—Moral and Religious: A History of the Baptist Mission in British Honduras and of the Introduction of the Bible Into the Spanish American Republic of Guatemala.* London: Gilpin, 1850.

Cruz, Serapio. *A los guatemaltecos.* Guatemala: Imprenta del Exercito, June 26, 1848. AHAG 1848.108, box T2.96.

de Cambrils, Ignacio. *Cronicón de la misión de pp. capuchinos en Centro América o fundación y propagación de la religión capuchina en la América Central.* Barcelona: Imprenta y Librería de la Inmaculada Concepción, 1888.

de Ciáurriz, Ildefonso. *Vida del siervo de Dios P. Fr. Esteban de Adoain, capuchino misionero apostólico en América y España.* Barcelona: Herederos de Juan Gili, 1913.

Documentos relativos al establecimiento de la Compania de Jesus en la Republica de Guatemala. Guatemala: Imprenta de la Aurora, 1851.

Dominguez, José Mariano. *Bernado Domingues padre del presbítero D. José Mariano Dominguez doctor en sagrada teología, licenciado en derecho civil, catedratico de instituta de esta universidad nacional, y abogado de la audiencia territorial de Guat. En demostración de su paternal amor, da a luz el discurso de su hijo, ó sermon pronunciado en esta Santa Iglesia Catedral el 24 de junio, con motivo de la augusta ceremonia de la instalación del Soberano Congreso de estas provincias; encomendado por el Illmó. y Rmo. Sór. Arzpo. Dr. Mtró. D. Fr. Ramón Casáus y Torres.* Guatemala, 1823.

Dunn, Henry. *Guatimala: or, The Republic of Central America, in 1827–8: being sketches and memorandums made during a twelve months' residence.* Detroit, Mich.: Blaine-Ethridge Books, 1981 [1829].

Echeverria, Manuel. *Discurso que el 15 de setiembre de 1844, Aniversario XXIII de la Independencia de Centro-América, pronunció el Sr. Ldo. Manuel Echeverria en el palacio del supremo gobierno del Estado de Guatemala.* Guatemala: Imprenta de la Paz, 1844.

El Coronel Galinier al Presidente Carrera. San Salvador: Imprenta del Gobierno, 1863.

Escoto, Luis. *Sermón que en la acción de grácias que el comercio de la ciudad de Guatemala tributó a Maria Santísima por haber libertado ambas Españas Europea y Americana de las asechanzas y tirania de Napoleon.* Guatemala, 1808. BLAC.

Facsimile del Acta de Independencia de Centro América. Firmada en la ciudad de Guatemala el 15 de septiembre de 1821. Guatemala: Tipografía Nacional, 1934.

Gálvez, Mariano. "[Discurso. 15 Septiembre 1832]." *Boletín extraordinario. Segunda parte,* September 30, 1832. CB.

García Peláez, Francisco de Paula. *A nuestros amados diocesanos los fieles del distrito de las parroquias de Santa Rosa, Jutiapa, Sansaria y Jalapa, salud en Nuestro Señor Jesu-Christo.* Guatemala, June 19, 1848. AHAG, box T3.80.

———. *Discurso pronunciado el 15 de setiembre de 1856 XXXV Aniversario de la Independencia de Guatemala.* Guatemala: Tipografía de la Paz, 1856.

———. *Nos el Dr. Don Francisco de Paula García Peláez, por la gracia de Dios y de la santa* 167 *sede apostólica, arzobispo de esta Santa Iglesia Metropolitana de Santiago de Guatemala, a los venerables párrocos y demás clero, y á todos los fieles de este arzobispado: salud en Ntro. Señor Jesucristo.* Guatemala, September 22, 1850. AHAG, box T2.100.

———. *Nos el Doctor D. Francisco de Paula García Peláez por la gracia de Dios y de la Santa Sede Apostolica, Arzobispado de esta Santa Iglesia Metropolitana de Santiago de Guatemala. Al venerable clero secular y regular y demás fieles de la Diocesis: salud en nuestro Jesu-Christo.* Guatemala, January 4, 1851.

Gómez, Ignacio. *Discurso pronunciado en la solemne clausura de las sesiones de la lejislatura de Guatemala, el 5 de agosto de 1838 por su presidte. Ldo. Ignacio Gomez.* Guatemala: Imprenta de la Academia de Ciencias, 1838.

González Lobos, F., and M. Figueroa. *Boletín Oficial del Exercito.* Guatemala: Gobierno de Guatemala, 1844. AHAG 1844.58.6, box T2.86.

González Lobos, Francisco. "A los gefes oficiales y soldados del General Rafael Carrera." Mataquescuintla, November 6, 1838. AHAG 1838.108.20, box T1.83.

———. *Antigueños.* Guatemala, September 2, 1838. AHAG 1838.108.5, box T1.83.

———. *Contestación* [al Francisco Malespin]. Guatemala, May 29, 1844. AHAG, box T2.56.

———. *Contestación* [al Manuel Serrano]. Guatemala, May 29, 1844. AHAG, box T2.56.

Guatemala. Comisión de Negocios Eclesiásticos. *Dictamen que la comisión de negocios eclesiásticos presentó al congreso constituyente del Estado de Guatemala en 29 de abril de 1845, en el cual, por los justos motivos que se espresan, se propone la derogatoria del decreto de 3 de julio de 1843, espedido por la asamblea constituyente del mismo, permitiendo la venida de los padres de la Compañia de Jesús.* Guatemala: Imprenta del Gobierno, 1845.

———. *Tabla general de los departamentos, distritos, ciudades, villas, pueblos, y demás lugares, con el número de habitantes respectivos, que componen el territorio del Estado de Guatemala, formada de órden del Gobierno con presencia de los censos más modernos, y arreglada á la división hecha por el decreto de su Asamblea de 12 de octubre de 1825.* Guatemala: Imprenta Mayor, 1825.

Herrarte, José Mariano. *Sermón predicado el quince de setiembre de mil ochocientos cuarenta Aniversario XIX. de nuestra Independencia del Gobierno Español en la Santa Iglesia Catedral.* Guatemala: Imprenta del Gobierno, 1840.

Larrazábal, Antonio. *Antonio Larrazábal, penitenciario de esta Santa Iglesia Metropolitana, y provisor, vicario capitular y gobernador del Arzobispado de Guatemala. A todos los fieles habitantes de este estado: salud en nuestro Señor Jesus Cristo.* Guatemala: Imprenta del Exército, March 16, 1841.

———. *Edicto, con el breve pontificio relativo á la disminución del número de dias festivos.* Guatemala: Imprenta del Exercito, 1840.

———. *El Gobierno del Estado en decreto de 22 del corriente, tributa á Dios la mas profunda acción de grácias por la bondad con que ha salvado á su pueblo.* Guatemala, 1840.

———. *El pueblo de la capital de Guatemala a sus hermanos los demás pueblos de Centro-América.* Guatemala: Imprenta de la N. Academia de Estudios, 1838.

———. *Ejercicio devoto a Señor San José, en acción de gracias por su protección á Goatemala destinado principalmente para el dia de su patrocinio: aplicable a sus demás fiestas y al dia 19 de cada mes.* Guatemala: Imprenta del Exercito, 1840.

168 ————. *Exhortación cristiano que el vicario capitular, de este arzobispado dirige á los pueblos que, engañados y seducidos, hacen la guerra a sus hermanos, y á los demás pueblos pacíficas del Estado, para que no se dejen engañar con falsos pretextos de religion.* Guatemala: Imprenta de la Academia, 1838.

————. *Memoria documentada, que al Illmo. Sr. Arzobispo Coadjutor de esta Santa Iglesia, Dr. Francisco Garcia Peláez, presenta el Dr. Antonio Larrazábal, canonigo penitenciario, al cesaren el cargo de Vicario Capitular Gobernador de este Arzobispado.* Guatemala: Imprenta del Exército, 1844.

————. *Siendo muy justo que el venerable clero solemnize con su asistencia la acción de grácias, que conforme al decreto de 17. de agosto último, expedido por la Asamblea Constituyente, se verificará en la Santa Iglesia el próximo viernes 19, por el feliz exito que tuvo la defensa de esta ciudad en aquel dia y mes del año anterior de 1840.* Guatemala, 1841.

Libro 2. de ingresos de la renta decimal, con arreglo á el acuerdo de el Mui Ilustre y Venerable Cabildo de esta Sta. Iglesia Metropolitana, de veinte y siete de julio de mil ochocientos quarenta y siete se formó. Guatemala: 1848–1859. AHAG, box T5.137.

[Los Lucios]. *A los pueblos de Guatemala.* Jalapa: Imprenta del Exercito, 1848. AHAG 1848.119.1, box T2.96.

————. *Manifestación del ejercito de los pueblos a los Chiquimultecos.* Sansur: Imprenta del Ejercito, 1848. AHAG 1848.118.3, box T2.96.

Malespin, Francisco. *Carta que dirige el Sr. General Presidente del Estado del Salvador, al Sr. Presbítero Franciscano González Lobos.* Guatemala, May 24, 1844. AHAG, box T2.56.

Marure, Alejandro. *Efeméridas de los hechos notables acaecidos en la República de Centroamérica desde el año de 1821 hasta el de 1842.* Biblioteca Guatemalteca de Cultura Popular, vol. 9. Guatemala: Ministerio de Educación Pública, 1956 [1895].

————. *Memoria sobre la insurrección de Sta. Rosa y Matesquescuintla en Centro-America, comparada con la que estalló en Francia, el año de 1790, en los departamentos de la Vendée* Guatemala: N.p., [1838].

Milla, José. *Esplicación de algunos de los conceptos contenidos en el discurso pronunciado en el salon del Supremo Gobierno del Estado de Guatemala, el dia 15 de septiembre de 1846, Aniversario XXV de la Independencia Nacional.* Guatemala: Imprenta de la Paz, 1846.

Ministerio del Gobierno de Guatemala. *Acuerdos del Minist. de Gobn. de los años de 1854 y 1855.* Guatemala, 1854–1855.

Molina, Pedro. *Discurso acerca de la utilidad de la Independencia de Centro-America.* Guatemala: Imprenta del Gobierno, 1837.

————. *Pensamiento filosoficos-politicos del Dr. P. Molina, borrador dedicado el 15 de setiembre de 1846, a su hijo R.* Guatemala: Tipografica el Progreso, 1877 [1846].

Molina, Vicente. *Discurso pronunciado el 15 de septiembre de 1845 vigesimo cuarto Aniversario de la Independencia de Guatemala en el salon del supremo poder ejecutivo.* Guatemala: Imprenta de la Paz, 1845. AHAG T4.58.

Montúfar, Lorenzo. *Reseña histórica de Centro América.* 7 vols. Guatemala: Tipografico el Progreso, 1878–1887.

Navarro, José María. *Estado actual de esta parroquia de Concepción de Villa Nueva, formado por el presbítero Jose Maria Navarro su cura encargado en 1864.* Cesar Brañas 3138. Guatemala, [1864].

————. *Memoria del estado actual de la parroquia de San Martin Xilotepeque formada por su*

cura encargado presbítero Jose Maria Navarro para presentarla en la visita canónica al 169
*Ilmo. y Rmo. Sr. Arzobispo Dr. Francisco de Paula García Peláez dignísimo prelado de
la diocesis de Guatemala. Comprende los años de 1857 a 1859.* Cesar Brañas 3137.
Guatemala: Imprenta de Luna, 1861.

*Noticia de las funciones con que se celebró la definición dogmática de la Immaculada Concepción
de la Santísima Virgen María, en la S.M.I. de Santiago de Guatemala por disposición
del Ilmo. Sr. Arzobispo Dr. D. Francisco García Peláez y del venerable clero, en los días
20, 21, 22 y 23 de julio de 1855.* Guatemala: En la Oficina de L. Luna, 1855.

Pérez, Rafael. *La compañia de Jesús en Colombia y Centro-América despues de restauración. Desde
el restablecimiento de la compañia de Jesús en Guatemala en 1851 hasta su segunda ex-
pulsión de la Nueva Granada en 1861.* Part 2. Valladolid: Imprenta Castellana, 1897.

Piñol, Bernardo. *Discurso pronunciado en la Santa Iglesia Catedral el 15 de setiembre de 1849 en
el vigesimo octavo Aniversario de la Independencia.* Guatemala: Imprenta de la Paz,
1849.

———. *Discurso que en la solemne acción de grácias que mandó celebrar el supremo gobierno
de la República de Guatemala, en la S. I. Metropolitana, por el restablecimiento de la
paz el día 11 de febrero de 1849.* Guatemala: Imprenta de la Paz, 1849.

———. *Sermón predicado por el Sr. Dr. Dn. Bernardo Piñol cura de los Remedios de esta ciudad, en la misa de gracias que se celebró en la Santa Iglesia Catedral el domingo 30 de
setiembre de 1849 por los faustos sucesos que anuncian la proxima restitución de N. Smo.
Padre el Sr. Pio IX al Solio Pontificio.* Guatemala: Imprenta Nueva de la Aurora,
1849.

———. *Sermón que el día 29 de mayo de 1839 en la acción de grácias por la solemne instalación
de la asamblea constituyente del Estado de Guatemala, dijo en la Santa Iglesia Catedral.* Guatemala: Imprenta de la Academia de Estudios, 1839.

Pius IX. *Alocución de nuestro Santísimo Padre, por la divina providencia Papa Pio IX, pronunciada en consistorio secreto el dia 1. de diciembre de 1854.* Rome: 1854. AHAG, box
T2.100.

Porras, Basilio. *Discurso de ley pronunciado en el salón de sesiones de la Asamblea Constituyente,
el 15 de setiembre de 1841.* Guatemala: Imprenta del Gobierno, 1841.

Puertas, Prudencio. *Discurso político-religioso pronunciado en la Sta. Iglesia Catedral el 15 de
setiembre de 1854, XXXIII Aniversario de la Independencia de Guatemala.* Guatemala:
Imprenta de la Paz, 1854.

Quiñones, José Matías. *Al soldado ilustre de la patria. Al defensor de la libertad y de la constitución en 829. Al vencedor de Omoa en 1832. Al invicto general C. Agustín Gúzman el
bueno de Centro America, en el Aniversario de Nuestra Gloriosa Independencia.*
Guatemala: Imprenta de la Union, 1835.

———. *Sermon predicado en la parroquia de Totonicapan el dia 25 de diciembre de 1838, con
motivo de la instalación de la Asamblea Constituyente del Nuevo Estado de los Altos, de
la Union Centroamericana, por el parroco de la misma iglesia, ciudadano Doctor, Jose
Matías Quiñones.* Los Altos: Imprenta del Estado de los Altos, 1838. CB 3091.

*Relación de la fiesta que el colegio seminario dió al Excmo. Sr. Presidente de Guatemala, Don
Rafael Carrera, y a su ejército espedicionario, el 9 de marzo de 1864.* Guatemala: Imprenta de la Paz, 1864.

*Relación de las fiestas con que se celebró en los días 29 y 30 de noviembre, 1 y 2 de diciembre, el re-
greso a la capital del Exmo. Señor Presidente y de las fuerzas expedicionarias.*
Guatemala: Imprenta de la Paz, 1864.

170   *Resolución modificando el cobro del diezmo: memoria sobre el destino de sus productos; y sobre la situación de esta Santa Iglesia Metropolitana, y manifiesto del venerable cabildo de la misma, y del Sr. Vicario Capitular Gobernador, publicando estos documentos.* Guatemala: Imprenta del Exército Acargo de F. Tellez, 1841.

Serrano, Manuel. *Carta del Sr. Vicario del exército salvadoreño al Sr. Cura de Jalapa Francisco Gonzalez Lobos.* Jutiapa, May 24, 1844. AHAG, box T2.56.

Sicilia y Montoya. "Oración eucarista que pronunció el Sr. Dr. D. Sicilia y Montoya arcediano de esta Santa Iglesia Metropolitana el martes 13 de diciembre de 1808 en la solemne acción de gracias que celebró la M.N.Y.M.L. Ciudad de Guatemala por la exaltación del Sr. Rey D. Fernando VII al trono de las Españas." In *Guatemala por Fernando Septimo el dia 12 de diciembre de 1808.* Guatemala, 1808. BLAC.

Stephens, John L. *Incidents of Travel in Central America, Chiapas and Yucatan.* 2 vols. New York: Dover Publications, 1969 [1841].

Suarez, Manuel. *Aniversario XL de la Independencia de Centro-America. Discurso pronunciado en el salon del Supremo Poder Ejecutivo de la Republica del Salvador por el Lic. Dn. Manuel Suarez, gefe de sección del ministerio de hacienda y guerra, y consejero de instrucción pública el 15 de setiembre de 1861.* San Salvador: Imprenta del Gobierno, 1861.

Suaso, Tomás. *Sermón predicado el quince de setiembre de mil ochocientos cuarenta y uno, Aniversario XX. de nuestra Independencia del Gobierno Español, en la Santa Iglesia Catedral de Guatemala.* Guatemala: Imprenta del Exército, 1841.

Un Militar. *Observaciones sobre el discurso pronunciado por el Bachiller José D. Milla, en el Aniversario de la Independencia de Centro-América.* Guatemala: Imprenta de la Aurora, 1846.

Unos Salvadoreños. *Observaciones al discurso pronunciado por el presbítero Don Prudencio Puertas en la catedral de Guatemala el 15 de Setiembre de 1854.* San Vicente: Imprenta de Dia, 1855.

Urrutia, José Antonio. *Aniversario XLVII de la Independencia de Guatemala. Discurso religioso pronunciado en la Santa Iglesia Catedral el 15 de setiembre de 1868.* Guatemala: Imprenta de la Paz, 1868.

———. *Exhortación dirigida al pueblo de Guatemala en el llano del incienso por el Presbítero Br. Sr. D. José Antonio Urrutia. En la fusilación de Feliciano Masariegos. El dia 3 de mayo de 1849.* Guatemala: Imprenta de Basilio Samayoa, 1849.

U.S. Department of State. *Despatches from United States Ministers to Guatemala, 1824–1906.* Microfilm.

Valenzuela, Pedro José. "Decreto." *Boletín Oficial* 35, April 15, 1834.

———. "Decreto." *Boletín Oficial* 41, August 22, 1834.

———. "Discurso sobre la igualdad de clases y diferencias de aptitudes." *Boletín Oficial,* September 1, 1831, 127–40.

Vasconcelos, Simon. "[Discurso] 15 de Setiembre." *Boletín Oficial,* no. 88, September 15, 1835, p. 876. Guatemala.

Velez, Manuel Francisco. *Discurso político-religioso pronunciado en la S.I. Catedral el 15 de setiembre de 1869. XLVIII Aniversario de nuestra Independencia de la Monarquia Española.* Guatemala: Imprenta de la Paz, 1869.

Zacarías Velásquez, Manuel. *Discurso político-religioso pronunciado en la Santa Iglesia Catedral de Guatemala el día 15 de septiembre de 1844, delante de las autoridades de la iglesia y*

del estado por el M. P. Fr. Manuel Zararías Velasquez del Sagrado Orden de Predi- 171
cadores. Guatemala: Imprenta del Exército, 1844.

Zeceña, Basilio. *Discurso pronunciado en la Catedral de Guatemala el día 15 de setiembre de 1839,*
Aniversario 18 de la Independencia, por el Presbítero Doctor Basilia Zezeña, represen-
tante a la Asamblea Constituyente. Guatemala: Imprenta del Gobierno, 1839.

———. *Oración pronunciada en la Santa Iglesia Catedral en el XXX Aniversario de la Inde-*
pendencia. Guatemala: Imprenta de la Paz, 1851.

———. *Sermón que en la función de grácias celebrada el día 1 de enero de 1844 en la Sta. Igle-*
sia Catedral antes las Supremas Autoridades del Estado Guatamalteco. Guatemala: Imprenta de la Paz, 1844.

Zepeda, Juan de Jesus. *Descripción del Templo de San Francisco de Guatemala, concluido el 22*
de febrero de 1851, continiendo con una oración pronunciada por el R. P. Guardian F.
Juan de Jesus Zepeda. Guatemala: Imprenta de la Paz, 1851.

SECONDARY SOURCES

Adams, Richard Newbold. *Crucifixion by Power: Essays on Guatemalan National Social Struc-*
ture, 1944–1966. Austin: University of Texas Press, 1970.

———. "Comunidad, y cultura en el proceso étnico-estado." In *De la etnia a la nación.*
Guatemala: AVANCSO, 1996.

Ahlstrom, Sydney E., ed. *Theology in America: The Major Protestant Voices from Puritanism to*
Neo-Orthodoxy. Indianapolis: Bobbs-Merrill, 1967.

Alvarez-Lobos Villatoro, Carlos Alfonso. "Doctor Francisco González Lobos." *Revista de la*
academia guatemalteca de estudios genealógicos, heráldicos e históricos, no. 8 (1983):
193–94.

Anderson, Benedict. *Imagined Communities: Reflections on the Origin and Spread of National-*
ism. London: Verso, 1983.

Arriola, Jorge Luis. *Gálvez en la encrucijada. Ensayo crítico en torno al humanismo político de*
un gobernante. Mexico: Editorial B. Costa-Amic, 1961.

Batres Jáuregui, Antonio. *La América Central ante la historia 1821–1921. Memorias de un siglo.*
3 vols. Guatemala: Tipografía Nacional, 1949.

Bauman, Zygmunt. *Hermeneutics and Social Science.* New York: Columbia University Press,
1978.

Beltranena Sinibaldi, Luis. *Fundación de la República de Guatemala.* Ediciones del Sesquicen-
tenario de la Independencia. Guatemala: Tipografía Nacional de Guatemala, 1972.

———. *La tragedia de Chalchuapa.* Guatemala: Sociedad de Geografía e Historia de
Guatemala, 1979.

Bendaña Perdomo, Ricardo. *La iglesia en Guatemala. Síntesis histórico del catolicismo.*
Guatemala: Librerías Artemis-Edinter, 1996.

Blacbourn, David. *Marpingen: Apparitions of the Virgin Mary in Nineteenth-Century Germany.*
New York: Alfred A. Knopf, 1994.

Borbridge, David Charles. "The Return of the Jesuits to Chile, 1836–1866." Ph.D. diss., University of California, Berkeley, 1979.

Brading, David A. *The First America: The Spanish Monarchy, Creole Patriots, and the Liberal*
State, 1492–1867. Cambridge: Cambridge University Press, 1992.

172   Burgess, Paul. *Justo Rufino Barrios*. Bryn Mawr, Pa.: Dorrance, 1926.

Burns, E. Bradford. *The Poverty of Progress: Latin America in the Nineteenth Century*. Berkeley and Los Angeles: University of California Press, 1980.

Cambranes, Julio C. "El derrocamiento de la dictadura conservadora." *Estudios* 6 (1975): 31–54.

Carmack, Robert M. "State and Community in Nineteenth-Century Guatemala: The Momostenango Case," in *Guatemalan Indians and the State, 1540 to 1988*, edited by Carol Smith, 116–36. Austin: University of Texas Press, 1990.

Carmack, Robert M., ed. *Harvest of Violence: The Maya Indian and the Guatemalan Crisis*. Norman: University of Oklahoma Press, 1988.

Chandler, David Lee. *Juan José de Aycinena, idealista, conservador de la Guatemala del siglo XIX*. Centro de Investigaciones Regionales de Mesoamérica, no. 4. Antigua, Guatemala, 1988.

Chartier, Roger. *Cultural History: Between Practices and Representations*. Translated by Lydia G. Cochrane. Ithaca, N.Y.: Cornell University Press, 1988.

Clendinnen, Inga. *Ambivalent Conquests: Maya and Spaniard in Yucatan, 1517–1570*. Cambridge Latin American Studies, gen. ed. Simon Collier. Cambridge: Cambridge University Press, 1987.

Cross, F. L., ed. *The Oxford Dictionary of the Christian Church*. London: Oxford University Press, 1957.

de Cogollos Vega, Padre Buenaventura. *Los capuchinos en Guatemala*. Spain: El Adalid Seráfico, 1972.

de Estello, Gumersindo. *Historia y empresas apostólicas del siervo de Dios P. Esteban de Adoain*. Pamplona, Spain: Editorial Aramburu, 1944.

Demerath, N. J. III, and Rhys H. Williams. *A Bridging of Faiths: Religion and Politics in a New England City. Studies in Church and State*. Princeton, N.J.: Princeton University Press, 1992.

Diez de Arriba, Luis. *Crisis*. In *Historia de la iglesia católica en Guatemala*. Vol. 1, Guatemala: N.p., 1988. Vol. 2, Guatemala: N.p., 1989.

Durkheim, Emile. *The Elementary Forms of the Religious Life*. New York: The Free Press, 1915.

Dussel, Enrique D. *Introducción general a la iglesia en América Latina*. Vol. 1 of *Historia general de la iglesia en América Latina*, edited by Dussel. Salamanca: Ediciones Sígueme, 1983.

Dussel, E., R. Cardenal, R. Bendaña, J. E. Arellano, M. Carias, M. Picado, and W. Nelson. *América Central*. Vol. 6 of *Historia general de la iglesia en América Latina*, edited by E. Dussel. El Peso de los Días. Salamanca: Ediciones Sígueme, 1985.

Escalante Arce, Pedro Antonio. *Brasseur de Bourbourg. Esbozo biográfico*. San Salvador: Talleres Gráficos, 1989.

Estrada Monroy, Agustín. *Datos para la historia de la iglesia en Guatemala*. Sociedad de Geografía e Historia de Guatemala. 3 vols. Guatemala: Tipografía Nacional, 1972–1979.

Farriss, Nancy M. *Maya Society Under Colonial Rule: The Collective Enterprise of Survival*. Princeton, N.J.: Princeton University Press, 1984.

Ford, Caroline. *Creating the Nation in Provincial France: Religion and Political Identity in Brittany*. Princeton, N.J.: Princeton University Press, 1993.

Geertz, Clifford. *The Interpretation of Cultures*. New York: Basic Books, 1973.

Griffith, William J. *Empires in the Wilderness: Foreign Colonization and Development in*

Guatemala, 1834–1844. Chapel Hill: University of North Carolina Press, 1965.   173

Gruzinski, Serge. *Man-God in the Mexican Highlands.* Stanford: Stanford University Press, 1989.

Gudmundson, Lowell, and Héctor Lindo-Fuentes. *Central America, 1821–1871: Liberalism Before Liberal Reform.* Tuscaloosa: University of Alabama Press, 1995.

Handy, Jim. *Gift of the Devil: History of Guatemala.* Toronto: Between the Lines, 1984.

Hernández, Shannon. "Charity, the State, and Social Order in Nineteenth-Century Guatemala." M.A. thesis, University of Texas at Austin, 1992.

Hernández de Leon, F. *El libro de las efeméridas. Capitulos de la historia de la América Central.* Vol. 1. Guatemala: Tipografía Sanchez y de Guiso, 1925.

Hobsbawm, Eric J. *Nations and Nationalism Since 1780: Programme, Myth, Reality.* Cambridge: Cambridge University Press, 1990.

Hobsbawm, Eric, and Terence Ranger, eds. *The Invention of Tradition.* Cambridge: Cambridge University Press, 1983.

Holleran, Mary. *Church and State in Guatemala.* New York: Columbia University Press, 1949.

Ingersoll, H. M. B. "The War of the Mountains: A Study of Reactionary Peasant Insurgency in Guatemala, 1837–1873." Ph.D. diss., George Washington University, 1972.

Kendall, Carl. "The Politics of Pilgrimage: The Black Christ of Esquipulas." In *Pilgrimage in Latin America,* edited by N. Ross Crumrine and Alan Morinis. New York: Greenwood Press, 1991.

Latourette, Kenneth Scott. *A History of Christianity.* New York: Harper and Row, 1953.

Lazaro de Aspurz, P. *Esteban de Adoain llevó el evangelio de la paz a siete naciones. Restauró la Orden capuchina en España.* Pamplona, Spain: Ediciones Navasal, 1980.

MacLeod, Murdo. *Spanish Central America: A Socioeconomic History, 1520–1720.* Berkeley and Los Angeles: University of California Press, 1973.

Mallon, Florencia E. "Nationalist and Antistate Coalitions in the War of the Pacific: Junín and Cajamarca, 1879–1902." In *Resistance, Rebellion, and Consciousness in the Andean Peasant World, Eighteenth to Twentieth Centuries,* edited by Steve J. Stern. Madison: University of Wisconsin Press, 1987.

Marroquín Rojas, Clemente. *Francisco Morazán y Rafael Carrera.* Guatemala: Editorial José de Pineda Ibarra, 1971.

Martínez Peláez, Severo. *La patria del criollo. Ensayo de interpretación de la realidad colonial guatemalteca.* 8th ed. Guatemala: Editorial Universitaria Centroamericana, 1981.

Marx, Karl, and Friedrich Engels. *On Religion.* Moscow: Progress Publishers, 1975.

McCreery, David. *Rural Guatemala, 1760–1940.* Stanford, Calif.: Stanford University Press, 1994.

Mecham, J. Lloyd. *Church and State in Latin America: A History of Politico-Ecclesiastical Relations.* Chapel Hill: University of North Carolina Press, 1934.

Menchu, Rigoberta. *I, Rigoberta Menchu: An Indian Woman in Guatemala.* Translated by Ann Wright. New York: Verso, 1984.

Miceli, Keith L. "Rafael Carrera: Defender and Promoter of Peasant Interests in Guatemala, 1837–1848." *The Americas* 31 (July 1974–April 1975): 72–95.

Miller, Hubert J. *La iglesia católica y el estado en Guatemala, 1872–1885.* Guatemala: Universidad de San Carlos de Guatemala, 1976.

Montúfar, Lorenzo. *Reseña histórica de Centro América.* 7 vols. Guatemala: Tipografía el Progreso, 1878–1887.

174 Oss, Adriaan C. van. *Catholic Colonialism: A Parish History of Guatemala, 1524–1821.* Cambridge Latin American Studies. Cambridge: Cambridge University Press, 1986.

Palma Murga, Gustavo Enrique. "Algunas relaciones entre la iglesia y los grupos particulares durante el período de 1860 a 1870. Su incidencia en el movimiento liberal de 1871." Tesis de licenciado, Universidad de San Carlos, Guatemala, 1977.

Palmer, Richard E. *Hermeneutics.* Evanston, Ill.: Northwestern University Press, 1969.

Palmer, Steven Paul. "A Liberal Discipline: Inventing Nations in Guatemala and Costa Rica, 1870–1900." Ph.D. diss., Columbia University, 1990.

Pattridge, Blake D. "La Universidad de San Carlos de Guatemala en el regimen conservador, 1839/1871. Penuria, reforma, y crecimiento." En Aportes a la Docencia, Instituto de Investigaciones históricas, antropológicas y arqueológicas. Guatemala: Escuela de Historia de San Carlos, 1995.

Paz Solorzano, Juan. *Historia del Señor crucificado de Esquipulas.* Guatemala: N.p., 1916.

Pinto Soria, Julio. *Centroamérica de la colonia al estado nacional (1800–1840).* Guatemala: Editorial Universitaria, 1986.

Poole, Stafford. *Our Lady of Guadalupe: The Origins and Sources of a Mexican National Symbol, 1531–1797.* Tucson: University of Arizona Press, 1995.

Prado, Eliadio. *La orden franciscana.* San José: Editorial Costa Rica, 1983.

Prien, Hans-Jürgen. *La historia del cristianismo en América Latina.* Salamanca: Ediciones Sígueme, 1985.

Quesada S., Flavio J. *Estructuración y desarrollo de la administración política territorial de Guatemala en la colonia y la época independiente.* Guatemala: Editorial Universitaria de Guatemala, 1983.

Quijada, Mónica. "Qué nación? Dinámicas y dicotomías de la nación en el imaginario hispanoamericano del siglo XIX." In *Imaginar la nación,* edited by François-Xavier Guerra and Mónica Quijada. Hamburg: LIT, 1994.

Reis, João José. *A morte é uma festa. Ritos fúnebres e revolta popular no Brasil do século XIX.* São Paulo, Brazil: Companhia dos Letras, 1991.

Ricoeur, Paul. "The Task of Hermeneutics." *Philosophy Today* 17: 112–29.

Rosenberg, Charles E. *The Cholera Years: The United States in 1832, 1849, and 1866.* Chicago: University of Chicago Press, 1962.

———. *Explaining epidemics and other studies in the history of medicine.* Cambridge: Cambridge University Press, 1992.

Schäfer, Heinrich W. "Identidad de iglesia entre represión y liberación. La Iglesia Presbiteriana en Guatemala." Manuscript submitted for publication. Studies from the World Alliance of Reformed Churches, 1988.

Schele, Linda, and David Freidel. *A Forest of Kings: The Untold Story of the Ancient Maya.* New York: William Morrow, 1990.

Simpson, Alan. "The Covenanted Community." In *Religion in American History: Interpretive Essays,* edited by John M. Mulder and John F. Wilson. Englewood Cliffs, N.J.: Prentice Hall, 1978.

Smith, Carol, ed. *Guatemalan Indians and the State, 1540–1988.* Austin: University of Texas Press, 1990.

Smith, Robert S. "Indigo Production and Trade in Colonial Guatemala." *Hispanic American Historical Review* 34 (May 1959): 181–211.

Solórzano, Juan Carlos. "Rafael Carrera. Reacción conservadora o revolución campesina? Guatemala, 1837–1873." *Anuario de Estudios Centroamericanos (Universidad de Costa*

Rica) 13 (1987): 5–35. 175

Sperber, Jonathan. *Popular Catholicism in Nineteenth-Century Germany.* Princeton, N.J.: Princeton University Press, 1984.

Stark, Rodney, and William Bainbridge. *The Future of Religion.* Berkeley and Los Angeles: University of California Press, 1985.

Stoll, David. *Is Latin America Turning Protestant? The Politics of Evangelical Growth.* Berkeley and Los Angeles: University of California Press, 1990.

Sullivan-González, Douglass. "Piety, Power, and Politics: The Role of Religion in the Formation of the Guatemalan Nation-State, 1839–1871." Ph.D. diss., University of Texas at Austin, 1994.

Taracena Flores, Arturo. "Oradores oficiales en las celebraciones de la independencia desde el año de 1831." Photocopy. CB 41052.

Taylor, William B. *Magistrates of the Sacred: Priests and Parishioners in Eighteenth-Century Mexico.* Stanford: Stanford University Press, 1996.

Thompson, Leonard. *The Political Mythology of Apartheid.* New Haven: Yale University Press, 1985.

Tobar Cruz, Pedro. *Los montañeses.* Guatemala: Imprenta Hispania, 1958.

———. *Los montañeses. La facción de los lucíos, y otros acontecimientos históricos de 1846 a 1851.* Guatemala: Editorial Universitaria, 1971.

Torres, Jaime. *Liberalismo y rebeldía campesina, 1820–1823.* Barcelona: Ed. Ariel, 1976.

Torres Rivas, Edelberto. *History and Society in Central America.* Translated by Douglass Sullivan-González. Austin: University of Texas Press, 1993.

Turner, Victor. *Dramas, Fields, and Metaphors: Symbolic Action in Human Society.* Ithaca, N.Y.: Cornell University Press, 1974.

Weber, Max. *The Sociology of Religion.* Boston: Beacon Press, 1922.

Woodward, Ralph Lee Jr. *Central America: A Nation Divided.* Latin American Histories. New York: Oxford University Press, 1985.

———. *Class Privilege and Economic Development: The Consulado de Comercio of Guatemala, 1793–1871.* Chapel Hill: University of North Carolina Press, 1966.

———. "Liberalismo, conservadurismo, y la actitud de los campesinos de la montaña hacia el gobierno de Guatemala, 1821–1850." *Anales de la Acadêmia de Geografía e Historia de Guatemala* 56 (January–December 1982): 195–210.

———. "Population and Development in Guatemala, 1840–1879." *Journal of the Southeastern Council on Latin American Studies* 14 (March 1983): 5–18.

———. *Rafael Carrera and the Emergence of the Republic of Guatemala, 1821–1871.* Athens: University of Georgia Press, 1993.

Wuthnow, Robert. *Meaning and Moral Order: Explorations in Cultural Analysis.* Berkeley and Los Angeles: University of California Press, 1987.

Index

Abella, Pedro, 46
Adoáin, Esteban de, 57–58, 123
Aguado, Fernando, 45
Ahpop, Tomás, 47
Alfaro, Julian, 75
Alta Verapaz, 5, 28
Alvarado, Pedro, 4
Anderson, Benedict, 15–16
Antigua, 69, 83, 93; Antiguans, 123
Aqueche, Francisco, 55–56, 82–84, 86, 125
Aragan, Francisco, 97
Arellano, José Nicolás, 63, 86, 99, 102, 105
Arendal, Juan de, 78
Argueta, Ygnacio, 97
Arriasa, Florencio, 83
Asunción Mita, 23, 112, 116
Atitlán, 82
Aycinena y Piñol, Juan José: 11, 80, 112; and covenant, 2, 64–67, 150n65; Independence sermons, 62–75, 124; death of, 120

Baja Verapaz, 5, 28, 75
Baldwini, Baltazar, 41, 80
bananas, 7
Barrios, Justo Rufino, 10, 131; and Catholic church, 121–23; and historiography, 11
Barrutia, José María, 75
Barrutia y Croquer, José, 74
Belice, 132
beneficed parishes (*cura propio*). *See* Catholic church, beneficed parishes.
Betancourt, Felipe de Jesus, 56
Black Christ, 151n74
Blanco, Nicolás, 75
Bourbons, 20, 63
Brasseur y Bourbourg, Carlos, 73
Brazil, 40, 132
Burgess, Paul, 121–22
Burns, E. Bradford, 10

Cabildo Eclesiástico. *See* Catholic church, Church council
Cabrera, Juan, 77–78
cacao, 7
Cacul, Joseph, 78
Cahabón. *See* Santa María Cahabón
Cájola, 43–44
Calvin, John, 66, 70
Camapa, 112
Cambrils, Ignacio, 69
cantores. *See* Catholic church, chanters
Cap, Ambrosio, 78
Capuchins, 56–58, 69, 123
Carmack, Robert, 128–29
Carrera, Rafael, xii, 1, 3, 10, 34; and Antonio Larazábal, 19, 83, 88; and Catholic church 2, 9, 17, 19–20, 27–28, 31, 53, 62, 81, 124–32; and cemetery revolts, 35, 40–46; and cholera epidemic, 8, 34, 53–59; and Civil War, 98–106; and clergy 3, 10, 31, 51, 60–62, 67; and clergy in insurrection, 82–87; and clergy in 1840s, 87–98; and clergy in civil war, 101–03; and clergy and the nation, 106–19; and clergy sermons about, 62, 71–72; and cofradías, 50–52; and El Salvador, 9, 14, 68–69, 106–12; and Francisco de Paula García Peláez, 23, 65, 76, 89–91, 112, 114, 117–19; and Francisco González Lobos, 1; and Francisco Morazán, 8, 72; his death, 9, 120; and historiography, 10–13; and Indians, 3, 10, 37–42, 108–09, 126–27; and Jesuits, 91, 114; and La Arada, 9, 106–12; and ladinos (mestizos), 4; and Mariano Gálvez, 8; and nation, 2, 106–12; and religion, 2, 80, 85; as President, 9, 114–15
Carrillo, Antonio, 38
Casarola, José Pablo, 90
Casasola, Pablo José, 83

DATE DUE